O9-BUB-255

PURSUING the FULL KINGDOM POTENTIAL
of Your Congregation

Also from
Lake Hickory Resources

James H. Royston, Executive Editor
George W. Bullard Jr., Senior Editor
SeniorEditor@LakeHickoryResources.org

**Spiritual Leadership in a Secular Age: Building Bridges
Instead of Barriers**

Edward H. Hammett

**Operation Inasmuch: Mobilizing Believers beyond
the Walls of the Church**

David W. Crocker

**Seeds for the Future: Growing Organic Leaders
for Living Churches**

Robert D. Dale

Available at
www.lakehickoryresources.com

PURSUING the FULL KINGDOM POTENTIAL
of Your Congregation

GEORGE W. BULLARD JR.

Lake Hickory RESOURCES
ST. LOUIS, MISSOURI

© Copyright 2005 by George W. Bullard Jr.

All rights reserved. For permission to reuse content, please contact Copyright Clearance Center, 222 Rosewood Drive, Danvers, MA 01923, (978) 750-8400, www.thenewcopyright.com.

Cover art: GettyImages
Cover and interior design: Elizabeth Wright

See more Lake Hickory resources at
www.lakehickoryresources.com.

10 9 8 7 6 5 4 3 2   06 07 08 09

Library of Congress Cataloging–in–Publication Data

Bullard, George, 1950-
   Pursuing the full kingdom potential of your congregation / George
W. Bullard, Jr.
      p. cm.
   Includes bibliographical references (p.   ).
   ISBN-10: 0-827229-84-4 (pbk. : alk. paper)
   ISBN-13: 978-0-827229-84-6
   1. Church growth. I. Title.
BV652.25.B85 2005
254'.5–dc22
                    Printed in the United States of America

Contents

Editors' Foreword

Inspiration and Wisdom for Twenty-First–Century Christian Leaders

You have chosen wisely in deciding to study and learn from a **Lake Hickory Resources** book. Lake Hickory Resources publishes for

- congregational leaders who desire to serve effectively
- Christian ministers who pursue excellence in service
- members of a congregation that desires to reach its full Kingdom potential
- denominational leaders who want to come alongside affiliated congregations in a servant leadership role

Lake Hickory Resources is an inspiration- and wisdom-sharing vehicle of Lake Hickory Learning Communities. LHLC is the web of relationships developing from the base of Hollifield Leadership Center (www.Hollifeld.org) near Hickory, North Carolina. LHLC addresses emerging strategic issues of leadership development for congregations, denominations, and parachurch organizations.

The mission of **Lake Hickory Resources** currently is being expressed through two meaningful avenues. First, George Bullard, executive coach for Lake Hickory Learning Communities, also is senior editor for *Net Results* magazine (www.NetResults.org), a national, transdenominational publication that appears monthly in print and electronic form.

Second, **Lake Hickory Resources** publishes books in partnership with Christian Board of Publication. Once this partnership is in full production it will produce eight to twelve new books each year.

We welcome your comments on these books, and we welcome your suggestions for new subject areas and authors we ought to consider.

James H. Royston, Executive Editor
George W. Bullard Jr., Senior Editor
SeniorEditor@LakeHickoryResources.org

Lake Hickory Learning Communities is a ministry of
www.NorthCarolinaBaptists.org

Preface

This book flows out of my life journey of thirty-seven years of ministry among congregations and denominations. Those years were preceded by eighteen years of growing up inside congregations and denominational organizations 24/7/365.

This journey is the result of a ministry filled with passion to help congregations reach their full Kingdom potential. This book is a direct result of personal work in the area of consulting, coaching, and teaching congregations the things they need to experience if they are to know how to pursue and sustain a vital Christian ministry.

For parts of four decades, I have worked in the areas of research, writing, teaching, consulting, and coaching in the processes written about in this book. The material in this book has been used throughout North America among more than thirty different denominations– from Assembly of God to Episcopalian, from Presbyterian to Lutheran, from Wesleyan to Methodist, from Disciples to Evangelical Free, and from American Baptist to Southern Baptist to European Baptist.

One major launching pad was a seminary graduate research project on one hundred churches in fifteen different cities. This project sought to discover what produces effectiveness in congregations facing multiple issues of transition and change. This research showed that three words illustrate the difference between congregations who diminish and congregations who thrive in the midst of great challenge. These words are: *Vision Plus Intentionality.*

I followed up this research with an in-depth investigation of what a consultation process might look like that would increase the chances that congregations could thrive rather than diminish. Since that research almost three decades ago, I have worked as a consultant, coach, or teacher to more than a thousand congregations and five hundred denominational organizations. I have lectured in numerous seminaries or divinity schools in various North American locations on subjects related to this book. I have also trained almost a thousand consultants and/or coaches in strategic processes related to congregations. Now it is time to put this information in book form for sharing with a larger audience.

Who Made This Journey Possible?

Many people and numerous experiences have served as my mentors and coaches. Without them, I would not have developed the knowledge and experience base that makes this book possible. Their contributions to my life fill the depths of this book. Five different types of mentors or coaches have contributed to my ability to share the insights in this book.

First, other consultants and coaches taught me how to do assessment, intervention, and learning with congregations. Chief among these is Lyle Schaller. I began reading his books and learning from him almost forty years ago. Although I corresponded with Lyle during my seminary research, my first opportunity to learn from him face-to-face was twenty-seven years ago when I spent a week with him at The Yokefellow Institute in Richmond, Indiana. Lyle will be the most surprised that I finally got around to completing a book.

During my early years of congregational work, Speed Leas was close behind Lyle Schaller in his influence on my consulting and intervention style. I began reading his writings on conflict management more than thirty years ago, corresponded with him during my seminary research, and began taking training from him twenty-four years ago.

Second, many ministry colleagues have influenced my work. Robert [Bob] Dale showed up on my radar screen when his book *To Dream Again* was published in 1981. A colleague, Jere Allen, and I had also been working on the type of life cycle approach to congregational life that Bob popularized in his book. I continue to work on this life cycle approach, which you will see introduced in chapter 5.

Jere Allen, the colleague with whom I wrote the manual *Shaping a Future for the Church in the Changing Community*, has been a friend over the past four decades. Wow, that is hard to believe! His passion for the church has always been a strong motivation for me.

Don Hammer believed in me early in my ministry. Perhaps at first his belief was based on the recommendation of others. Very quickly, however, Don showed that he trusted me to act quickly and decisively to help congregations and local denominational organizations—known as *associations* in Baptist life—soar with their calling, gifts, and strengths. He gave me a challenge in 1981 that resulted in a very fulfilling strategy known as Mega Focus Cities. This strategy concentrated Baptist resources on the fifty largest metropolitan areas in the continental United States.

Third, mentors and teachers encouraged me along my own journey. Willis Bennett was my academic mentor during my ten years of seminary work in Louisville, Kentucky. He was my advocate who found ways to gain permission for me to try things that did not exactly fit the catalogue, but made more sense than those things that did.

Larry McSwain, a colleague of Willis Bennett and a primary academic and professional coach to me, still challenges me today as we collaborate on various projects. What I know about intervention into systems I learned best from Larry in the classroom while serving as a student assistant to him, and when challenged by his presentations and dialogue through the years. We are still collaborating on projects of support to the work of God's kingdom on earth.

Fourth, two congregations are highly significant to me. Gregory Memorial Baptist Church in Baltimore, Maryland, nurtured me from the first through tenth grades, and then tolerated me as a member for a couple of years as a young adult. These caring people provided me a foundation of biblical, spiritual, Christian understandings and practices that prepared me for the challenges of my adult ministry. They even allowed me to practice–however badly–my emerging consultation skills on them during my early years of consulting. Granted, my father was the pastor, but it was more than Dad. It was a collection of gifted people who were not afraid to expose me to the good, bad, and ugly of congregational life and dare me to learn from it in a way that I could serve other congregations.

Everything I really needed to know about Christian ministry I learned at West Side Baptist Church in the Portland community of Louisville, Kentucky. I served this congregation as community minister and then pastor during my core seminary years. They taught me so much. I still love telling the stories of that congregation and its people.

Many of the significant things I learned were unrealized at the time, but blossomed in later years. Often I have enjoyed playing "Monday morning quarterback" on so many ministry situations I encountered. They were a rich laboratory where I learned through action and then reflection.

It is no trite statement that my parents–G.W. and Mozelle Bullard–taught me phenomenal things about congregational life and ministry and are my fifth category of mentors and coaches. I learned so much at the breakfast, lunch, and supper table of my minister, missionary, and denominationally dedicated parents. By adulthood, I felt like I already had a generation of experience in the dynamics of congregations and denominations. As a colleague–Bob Wiley–says about our common background, we learned many things about religious organizational life from our families, yet we have no idea where or when we learned them. We just know them.

I have spent so much time sharing my mentor and coach heritage in order that you and I both are reminded that very little we know comes to us without cumulative experience and interaction with real people and real situations. None of us are born experts, and perhaps the longer we live, the more we realize the less we really know that fits the category known as "expertise." We are all on a humble journey dependent on the Triune God.

It is in this spirit that I seek in this book to share with you all the really important things I remember about helping congregations reach their full Kingdom potential. Hang on. The ride is fast. The fire hydrant of learning is open, and I am asking you to take a sip or two of water.

What Kind of Journey for What Kind of Congregation?

Welcome to a journey! A spiritual strategic journey for your congregation. Hang on. It may be a wild journey. It will at least be a journey with opportunities for insights, reflections, actions, and accountability about your congregation's journey. My hope is that it will be a journey in the direction of the full Kingdom potential for your congregation in response to a God-called, Christ-centric, faith-based sense of mission and vision.

All kinds of congregations will benefit from this material. Smaller membership congregations, as well as very large congregations, will find affirmations and challenges for their journeys. The journey will be different for each congregation. Your congregation is a unique fellowship of people with varying spiritual gifts, life skills, and personality preferences. This book suggests processes to help you assess your unique characteristics and travel forward into God's future for your congregation.

My generation has explored many unique strategies and methods to help congregations losing ground in our nation's culture wars. Contextual performance categories became popular during the 1960s. Growth and strategy planning performance categories rose to popularity during the 1970s. Size performance categories were in vogue during the 1980s. Health performance categories of various types had ascendancy during the 1990s.

For me the current decade is characterized by performance categories that center on the spiritual and strategic journey of congregations. Using categories to think spiritually and strategically about congregations does not mean I stereotype them. It means that I benchmark them against certain Kingdom standards of performance.

How Will This Journey Help Your Congregation Pursue Its Full Kingdom Potential?

The purpose of this book is to help congregational and denominational leadership empower congregations along a spiritual strategic journey. The book provides clear approaches to assessment, learning, and action that congregations must take along their spiritual and strategic journey, a journey toward reaching their full Kingdom potential.

The number of plateaued and declining congregations throughout North America is at an all-time high. So unfortunately, this book has a growing market. An increasing number of congregations are ready for approaches that are effective and lasting. This book gives such congregations maps for the journey to use to meet the outreach and growth potential of their congregations in the postmodern context of the twenty-first century. I have seen congregational and denominational leaders use this material to help congregations soar. You can, too!

This book offers a new paradigm for churches wanting to grow. This is not just another process for congregational redevelopment. It learns from the past but does not simply repackage strategic planning models from the past four decades. It uses a journey motif that is open-ended, custom-made, and locally owned, rather than a closed process that is intended to work for any congregation. The focus is on capacity building in each congregation, so that learning what works and how to hardwire new learning into the congregation is a strong component of the process recommended.

This book is a twenty-first–century process, aware that an increasing number of processes relevant to congregational life are right-brained in orientation rather than left-brained, and postmodern rather than modern. This calls for congregations to take a narrative approach to their futuring as they respond to the new thing God is seeking to do in and through them.

This book will help pastors, staff ministers, lay leaders, denominational servants, parachurch leaders, and consultants or coaches to understand the spiritual and strategic journey in which congregations must engage to be able to reach their full Kingdom potential. You should use this book as a guide to assess your congregation and to launch a spiritual strategic journey. Properly taken, this journey will improve the internal and external ministries of your congregation. You will be more effective in evangelism, new member recruitment and assimilation, discipleship development, leadership development, and ministry mobilization. Your congregation will learn to act in ways that carry out the mission you perceive God has for your congregation.

How Is This Book Organized?

Chapter 1 provides an overview of the stated and implied processes for helping a congregation reach its full Kingdom potential. Chapters 2 through 10 talk in specifics about the processes for helping a congregation reach its full Kingdom potential. Chapters 11 and 12 deal with two special issues: the process of coaching congregations to pursue their full Kingdom potential, and the implications of this book for denominational organizations.

Each chapter follows a specific organizational outline:

1. A short executive summary
2. The chapter's main text with a coaching break
3. "Coaching Insights"
4. "Personal Reflections"

The short executive summary provides insight into the key content of each chapter. The main text takes you another step along the journey to your congregation's full Kingdom potential. Somewhere along the way we take a coaching break. "Coaching Insights" provide questions for readers to answer about themselves and their congregation in light of the chapter's main text. "Personal Reflections" invite you to journal your reflections on the material presented in the chapter and to list the actions you need to take about your life, ministry, and/ or congregation based on the material the chapter presents. These "Personal Reflections" also challenge you to indicate how and by whom you want to be held accountable for taking these actions. The bias is for transformational action to occur in the life and ministry of your congregation.

Where Can I Find More Up-to-Date Information?

Several barriers have kept me from writing this book for about twenty years. First, I wanted to be sure I had enough right stuff to say that would really contribute. Because of the encouragement of others, I think I finally have that.

Second, I try to always be learning, and I could not feel good about the year it takes to get a traditional book out. Often I felt that by the time the book came out I would be down the road past that material and not be proud of the actual book. Well, I have learned to accept that, and I have discovered web logs, or "blogs."

If you want to know my current thoughts about what I am saying in this book, go to www.BullardJournal.org and check out the category with this book's title. I invite you to use that site to comment on what you read in this book. It will help me improve my next book manuscript.

COACHING INSIGHTS

As you weave your way through this book, it is important to understand your beginning point. Consider these issues:

■ What are the current signs of health and strength in your congregation on which you can build an excellent, effective future?

■ Is your congregation currently traveling along a spiritual strategic journey? If so, what characterizes that journey? Does your congregation have *Vision Plus Intentionality* as a part of its journey?

■ What is the full Kingdom potential of your congregation? Is your current journey sufficiently spiritual and strategic to pull you forward to your full Kingdom potential?

■ Who has made your personal journey possible? What are their contributions to your life and ministry? Who is your coach for your current journey?

■ What factors make your congregation's journey possible? What are the contributions of the past and present of your congregation that give you both heritage and hope in God's future for your congregation? Who is your congregation's coach for your current spiritual strategic journey?

PERSONAL REFLECTIONS

YOUR REFLECTIONS: What are your reflections on the material presented in this introduction?

_____

_____

_____

_____

_____

YOUR ACTIONS: What actions do you need to take about your life, ministry, and/or congregation based on the material presented in this introduction?

_____

_____

_____

_____

_____

YOUR ACCOUNTABILITY: How and by whom do you want to be held accountable for taking these actions?

_____

_____

_____

_____

_____

CHAPTER 1

Understanding the Full Kingdom Potential of Your Congregation

---

EXECUTIVE SUMMARY

The purpose of this chapter is to provide a conceptual framework for helping a congregation reach its full Kingdom potential. It deals with the difference between church growth, church health, church faithfulness, church success, and church transformation. It seeks to position the full Kingdom potential of a congregation as a journey rather than a destination. It seeks to help congregations realize that they must be molded in God's image rather than in the image of humankind.

It's Not about Closing the Gap

Let's get right to it. One caution. Do not be turned off by these first few paragraphs. Stay with the meaning of the text and read below the surface. The implications for your congregation are earthshaking.

In this book I have no interest in several common approaches to congregational vitality. *I am particularly not interested in closing the gap between where a congregation finds itself and where it wants to push forward to become.* Look with me at the difference between closing gaps and taking a journey to reach your congregation's full Kingdom potential.

Church Growth

I am not interested in the growth of your congregation. It really does not matter to me whether or not your congregation is growing numerically. At its best church growth is an outward expression of a desire for a local congregation to attract as many people as possible into the Kingdom of God and into their congregation with its discipleship practices.

Church growth at its worse is a self-serving, competitive desire to win. The other side of the will to win is a willingness for other congregations to lose. Church growth zeroes in on individuals you want to participate in your congregation. In so doing church growth risks treating these persons as objects rather than as persons of worth created in the image of God to live and to love.

Growth can shape a congregation into a business that is trying to make a profit. Church growth sells meaning to achieve profit or to close the gap between the current size of the church and the potential size of the church. But Kingdom potential is not about closing the gap.

Church Health

I am not interested in the health of your congregation. Church health has at least two current meanings in the North American church. Church health can mean emotional or family systems health. The emotional quotient of a congregation is important. Congregational members need to be persons who are healthy psychologically and spiritually. However, an overemphasis on this type of church health can result in a healthy congregation in neutral with no sense of destination or journey. Health becomes an end result.

Church health can also mean a congregation with a healthy balance of worship, evangelism, discipleship, fellowship, and ministry. Such a congregation has the programs and systems of congregational life aligned with theological understandings of what a congregation ought to be. Some of these congregations soar with great excellence and effectiveness. Church health approaches may lead to emotionally healthy congregations and healthy, balanced congregations who have closed the gap between being unhealthy and being healthy. But Kingdom potential is not about closing the gap.

Church Faithfulness

I am not interested in the faithfulness of your congregation. Congregational faithfulness often focuses on the past. It centers attention on what the church has always done, always believed, or forever refused to do. It presents present patterns of the congregation, its denomination, the historic Christian church, or the core values of a movement within the denomination or historic church. Congregational faithfulness is seldom a proactive position. Rather, most often congregational faithfulness becomes a passive position seeking to protect that congregation from patterns of thought or action that do not fit the paradigm of the long-term leadership of the congregation. Faithfulness is often the rallying cry of aging, plateaued, and declining congregations.

Church faithfulness forgets that faithfulness alone is insufficient. It must also have effectiveness and innovation to be complete. Faithfulness focuses around substance. For faithfulness to be complete, congregations must also close the gap with effective structures and innovative styles. But Kingdom potential is not about closing the gap.

Church Success

I am not interested in the success of your congregation. Church success usually focuses on the organizational success of the congregation and not the spiritual fulfillment of the congregation. Church success often relates to management goals such as reaching the budget, achieving a certain membership or attendance size, surviving another year to minister, or thriving once again as the congregation did in the past.

Church success forgets that success is nothing without moving from success to significance in ministry on one hand, and surrender in service to God's Kingdom on the other. But Kingdom potential is not about closing the gap.

Church Transformation

While I may be very interested in the transformation of your congregation, this is not the destination I see for your congregation. Congregations do need to transition, change, and transform. These three concepts are highlighted throughout this book. Chapter 6 will particularly focus on them. Transformation, however, implies a destination. It is an act or process that can be finished. Once done, it does not have to be done again in the eyes of many people. Thus, a transformed congregation claims permanent transformation. Following the transformation, it does not have to continue to work on transformation issues.

Many congregations have used transformation processes borrowed from the outside or those developed internally. Eventually most churches reach a point where they feel the transformation process is complete. They stop following the act or process of transformation.

They do not realize that transformation is an ongoing spiritual process that is leaving them behind. The transformed congregation loses track of its ever-changing context and no longer follows a sense of spiritual vision. Soon they discover or ignore a gap between where they are and what it means to be transformed. But Kingdom potential is not about closing the gap.

Transformation within a congregation is very similar to the individual Christ-centric, faith-based journey. If a person stops a personal transformational journey at the point he or she discovers and embraces what it means to have a life-changing relationship with God through Jesus Christ, then that person remains spiritually immature and shallow, never experiencing the joys of a life fully dedicated to a spiritual strategic journey focused on the Triune God. But Kingdom potential is not about closing the gap.

It's All about Your Full Kingdom Potential

Church growth, health, faithfulness, success, and even transformation all tend to have a focus on closing the gap between where congregations are and where they want to be. This is a philosophy known as *Gapology*. Gapology is the constant desire to close the gap between where you are and where you want to be, which is primarily transactional change. It may also be transformational change if transformation is seen as a static destination. Gapology certainly does not empower your church to live continually into your full Kingdom potential.

In economics, Gapology relates to supply and demand. For a company to realize profits, the gap between supply and demand must always be as small as possible. Theologically Christianity falls into a Gapology approach when it seeks to define God as being in the gap between the known and the unknown. Such a God only fills in the gaps scientific knowledge leaves. Such an approach reduces and marginalizes our understanding of God.

Strategic approaches often seek to push forward or close the gap in congregations. They are often problem-solving approaches that reduce and marginalize a congregation's core mission. These approaches seek to discern and discover what is wrong, weak, and missing and then make them right, strong, and present. Dialogue is around the number of "No" votes present rather than the number of "Yes" votes present.

The tendency in many approaches is for the destination to be a static location. These approaches look for the areas of deficiency that need to be corrected in order to bring the congregation to its desired location. Often these actions focus on issues of programs and management. For example, the youth program needs fixing, the worship services are dead, the finances are static, the membership and attendance have plateaued, or long-tenured members are controlling the direction of the congregation.

Gapology focuses on what is thinkable, doable, and controllable. As opposed to this, a spiritual strategic journey toward a congregation's full Kingdom potential can lead congregations to focus on the unthinkable, the undoable, and the uncontrollable. Such focus comes not by following strategic approaches but by following the leadership of God. Kingdom potential *pulls* the congregations forward rather than *pushing* it forward.

Empowering Congregational Futures

I am interested in empowering congregational futures. I am interested in helping your congregation pursue, perfect, and be pulled toward its full Kingdom potential. This involves a spiritual strategic journey toward God's ideal or perfect destination for your congregation. I am interested in helping your unique Christ-centric, faith-based community. I want your community to utilize fully its collective spiritual giftedness, its life skills and strengths, and its personality and cultural preferences so you can soar in response to God's ideal or perfect leading. This means you must visualize God's future for your specific congregation.

The full Kingdom potential for congregations must be discerned, discovered, and developed one congregation at a time. Each congregation must follow God's leadership and find solutions in a manner unique to the opportunities and challenges they face. While God's eternal mission for congregations remains the same, the everlasting historic purpose, the enduring core values, and the empowering vision of each congregation is unique.

I am interested in your congregation being reimaged in the image of God. All too often we find congregations being reimaged in the image of the latest church growth, health, faithfulness, success, or transformation process of humankind. I am interested in helping your congregation understand the context in which you find yourself and then to fully, sacrificially, lovingly, and unconditionally minister among the people in that context. At times that is a geographically defined context; at other times it has a cultural, affinity groups, or target group definition. Any of these are fine as long as they are the context to which God has given you gifts, skills, and preferences for exceptional ministry.

I am interested in helping your congregation walk in the spirit of 2 Corinthians 5:7 that calls for Christians to "walk by faith, not by sight." That involves being embraced and captivated by God's ideal or perfect will for your congregation. This involves placing more emphasis on visionary leadership and relationship experiences with God, with one another, and with the context in which you serve than it does on programs and management of your congregation.

Foundationally, *my interest in this book is all about your full Kingdom potential. Full* refers to that which is comprehensive, far-reaching, and thorough. *Kingdom* implies that which embraces the reign of God as a focus rather than the realm of humankind. It implies a broad Christian worldview rather than being concerned only about a single local congregation. *Potential* refers to that which is impossible except for the promise of God.

Are These Congregations Reaching Their Full Kingdom Potential?

How do you know a congregation is reaching or has reached its full Kingdom potential? What are the signs or characteristics? How is this measured? The reality is that full Kingdom potential must be defined one congregation at a time and probably cannot be objectively measured. Even if you know the full and final story of a congregation's life and ministry, you may find it difficult to know if the congregation ever reached its full Kingdom potential. A combination of congregational participants, sister congregations in a same or similar context, and other outside observers might be able to discern if a congregation ever reaches its full Kingdom potential.

Probably no congregation ever truly reaches its full Kingdom potential. It may have periods of prime in its life, but each prime or summit represents a beginning point for the next dimension of ministry challenge. Study the following stories of several congregations as examples of those who strove to reach their full Kingdom potential.

New Region Congregation

During the generation following World War II, a major Protestant denomination started a new congregation in a region of the country where they had never had congregations before. This congregation was primarily composed of people from this denominational tradition. Their jobs and education programs had taken them to this region. From the beginning this was a reproducing congregation. It would regularly send out groups from within its congregation to start new congregations throughout the region. It would also sponsor, nest, or adopt new congregations of its denomination that began to emerge from other efforts.

More than fifty years since the start of this congregation, almost 300 congregations of the denomination exist within a fifty-mile radius of where this congregation started. More than 80 percent of the congregations are primarily composed of non-Anglo Americans, making this one of the most culturally diverse regions of this denomination in North America.

However, "New Region Congregation" no longer exists. It only thrived for one generation, going out of existence when it was twenty or so years old. It continually gave away its members to start new congregations until it had no more people to give. It died serving its context.

Did this congregation reach its full Kingdom potential? What was its potential? Could it have balanced sacrificial mission and ministry with efforts to attract new people to the founding congregation, and continued its life as a flagship congregation of its denomination in its region? Perhaps.

Small Rural Congregation

The "Small Rural Congregation" is one of five congregations located in an unincorporated community of around 200 people. Each of these five congregations averages between thirty-five and fifty-five people for Sunday worship. It is estimated that only five families in the community do not have some connection with one of these five congregations. Over the past several years, members from "Small Rural Congregation" have visited all five unchurched families several times, seeking to recruit them for attendance and membership in their church.

In one of the households, a woman from "Small Rural" discovered that neither the mother nor the father could read and write. She prepared herself for ministry by attending literacy missions training that her denomination offered. She went to this family and offered to teach the mother and the father to read and write with her newfound skill. The mother and father readily accepted. Over the next eighteen months to two years, she taught them to read and write at a level that increased their functioning in their workplace and in the community. She used a simplified version of the New Testament as one parallel reading source.

While tutoring the parents, she developed a close and meaningful relationship with them. Out of this, she had a natural, genuine opportunity to share the story of her personal Christian faith. Through this endeavor, the mother and the father both came to a faith relationship to God through Jesus Christ and became part of the Small Rural Congregation. Their four children also joined them in this new spiritual adventure.

Small Rural Congregation is, in Kingdom terms, a significantly growing church because they have figured out a need in their community and have effectively addressed this need. They have been able to move forward to reach their full Kingdom potential.

Nevertheless, have they reached that potential? What is their potential in this open rural setting? What are their next steps as a congregation in identifying other needs and addressing them? Should their ministry be confined to only their immediate geographic setting? Is their Kingdom potential much broader than they realize?

First Congregation

"First Congregation" is an extremely large "mega" congregation in an equally large metropolitan area of the United States. A metropolitan congregational strategist conducted research that surprised First Congregation. They were not reaching unchurched people. Their long list of new members and attendees did not include many people who previously had not been involved in a Christ-centric faith-based relationship at a local congregation. They were primarily reaching people who transferred from other congregations, or were the children of their existing members and regular attendees.

The research showed that some local congregations were indeed reaching people new to a Christ-centric faith-based relationship through a local congregation. These were the small-to-medium-sized congregations throughout the metropolitan area that First Congregation served. Still, many of these congregations were suffering numerically. They could trace their loss of members to two sources. First, massive multicultural transition was occurring in this metropolitan area. But second, many of the new people these smaller congregations had brought into church life did not stay in the smaller churches. Instead, they left in a few years to join one of the several different mega congregations, including First Congregation, because these larger churches offered an attractive diversity of excellent programs, ministries, and activities.

First Congregation realized that for them to continue reaching people new to the Christian faith they needed to be also concerned about the small-to-medium-sized congregations in the community, particularly those who were suffering in some way or another. They needed to help these congregations renew, reinvent, or resurrect vitality. In response to this challenge, the pastor of First Congregation made a bold commitment to lead his congregation to renew, restore, or restart one hundred congregations over the next twenty years. They began movement in this direction approximately twenty years ago and have now achieved this goal. This resulted in the continual growth of First Congregation, significant diversity of its ministry, the renewal, restoration, or restarting of congregations relevant to the context in which the facilities were located, and many persons launching and sustaining a Christian discipleship journey.

As great as this sounds, does this really represent the full Kingdom potential of this congregation? Is this effort too focused on the growth of First Congregation? Where is the evidence of a more complete ministry that looks at the physical, spiritual, social, and emotional needs of people? Maybe it was present, but was it enough of a major focus to inspire others to a balanced ministry? What has First Congregation done to be a teaching model that would share information and inspire this type of service mentality in other congregations? Could it be that First Congregation could make significant to sacrificial progress toward its full Kingdom potential by giving away to others what it has learned?

Emerging Congregation

"Emerging Congregation" came into existence when its pastor's family and three other families moved 1100 miles from another part of North America to a fast-growing suburban area populated by significant numbers of twenty-somethings and thirty-somethings. These four families formed the initial leadership community for a new postmodern congregation. From its beginning this congregation focused on reaching people who are turned off by the traditional church, who are looking for a place with an emphasis on helping each person grow in faith, and who are searching spiritually without considering that a Christian faith would satisfy their searching.

The congregation's style is one of celebration, interaction, community, and service. Worship services are lively. Never-ending fellowship is contagious and builds a strong sense of community. Servant evangelism is a hallmark of their ministry.

The structure of the congregation focuses on an elder board of the pastor and six laypersons. A radical mobilization of the laypersons into leadership, along with collaborative and learning communities, drives the programs, ministries, and activities of the congregation. Growth has been rapid. Following almost a year of developing a faith and practice foundation for the congregation, public worship services were launched in a local middle school. Very quickly attendance grew to more than 300.

It was difficult to find adequate temporary meeting places for the congregation until they finally constructed their first building. Over the past decade the congregation has constantly been involved in a building expansion project, and thus in conducting capital fundraising efforts. Weekly worship attendance is now over 2500 as the congregation closes in on its tenth anniversary. More than 1300 adults are involved in weekly cell groups. Almost 700 people participate monthly in various servant evangelism activities.

Less than 20 percent of the worship attendees are over 40 years old. Only about half indicated they had a personal Christian faith prior to connecting with this congregation. With such effectiveness at reaching what are considered difficult target groups to involve in church, Emerging Congregation is seen as a role model of a congregation reaching people with a postmodern mindset. Surely they are reaching their full Kingdom potential!

Actually, we cannot know for sure about the full Kingdom potential of any of these four congregations, or that of many more examples about which we could have dialogue. The full Kingdom potential of a congregation is a journey—a spiritual strategic journey. It is not a destination. It is a beginning, but seldom an ending. It is ongoing for the vast majority of congregations.

COACHING BREAK

✔ Gaze out the window for a minute. Ponder the situation of your congregation. What images come to mind?

✔ Is your congregation reaching its full Kingdom potential? Or, is your congregation simply trying to close the gap, fix problems, be faithful, experience success, or show growth? If your congregation is seeking to reach its full Kingdom potential, what evidence do you see of its transformation and fulfillment of God's vision?

Pursuing Your Congregation's Full Kingdom Potential

For your congregation to reach its full Kingdom potential, reaching that potential must be your enduring passion and desire. Growth, health, faithfulness, success, and even transformation are finite goals. They focus on things from the beginning until now, plus what we can project with our sight. They focus on reimaging your congregation in the image of the author or advocate of growth, health, faithfulness, success, or transformation. These finite goals must not consume your passion.

The only image that will really work for your congregation is God's image. That image is found only in the future and is yet to be discerned, discovered, and developed. Only your full Kingdom potential is an eternal goal. It focuses on pulling you forward to a future God already knows. Only this goal is worthy of your passion.

If you have difficulty getting your arms around the theological concept of your full Kingdom potential, let me share a familiar tale. Do you remember Merlin the Magician in the story of Camelot, King Arthur, and the Round Table? Merlin had a mysterious ability to know the future. It seems that he was born in the future and lived "backwards," thereby acquiring the ability to "look back" on the future from the present. In 1994 Charles E. Smith published an interesting article in *Business Strategy Review* entitled "The Merlin Factor: Leadership and Strategic Intent."[1] I have rewritten a key part of his article in terms relevant to congregations while at the same time remaining faithful to Smith's strategic intent:

> The Merlin Factor is the capacity to discern, discover, and develop the potential of the present from the point of view of the future. It is the gift and skill to enlist people throughout your congregation as advocates who listen, speak, and act on behalf of a progressive understanding of God's future. It is an absolute commitment to a spiritual strategic journey that increases existing possibilities geometrically to empower world-shattering transformation in response to the pulling of God toward the full Kingdom potential for your congregation.

It is extremely important that your congregation is complete in the image of God, rather than in the image of the latest program, project, or process. When a congregation is complete in the image of the latest program, project, or process, they seldom make the revolutionary progress necessary to reach their full Kingdom potential. They are often stuck in being an emulating congregation that only seeks to copy what they see as successful in other congregations. Only when a congregation engages in a spiritual strategic journey to discern, discover, and develop their unique journey in the image of God will the congregation be able to begin approaching full Kingdom potential.

What Does a Spiritual Strategic Journey Involve?

It involves a focus on a spiritual strategic journey, and not a program or project. My early ministry was built around strategic planning that is linear and left-brained. It took me a long time to realize that the societal models are shifting. This requires that a different approach to planning be added to the collection of planning models. This approach must be both spiritual and strategic in nature.

I had to overcome one point of resistance. Some prognosticators of emerging models insisted on a tear down and build new approach. They suggested or at least implied that the era of strategic planning was over and that doing strategic planning was a bad thing for a congregation. I saw this new approach lived out in many congregations. These congregations shared something in common. They were already convinced that they did not want to do strategic planning, or that they could not do strategic planning, or that they were unable to stay focused on implementing any strategic plan they were a part of developing. These congregations suddenly had a reason to avoid planning because it was no longer the right thing to do.

Planning, at its best, is not a destination. It is a journey. It is a journey that is both spiritual and strategic. Thus, I call it a spiritual strategic journey. Such a journey is an ongoing movement rather than a static process. It focuses on building ownership and passion rather than documents and plans.

A spiritual strategic journey establishes a dynamic strategic framework with enough infrastructure and details to point people, a congregation, a denomination, or a parachurch organization in an effective direction. It frees a movement of people from its current location and empowers it to soar in the direction of a new location toward which God is pulling it.

A spiritual strategic journey is *spiritual* in that it assumes total reliance on God as individuals and as congregations. It assumes that unless the journey is of God, it is for nothing.

A spiritual strategic journey is *strategic* in that it focuses on those goals and actions that will make the most significant difference in a congregation's ability to serve in the midst of God's kingdom. It focuses on effective touch points.

A spiritual strategic journey is a *journey* in that it is ongoing. Philippians 3:12–16 talks about the journey of a Christian individual as being something that is never completed. Yet it is a journey into which we live at the level of maturity we have achieved today, knowing that we will achieve a higher or deeper level of maturity tomorrow. We never go back. We always press forward to God's high calling.

God may be calling your congregation to a very high calling that will cause you to break out of the box of past-to-present mediocrity. His high calling may give you freedom to see large numbers as success, but not as completion. His high calling may let you live into God's future rather than simply maintaining the gains of the past.

Too often business planning models are brought into congregations without translation. They cannot be used in congregational life because congregations are organisms that are living, breathing, moving, and constantly transitioning and changing. A spiritual strategic journey is a focus on how an organism functions rather than how an organization functions.

Congregations are also voluntary associations rather than hierarchical businesses. For example, in congregations, vision and direction cannot be imposed. Vision is not something you pitch to membership and they catch it. Business leaders can demand that their employee get the vision or leave their employ. The same is not true in a congregation. Congregations are more complicated and are dealing with core issues such as how eternity is approached.

Vision and direction is something congregational participants are caught by rather than something they catch. It captivates them. If they are not captivated by vision, it is unlikely they will support the journey of the congregation. In congregations the journey cannot be only strategic; it must also be spiritual. It must ultimately be based on the new thing God is doing in and through a congregation.

How Does Your Congregation Engage in a Spiritual Strategic Journey?

To understand the design of a spiritual strategic journey, you must start in the future. Start way far out on the pathways and passages of the journey. Yes, the distant unknown future, not the oppressive present, is the beginning point. You must start at the point in the future where you are maturing and soaring in your spiritual strategic journey. You must start by projecting a point at which you will experience the pull of God with ease and joy.

The desired end result of a spiritual strategic journey is that a congregation will develop a future story of its ministry into which it will seek to live. In projecting the future story of a congregation, empowering questions are important. Here are several such questions.

What, though seemingly impossible today, would transcend the current depth of our congregation's life and ministry and radically transform its ability to serve in the midst of God's kingdom? This would be a Gideon-type of experience. Only by the power of God could this happen in your congregation.

What is the future toward which God is pulling your congregation? From where you now stand, what does it look like? These questions take us into a Merlin factor experience.

What do you envision as God's full Kingdom potential for your congregation, and what is the future story of that potential for the next ten to twelve years? What will the ministry of your congregation be like on October 31, 2017, the 500th anniversary of Martin Luther nailing the 95 theses to the Wittenburg door? These are the spiritual strategic journey questions that seek to help us build the next steps on ministry based on a desire to reach our full Kingdom potential.

What Does the Full Kingdom Potential of Your Congregation Feel Like?

It feels like something your congregation owns for itself and not something that fulfills someone else's image for your congregation. It is when you have soared as a congregation in response to God's image for you, which pulls you forward. It is something that is felt or experienced, rather than claimed or measured.

It feels like something you will never reach because if you could, then it would not be your full potential. Your full Kingdom potential is always beyond your reach. It is always further up and further in.

In "The Chronicles of Narnia" volume *The Last Battle,* C. S. Lewis describes that potential which is further up and further in when he says, "This is the land I have been looking for all my life, though I never knew it until now."[2] He goes on to say that "the further up and the further in you go, the bigger everything gets. The inside is larger than the outside."[3]

He concludes the book with these words of great relevance to the ongoing nature of a congregation's Kingdom potential:

> And for us this is the end of all the stories, and we can most truly say that they all lived happily ever after. But for them it was only the beginning of the real story. All their life in this world and all their adventures in Narnia had only been the cover and title page: now at last they were beginning Chapter One of the Great Story which no one on earth has read: which goes on forever: in which every chapter is better than the one before.[4]

The full Kingdom potential of your congregation is in the process of being revealed to you as you travel toward it. From where you stand today, what does the full Kingdom potential of your congregation feel like? If you travel toward it, where you stand tomorrow will give you a different perspective on your potential.

You can best express the full Kingdom potential for your congregation in a dynamic narrative story that represents your current understanding of God's full Kingdom potential for your congregation. That narrative continues to evolve as your congregation lives into God's future. The closer you get to God's future, the further up and the further in it will appear to be. Your potential is always out in front of you. The longer you travel toward it, the more it exceeds what you could have conceived at the beginning or anywhere along the journey.

The future storytelling process is the subject of chapter 8. All the preceding chapters are a prelude to this creating experience. To the extent these prelude chapters imply a fixed process, here it is: My desire is that your congregation will develop the spiritual and strategic capacity to live into your current understanding of the story of God's ideal future for your congregation. This will be represented in a future narrative story you tell, live into daily, and update continually to keep it congruent with God's active leadership and with the new insights you gain along the spiritual strategic journey of your congregation.

Once your congregational story is crafted, living into your story becomes the focus on your congregational ministry. The details of living into your story are the subject of chapter 10.

COACHING INSIGHTS

■ Before today, on what has your congregation been focusing: church growth, church health, church faithfulness, church success, or church transformation? What has been satisfying for you about this focus? How has or has not this focus helped you achieve your full Kingdom potential?

■ What are your thoughts and feelings about how you can tell when a congregation is moving in the direction of its full Kingdom potential? What are the road signs along the way that help you know you are making progress? How is this measured? How can Kingdom progress best be measured in your congregation?

■ In what ways is your congregation seeking to push its way into the future? In what ways is your congregation aware of and responding to God's attempts to pull you forward into the future? What is the evidence of the Merlin factor in your congregation? Who are the visionaries who see the future, and what characterizes them?

- In the past, how has planning that is strategic in nature served your congregation well? How has it failed your congregation? What do you see as the promise of the approach being called a spiritual strategic journey?

- What, though seemingly impossible today, would transcend the current depth of your congregation's life and ministry and radically transform its ability to serve in the midst of God's kingdom?

- What is the future story of your congregation, inspired by God, into which you must live to approach the full Kingdom potential of your congregation?

PERSONAL REFLECTIONS

YOUR REFLECTIONS: What are your reflections on the material presented in this chapter?

_____

_____

_____

_____

YOUR ACTIONS: What actions do you need to take about your life, ministry, and/or congregation based on the material presented in this chapter?

_____

_____

_____

_____

YOUR ACCOUNTABILITY: How and by whom do you want to be held accountable for taking these actions?

_____

_____

_____

_____

CHAPTER TWO

Preparing Your Congregation for a Spiritual Strategic Journey

EXECUTIVE SUMMARY

The purpose of this chapter is to share the types of things congregations need to do to prepare for a spiritual strategic journey. The focus is on four elements of readiness: passion, spirituality, leadership, and strategy. The key thought concerns what it takes to be ready to transition and change in a manner that may achieve transformation. In addition, the five varieties of congregations are explained in relationship to the spiritual strategic journey. These five varieties of congregations are presiding, providing, preparing, pursuing, and perfecting.

I have been consulting and coaching with congregations for thirty years. After the first fifteen years of consulting with congregations, I became part of a learning community of consultants who sought to evaluate the effectiveness of the assessment and intervention that had been done with congregations from the mid-1970s forward. One of my ministry colleagues, Glenn Akins, had a phrase that fit our thoughts about the effectiveness of many consultations. He would say, "We ain't hurtin' 'em none."

The translation and application of Akins' phrase is that some of the congregations with which we worked were making significant, transformational progress. Some of the congregations with which we worked were making minor, transactional progress. Many congregations failed to make the hoped-for progress. Why? Over the next five to seven years I worked hard with my learning community to figure out the answers. Here are some of the answers that make the most sense to me.

Reasons Congregations Fail to Progress

Five reasons explain why even congregations with strategic plans fail to make progress toward God's potential for them.

First, often the senior pastor, staff ministers, and lay leadership were not personally prepared to lead the changes needed for the congregation to transform. They would intentionally or unintentionally undermine the transition and change process when it did not seem to head in a direction they wanted to or could lead it in.

Second, at times conflict arose in the middle of a strategic planning process, and the congregational leadership was not ready to deal with it. Conflict that is unhealthy will sidetrack a positive strategic planning process.

Third, resistance to transition and change was so strong in many congregations that although some leaders could conceive of effective strategies, they could not convince the majority of leadership to embrace the strategies.

Fourth, engaging congregations at levels of spiritual relationship with God and one another is a difficult task. Often a process could engage their heads, but engaging their hearts was more difficult.

Fifth, many times the impact of changes threatened the culture and cultural leaders in the congregation.

Each of these specific reasons could be summed up by the word *readiness*. Often congregations were not ready to engage in a transformational journey. Therefore, I began to investigate various approaches to readiness that could be applied to congregations.

One great business source that has numerous implications for congregations is *Leading Change* by John Kotter, which offers an eight-step linear process for change. In his early steps I found some clues to a readiness system for congregations.

Congregational Readiness for Transition and Change

The number one reason that transition and change efforts fail in congregations is that congregations do not engage in effective readiness activities before they launch a transition and change process.

External or interpersonal relationship factors too often drive congregational transition, change, and readiness activities.

External factors include a crisis in the context. These range from a natural disaster to a significant change in the demographic patterns such as a change in the socioeconomic or cultural patterns of the new residents moving into the area. A new denominational initiative or program may look inviting and become another reason to launch a transition and change process before readiness is achieved. Denominational leaders may exert pressure to participate without allowing the local congregation time to prepare and become spiritually ready.

Interpersonal relationship factors often jump start congregational transition and change processes. These factors include the coming of a new pastor, the leaving of the current pastor, or a major conflict in the congregation. Often a congregation is thrown into these situations without adequate preparation for transition and change.

Readiness may be achieved in two radically different ways. One is instant, and the other is incremental. The instant way is what I call *God's Triple D*–God does something *d*irect, *d*ramatic, and *d*ivine in the congregation. This usually creates instant readiness as a sense of renewal or revival sweeps through a congregation.

The incremental way is to carefully build a strong foundation for transition and change through four actions this chapter will explain:

1. Develop a sense of urgency for transition and change.
2. Create spiritual readiness.
3. Build leadership readiness.
4. Achieve strategic readiness.

We will look at each of these in turn.

Develop a Sense of Urgency for Congregational Transition and Change

Congregations that seek to engage in a transition and change process without first developing a strong sense of urgency are likely to fail in that effort. Without a strong sense of passion, congregations tend to be passive, to lack focus, and to grasp for fixes rather than solutions.

Urgent passion must support needed transitions and changes that may lead to transformation. Successful transition and change demands that strong, positive, passionate readiness concerning the future of the congregation exist among many persons within the congregation. This zealous sense of passion and urgency is derived from a positive feeling flavoring the future of the congregation. Such positive zeal must displace negative feelings.

Negative passion may lead to a future dysfunctional congregation with arrested development, rather than a transformed congregation reaching for its Kingdom potential. Godly passion must oppose or fight against any demon or negative factor in the congregation or in its context. Congregations must be passionate about the need for transition and change. Two things create such passion. Either people feel some great negative event will happen without transition and change, or the vision for a transformational future catches them.

Too often congregations are complacent and feel that *good enough is good enough.* This commitment to mediocrity dooms a large percent of congregations to a ministry of maintenance when they could participate in exciting mission. The pastor and other initiating leaders need to develop a clear understanding as to why the congregation needs transition and change. They must communicate this understanding to the congregation in a manner and with a message that inspires the congregation to be embraced by transition and change.

To develop a sense of urgency for transition and change, congregations must first determine the current level of urgency, figure out why the congregation may still be complacent about the need for transition and change, and then choose the appropriate methods for developing a sense of urgency.

DETERMINE THE CURRENT SENSE OF URGENCY FOR TRANSITION AND CHANGE

Creating a passion for congregational transition and change is a formidable task in a Christian congregation. The church of Jesus Christ is an organism that focuses on creating stability and assurance in response to an eternal Heavenly Father and to a Savior who is the same yesterday, today, and forever. The vast majority of people in the typical congregation do not perceive a need for transition and change. They are not ready to respond to a new generation of challenges they may be facing. They are seeking stability and acceptable predictability, not what could appear to be chaos and unacceptable unpredictability.

Complacency is generally high and has multiple sources in many congregations. Here are ten examples of the reasons or occasions for complacency:

1. The absence of a major crisis or a highly visible demon robs a church of motivation for change.

2. Apparent signs of success rob a church of motivation for change. Congregations generally do well at enabling the construction of beautiful buildings. With such a visible sign of success why should change be considered?

3. Low expectations rob a church of motivation for change. Members are comfortable with a congregation that meets their basic spiritual, fellowship, and cultural needs. Mediocrity is confused with excellence.

4. Limited perspective robs a church of motivation for change. Laypersons are rewarded for doing specific service jobs in the congregation and never look at the whole congregational system. They know their small group and their accountability areas, but do not see the direction forward or backward that the church is taking.

5. False measurements of success rob a church of motivation for change. Congregations measure success based on programs or budget achievement goals. Often the church is meeting these goals, at least in the eyes of leadership and the silent majority of supporters. Spiritual growth is not being measured.

6. Interpretation of statistics robs a church of motivation for change. It may surprise some people to know that often a few key leaders control the performance measurements in congregations. They put a spin on the figures that lead people to feel complacent about any perceived threats to the vitality of the congregation and thus about any need for change.

7. Rejecting criticism robs a church of motivation for change. Leaders treat people like lepers when they criticize the performance of the congregation. When the critics get frustrated and leave the congregation, no one goes after them. Leaders may even verbalize expressions of pleasure about their leaving.

8. Denial of reality robs a church of motivation for change. Many people simply deny that the congregation is not reaching its God-inspired potential. This is particularly true if they are already experiencing numerous life stresses and are codependent on the congregation as it currently exists.

9. False values rob a church of motivation for change. In more congregations than most people would like to admit, the pastor, staff, and key lay leaders value morale over mission. As such, they engage in what John Kotter of Harvard University calls happy talk. Such rhetoric is used to drown out what are called the voices of discontent.

10. Honoring revered leaders robs a church of motivation for change. Hardwired into the culture of many congregations that are more

than a generation old is the core value that maintaining the status quo in honor of the founders is a virtue. This founding fix is more powerful than many change agents perceive. It holds onto "traditions" rather than change to meet Kingdom potential.

METHODS FOR DEVELOPING A SENSE OF URGENCY

Secular models for creating urgency for transition and change have both ethical and unethical methodologies. Both are also seen in congregations. In the following suggestions, both are illustrated. Congregations will reveal their spiritual values, ethics, and approaches to transition and change by the methods they use to create urgency. In some cases, the methods chosen produce a healthy or functioning congregation, but others produce an unhealthy or dysfunctional congregation. As you read, decide which methods are most acceptable for your congregation.

First, create a crisis if one does not exist. Set up a demon that needs to be destroyed. Magnify a sin that needs to be eliminated. Exaggerate the scale of an evil to fight.

Second, allow the congregational facilities to get into disrepair. Reallocate a significant amount of budgeted funds for needed major repairs and renovations. Take away perks, privileges, and fringe benefits from the pastor and staff in response to the resulting short-term cash flow problems.

Third, cast a transformational vision that cannot be fulfilled with actions that represent "business as usual." Call for radical discipleship and commitment on the part of all core leaders and supporters.

Fourth, raise the level of accountability, and set measurable goals that require a new class of leadership actions. Help people to see how improvements in their areas of accountability can have a positive impact on the overall mission performance of the congregation.

Fifth, share the actual measurements of success, without the editing of spin-doctors, with a large percentage of the active members and attendees in the congregation. Point out the places where real time performance does not match the perceived image of success.

Sixth, set up exit interviews with people who leave the congregation to join other congregations in the same area, or otherwise join the ranks of the inactive. Share the results with appropriate leadership groups.

Seventh, use outside speakers, consultants, or congregational coaches to inject new information, knowledge, and wisdom into the congregational culture that will help the congregation to realize their potential.

Eighth, engage in more honest communication in the congregational fellowship about the reality of the congregation's present and future situation. Challenge the *happy talk* morale with some Kingdom-focused missional discussion.

Ninth, saturate the communication channels in the congregation with information on future opportunities and the inability of the congregation to address these opportunities without making significant transitions and changes.

Tenth, build a spiritual exploration movement within the congregation focused on individual, small group, and corporate prayer. This movement can focus on finding God's will for the congregation, spiritual awakening in the fellowship, or discovery of where God is at work in the congregation and its target communities.

Which of these methods for developing a sense of urgency are common to your congregation? Which ones are empowering your congregation, and which ones are controlling your congregation?

Create Spiritual Readiness for Congregational Transition and Change

Is God up to something transformational through your congregation? Is your congregation ready for this to happen? Then you need strong, positive spiritual readiness. This comes only through personal and congregational community spiritual processes. This spiritual readiness involves the full leadership community feeling that God is leading the congregation forward on an exciting spiritual strategic journey. Spiritual readiness will require the congregation to engage in an intentional spiritual emphasis over a period of time. You might choose *100 Days of Share and Prayer Triplets,* which we will discuss in chapter 7.

To create spiritual readiness, individuals and groups will have to engage in specific activities. These include dialogue, prayer, Bible study, and worship services focused on the future of the congregation. Congregational learning experiences must focus on inspiring encounters of dreaming and storytelling about the Kingdom potential of the congregation.

Congregational leaders and participants must feel that something new is happening in their community of faith and that it involves God's leadership. They do not have to understand all of the particulars, but they must be inspired by the possibility of a renewing spiritual strategic journey.

Readiness for transition and change in Christian faith-based organizations is different from readiness in non-faith-based organizations. Non-faith-based organizations feel no need to spend time creating spiritual readiness, whereas creating spiritual readiness is an essential first step for Christian faith-based organizations, including the local congregation.

A second difference is perhaps not so obvious. In congregations the flavor of spiritual readiness must be distinctively Christian. Some non-faith-based organizations pursue spirituality as a basis for their organization's values, but their spirituality may not necessarily be distinctively Christian in nature.

Third, in congregations the Christ-centered spiritual readiness must permeate all that happens. Spiritual readiness is not simply a launching pad for exploration. Spiritual readiness must be a continual part of the spiritual strategic journey. The congregation must constantly stand ready for God to reshape its theology, its history, it structures, and its culture.

How Can You Tell When a Congregation Is Spiritually Ready for the Journey Ahead?

Accurate measurement does not involve leaders. It involves the basic active membership, what we call *Quad A's*. Quad A's are the average number of active, attending adults present in worship in a congregation during a typical weekend of services. A congregation is spiritually ready when *21 percent of the Quad A's*, also known as the *People of Passion*, in a congregation have positive feelings that something new is happening in their faith community and that it involves God's leadership. The Quad A's do not have to understand all of the particulars, but they must be inspired by the possibility of a renewing spiritual strategic journey. You may follow many paths to create spiritual readiness in your congregation. It is spiritually myopic to suggest that there is one right way to create spiritual readiness. Still, each path will include the actions essential for spiritual readiness to occur in your congregation. We have isolated at least four essential actions:[1]

1. spiritual preparation of the pastor and other initiating leadership
2. rediscovery of the theology, history, and culture of the congregation
3. exploration concerning the Kingdom potential of the congregation
4. congregational involvement in a spiritual discovery and exploration process that creates a feeling that God is in the process of doing a new thing in their midst.

We will look at each of these in turn.

Spiritual Preparation of the Pastor and Other Initiating Leaders

The pastor and other initiating leadership of the congregation must spend quality time building spiritual community in preparation for leading the congregation in creating spiritual readiness. The initiating leadership is the 21 percent leadership community, also known as the *People of Position*, who must be united and passionate about the future of the congregation for truly transformational transition and change to occur. Without a passionately committed group of such size spiritually united around a future toward which God is drawing the congregation, attempts at a spiritual strategic journey will fail, or be a fix rather than a solution.

Obviously, the pastor's role in initiating the spiritual preparation process is extremely important. The pastor may need some personal time of preparation. This can occur through focused learning experiences, a peer learning group, a personal spiritual retreat, sessions with a spiritual coach, and other similar ways.

In a postmodern world, leadership is best expressed in community rather than through the individual effort. As soon as possible, the pastor must gather this first stage leadership community together and begin walking them through a spiritual pilgrimage until they catch the vision of God at work in their church's journey.

Rediscovery of the Theology, History, and Culture of the Congregation

For many people spiritual readiness will emanate from study and reflection on the theology, history, and culture of the congregation. This will generally be reflected in the mission, purpose, and core values of the congregation.

Congregations need to build a knowledge base together. Such learning experiences allow them to rethink or rediscover the overarching mission of New Testament congregations. Having reflected on the mission of congregations in general, they need to renew their understanding of the specific purpose for which this congregation was founded. They can do this by clarifying the congregation's founding story for themselves.

Finally, they need to test the congregation's culture, what has endured from the past to the present. They do this by examining the congregation's enduring core values. They can then determine if the current practice and values are consistent with the congregation's historical understanding of mission and purpose.

Exploration Concerning the Kingdom Potential of the Congregation

Spiritual readiness does not involve simply a willingness to engage in transition and change activities. It also involves the willingness to make a transformational difference in how the congregation serves in the midst of God's kingdom.

Spiritual readiness thus involves several things:

1. a willingness to let God transform the entire faith community and to let God draw the congregation toward a future that God is unfolding before the congregation
2. an understanding of the unique purpose of the congregation and what form the congregation might take if it reaches its Kingdom potential
3. an understanding of the people the congregation is best gifted, skilled, and willing to nurture in their faith journey
4. a radical commitment to discipleship that embraces the idea that God might even do something that is revolutionary through the congregation

Therefore, as a part of spiritual readiness the pastor and the various stages of leadership communities need to engage in some preliminary exploration concerning the Kingdom potential of the congregation. This can happen at a spiritual retreat, through brainstorming sessions, or by trying to tell the story of the future of the congregation in words, concepts, and frameworks that are genuine, meaningful, and exciting.

Involvement of the Congregation in a Spiritual Discovery and Exploration Process

The entire congregation does not have to be as spiritually passionate about the transition and change that can lead to transformation as are the various stages of leadership communities. However, it is important and even necessary to engage the active congregation in exercises of spiritual discovery and exploration.

These can be experiences in which everyone who desires to can participate. One example would include a series of worship services that focus on the spiritual strategic journey of the congregation and what the congregation might look like if it reaches it full Kingdom potential.

Another option would be a congregational learning experience with an outside leader that focuses on helping the congregation to think about itself now and in the future, and what its spiritual strategic journey might be if it reaches its Kingdom potential.

A third possibility is a series of directed Bible studies that might be used in Christian education or disciple-making experiences such as Sunday school or adult Bible study classes, small groups, or even in cell groups. Such Bible studies could look at the early church through frameworks provided by the Acts of the Apostles.

Prayer is an extremely important component for building a common sense of spiritual strategic passion for transition and change. The essence of this approach is the formation of share and prayer triplets. In these groups of three, people agree to meet ten times over 100 days for 100 minutes each time. In these meetings they share about their personal spiritual journeys and their journeys in relationship to the congregation, and talk and pray about the future of their personal and congregational journeys. The share and prayer triplets are the focus of chapter 7.

Build Leadership Readiness for Congregational Transition and Change

Strong positive leadership must be willing to exert empowering leadership. To achieve transformation and reach full Kingdom potential, church leadership must empower the congregation to make the required transitions and changes. Strong positive leadership is composed of *People of Pastoral Leadership, People of Passion, People of Position,* and *People of Participation.* These groups within a congregation will be discussed in-depth in chapter 3.

The *People of Passion* involve the pastor, any ministerial staff, and key lay leaders up to 7 percent of the *Quad A's* who have strong, positive, spiritual passion about the future of the congregation. In a small congregation, this can be three people. In a congregation of 1000 in attendance, this can be almost fifty people.

These *People of Passion* must understand in detail the transitions and changes the congregation should address and be passionately committed to them. They must be highly knowledgeable about, motivated by, and accepting of the Kingdom potential of the congregation. Most importantly, they must be captivated by the vision of the future toward which God is pulling the congregation.

The *People of Position* are 21 percent of the *Quad A's* who are knowledgeable of the transitions and changes that might occur and are included in the process of readiness through learning experiences. They feel that a future that involves transition and change is one filled with more significant and sacrificial ministry than would be possible without a new spiritual strategic journey.

They are willing to provide some tactical leadership to fulfill the journey through the waves of transition and change because they feel ownership of the future vision of the congregation. They can articulate the vision in their own words and are willing to align their Christian service in a manner that seeks to fulfill that vision.

The *People of Participation* are up to 63 percent of the *Quad A's*, and must *not* be opposed to transition and change. They do not necessarily have to embrace the specifics of the spiritual strategic journey, but they must have confidence in the people who are the leaders and workers on the journey.

They must understand why transition and change are necessary, and also understand some of the benefits for their personal spiritual walk, as well as the mission fulfillment of their congregation.

Achieve Strategic Readiness for Congregational Transition and Change

A core of initiating leadership must be fully aware of the types of strategies and tactics needed to make the necessary transitions and changes leading to transformation and to reaching the full Kingdom potential of the congregation. Leadership participates in learning experiences that help them develop the capacity to guide each step of the spiritual strategic journey with full knowledge of the necessary steps.

Achieving strategic readiness involves at least two actions by the *People of Position.* First, the *People of Position* must have full understanding and ownership of the task and of the relationship sides of the transition and change process. They must have engaged in mutual learning experiences in which they have created a sense of connectedness with one another as a leadership group of their faith community. They must be able to articulate a common vision, a challenging strategy, and be able to tell a consistent story of the future they feel that God is bringing forth in their midst.

Second, they must be committed to creating time and energy to empower the congregation to experience new relationships and tasks. They do this by diminishing the controlling aspects of the congregation's management systems. They must begin a movement from management to ministry. Only then can the first forward steps of transition and change take place. Achieving strategic readiness involves the deepest, most passionate, and most knowledgeable actions.

Understanding the Relationships and Tasks of Achieving Strategic Readiness

To achieve strategic readiness the *People of Passion* must have full understanding and ownership of the relationship and task sides of the transition and change process. They need to learn and/or do the following:

1. They must have engaged in mutual learning experiences in which they have developed an understanding of the transition and change process in congregations. Such a learning experience must help them understand readiness for transition and change in congregations, the length of time transition and change may take, and the roles they must play as an initiating leadership community.

2. They must feel a sense of urgency for transition and change, be spiritually ready, have skills as leaders, and have a long-term commitment to the congregation. A long-term commitment of five to seven years is essential for lay and clergy leadership to be present throughout the transition and change process. One huge factor that negatively impacts a transition and change process is the leaving of crucial leaders in the midst of the process. Certainly, other skilled leaders can take their places. The issue is that these new skilled leaders may not have been involved in the experiences of the journey to this point and thus have the necessary experience base to continue the journey with meaning and passion.

3. They must have engaged in mutual learning experiences in which they have created a sense of connectedness with one another as a leadership group within their faith community. This connectedness must symbolize and energize a multi-year journey.

4. They must be able to articulate a common vision, explain a challenging strategy, and tell a consistent tale of the future they feel that God is bringing forth in their midst. The common vision must be an evaluation filter used to consider the value of various actions. Actions that do not help the congregation fulfill their vision should be evaluated as to whether they need to be done. Often they should because they contribute to the basic foundation of congregational life. However, they should not be seen as high priorities, only as basic services.

5. They must work with the *People of Position* to develop a road map for the congregation's spiritual strategic journey. This road map must be appropriately challenging and must help the congregation fulfill its vision.

In some congregations, this road map will involve strategies that are consistent with the past practices of the congregation. This fits in situations in which a mild rate and pace of transition and change is sufficient to bring about the necessary transformation. Generally, this is appropriate in congregations that are growing or developing both qualitatively and quantitatively.

In other congregations, the road map will involve strategies that are discontinuous in regard with the past practices of the congregation. This fits in situations in which a significant rate and pace of transition and change are needed to bring about the necessary transformation. Generally, this is the case in congregations that are aging and find themselves in decline.

In a third group of congregations, this road map will involve strategies that are radical in regard to past practices of the congregation. This fits in situations in which congregations must make a dramatic change in their direction or they may not exist with vitality for much longer. *Vitality* is the key word. It does not mean that death of the congregation is close, but only that its vitality and ability to be recaptured by vision is threatened.

CREATING THE TIME AND ENERGY FOR ACHIEVING STRATEGIC READINESS

Leadership must be committed to creating time and energy for new relationships and tasks to happen in the congregation by diminishing the controlling aspects of the congregation's management systems.

First, as a part of readiness they must enable themselves and the congregation to begin moving from management to ministry. Only then can the first forward steps of transition and change take place. Often congregations are stuck in old patterns. Particularly if they are on the aging side of their life cycle, management systems may dominate the leadership's time and energy.

In many congregations, management systems control the congregation by absorbing the financial resources, the leadership resources, the time resources, and the spiritual energy of the lay leaders. Management systems can be so controlling because the congregation has grown accustomed to see each action as necessary for the survival of the congregation.

Often the congregation has no vision. This makes the managers afraid to give up control because they feel the congregation will fail if things are not done right. Also, over the years managers fall into patterns of thought that the management work is *the work* of the congregation.

Second, the *People of Passion*, supported by the *People of Position*, must determine ways to diminish the controlling aspects of management to free new time and energy for new actions. The *People of Position* need to discuss all that the congregation does. Each thing must be evaluated in terms of whether it needs to continue or be stopped.

Then they need to consider the new actions that need to be started so the congregation can move in new directions.

COACHING BREAK

✔ Gaze out the window for a minute. Ponder the situation of your congregation. What images come to mind?

✔ What are the implications of the need for a congregation to have readiness for transition and change? Was your congregation truly ready for transition and change the last time you tried to lead them through some type of renewal or transformation activity? Could that be why it did not achieve the renewal or transformation for which you had hoped? What would you do differently this time?

In What Performance Category Is Your Congregation?

The performance categories of congregations offer a way of evaluating congregational readiness for transition and change that may lead to full Kingdom potential. Recently I needed some new tires for my car. I searched online to check out the performance reviews for various tires. I was glad to see such categories as dry traction, wet traction, hydroresistance, snow traction, cornering stability, steering response, and–the all-important–ride comfort. The primary site I visited provided results of online surveys for more than 500 different tires.

Tires were categorized by the type of vehicle they were engineered for, their size, the composition of their materials, the tread style and wear patterns, their mileage rating, their temperature rating, and their price. These performance categories also indicated if they were primarily for highway performance, around town and commuting performance, off-road performance, or high-speed performance.

Performance category is a phrase that I apply to congregations. For thirty years, I have used various ways to categorize congregations to give me a perspective from which to think about them. In the current decade performance categories center on the spiritual and strategic journey of congregations. I use these categories to benchmark congregations against certain Kingdom standards of performance.

Currently I am working on a system with five dimensions of performance that result in five varieties or categories of congregations.

They are *Perfecting Congregations, Pursuing Congregations, Preparing Congregations, Providing Congregations,* and *Presiding Congregations.*

PERFECTING CONGREGATIONS

Perfecting Congregations are those congregations who are sustaining a spiritual strategic journey. They typically engage in great, excellent, sustainable ministry. Key concepts for them are perfecting their journey, sustaining excellence, and connecting with peer learning communities. The time focus of these congregations is almost exclusively the future. Their goal is to keep on reaching their full Kingdom potential.

These congregations typically score 80 to 100 on the *Congregational Issues for Generative Dialogue* initial assessment to be introduced in chapter 4 and also found at *www.SSJTutorial.org.* They are seeking to reach their unique full Kingdom potential. This category may include some new congregations fewer than seven years old.

PURSUING CONGREGATIONS

Pursuing Congregations are those congregations traveling along a spiritual strategic journey. These congregations are engaging in good ministry and striving for great ministry. Key concepts for these congregations are pursuing vital ministry, strategic capacity development, and coaching as a preferred style of learning and leadership. The time focus of these congregations is primarily the future, but they will also focus their passion on some elements of present ministry. Their goal is to reach a place at which they engage in great, sustainable ministry.

These congregations typically score 55 to 80 on the *Congregational Issues for Generative Dialogue* initial assessment. They are seeking to position themselves to be able to reach their full Kingdom potential. Generally, these congregations are either seven to twenty years old, or they are more than thirty years old and seeking to develop forward to a new dimension of their life as a congregation.

PREPARING CONGREGATIONS

Preparing Congregations are those congregations that are engaging in readiness activities for a spiritual strategic journey. They practice acceptable ministry and are preparing for better ministry. Key concepts for these congregations are preparing for a journey, spiritual preparation that builds new relationships with God and with one another, and expert consultation for their journey. The time focus of these congregations is the recent past to the present. Their goal is to be able to activate a spiritual strategic journey that pursues vital ministry.

These congregations typically score 30 to 55 on the *Congregational Issues for Generative Dialogue* initial assessment. Often these congregations are thirty-five or more years old.

PROVIDING CONGREGATIONS

Providing Congregations are those congregations who are satisfied with their current journey. They engage in maintenance, yet faithful, ministry. They do not feel an urgency to seek a more meaningful or effective ministry. Key concepts for them are providing faithful Christian ministry, satisfaction with ministry that helps people be warmed and filled, and the use of materials prepared by knowledgeable clinicians.

The time focus of these congregations is the reliable past of the congregation, which they may seek to emulate through appreciative inquiry. Their goal is to be found faithful. Their favorite hymns are *May Those Who Come Behind Us Find Us Faithful* and *I Am Satisfied.*

These congregations typically score 20 to 30 on the *Congregational Issues for Generative Dialogue* initial assessment, It is not unusual for many of these congregations to be at least fifty years old.

PRESIDING CONGREGATIONS

Presiding Congregations are surviving without a journey. They engage in cultural congregational practices characteristic of nominal or casual Christian ministry. They are unwilling to consider ministry that is more meaningful or effective. Key concepts for these congregations are preserving the past, surviving until all key leadership persons die, and geriatric chaplaincy. The time focus of these congregations worships the past. The goal of these congregations is survival, one year at a time.

These congregations typically score less than 20 on the *Congregational Issues for Generative Dialogue* initial assessment. These are preaching stations, chaplaincy outposts, cultural enclaves, or faithful family fellowships. Congregations may reach this performance category sometime between the sixtieth anniversary and eightieth anniversary. It is hard for these congregations to die, much less to kill them.

One last question: If congregations were cars, what tires would you want to install on them? Perfecting, pursuing, preparing, providing, or presiding?

COACHING INSIGHTS

■ Probably up to 60 percent of all congregations are not sufficiently ready for a spiritual strategic journey. How ready is your congregation for such a journey? Is there urgent readiness, spiritual readiness, leadership readiness, and strategic readiness?

■ What are several strong, positive characteristics of your readiness? What are some areas of challenge for your readiness? What would you suggest that your congregation do next to be ready for a spiritual strategic journey?

■ Congregations with a negative urgency for transition, change, and transformation are highly susceptible to being dysfunctional and unhealthy. Does your congregation move off of a positive or negative motivation for transition, change, and transformation? If negative, what can be done to modulate to a positive position?

■ In what performance category is your congregation? What does this say about the readiness of your congregation for transition, change, and transformation? What is the difference between the personal performance category of your pastor, your congregational leadership, and the congregation as a whole? What are the implications of this for the future of your congregation?

PERSONAL REFLECTIONS

YOUR REFLECTIONS: What are your reflections on the material presented in this chapter?

_____

_____

_____

_____

_____

YOUR ACTIONS: What actions do you need to take about your life, ministry, and/or congregation based on the material presented in this chapter?

_____

_____

_____

_____

_____

YOUR ACCOUNTABILITY: How and by whom do you want to be held accountable for taking these actions?

_____

_____

_____

_____

_____

CHAPTER THREE

Navigating the Spiritual Strategic Journey of Your Congregation

EXECUTIVE SUMMARY

The purpose of this chapter is to share the people groups and relationships that must be cultivated to provide the steering or navigation for a spiritual strategic journey. The concentric circles of people groups are *People of Pastoral Leadership, People of Passion, People of Position, People of Participation, People of Passivity.* Other related circles are *People of Perpetual Care* and *People of Potential.*

The key learning is around the first three of these people groups, who form the *Enduring Visionary Leadership Community.* They provide the steering or navigation for a spiritual strategic journey.

Navigating the spiritual strategic journey of your congregation is all about people and their relationship with God, with one another, and with the context in which they serve. That's right. It is not about the things we change! It's about the people who transition in response to God's leading of individuals, groups, and the congregation. It requires a transition–then change–approach, rather than a change–then transition–approach.

41

That is a hard lesson for many of us to learn, particularly those of us who, like myself, begin our thought processes as left-brain thinkers. In my younger life I was a true believer, a cause-oriented person who believed that my perspective and ideologies surrounding change were so right and important that regardless of the relationships with the people being impacted, the cause had to break through and win.

Short-term, this can work. People, groups, congregations, and denominations are often glad to have an idea presented to them that looks as if it will work. Many great ideas do work, as long as the person pushing the idea continues to push the people, and the people receiving the idea determine to embrace the idea-pusher rather than resist.

Too often the change then transition approach is a fix rather than a solution. In the short-term great things may happen with a push approach that is focused on the person or position of the leader, the expertise of the consultant, or the success of a particular program, project, or process.

In the long-term, when the leader leaves or loses effectiveness, when the consultant is finished, or when the program, project, or process is over, the congregation may either return to the patterns of the past or wonder what's next. This pattern can be seen in many congregations. They return to old patterns when a strong-willed pastor leaves. A congregation does not hardwire the patterns and practices a consultant recommends and so returns to old patterns when the consultant is no longer present to push them. They see satisfying the requirements of a program, project, or process as the goal rather than the intended changed behavior or outcomes being the goal.

Who Are the People Who Attend Your Congregation?

Focusing on people and transition rather than things and change makes it necessary to identify the types of categories of people present within your congregation. The purpose of using a typology of people is not to reduce your understanding of people to types or categories, but to have some handles for initiating a transition and change journey.

Another way to say this is that as you look at the crowd of people who make up your congregation, how do you know where to begin, and why you are beginning at this point? In either case, you have to decide what entry point is most meaningful to you.

So, what types of people attend your congregation? How do you categorize them? Are they primarily young, middle-aged, senior adult, or a balance of various age generations? Are they wealthy, poor, middle-class, or spread throughout various socioeconomic levels? Are they African Americans, Anglo Americans, Asian Americans,

Hispanic Americans, Native Americans, or are you a multiethnic, multicultural congregation?

What about the Following Categories?

Are they new Christians? lifelong Christians and church members? church members from another church of your denomination? church members from another Protestant or Catholic tradition? from a Jewish tradition? from an Islamic tradition? Or do you have a blend of these backgrounds? Are they spiritually mature, spiritually searching, spiritually growing, or spiritually indifferent? Are they natural congregational leaders, natural followers, people desiring basic leadership development, or people oblivious to any need to contribute to the leadership base of your congregation?

How do the people who attend your congregation measure up in terms of their connectedness with the congregation? Are they periodic attendees; regular attendees who are connected with some program and relationship groups in your congregation; members of the congregation who have participation in programs, relationships, and leadership roles; or core members of the congregation who provide significant leadership and tithe their gross income through the congregation?

What about Their Thinking or Processing Style?

First, are they people who approach situations with character, and focus on values, visions, and ideals? Do they tell stories that focus on meaning and significance? Do they tend to embrace the Gospel of Luke?

Second, are they people who approach situations with a desire for connectedness, and focus on experiences, relationships, and the rush and thrill of spiritual life? Do they want to experience the real Jesus in each person? Do they tend to embrace the Gospel of Mark?

Third, are they people who approach situations with competence, and focus on strategies, systems, and structures? Do they work hard on well-thought-out programs, ministries, and activities of change? Do they tend to embrace the Gospel of John?

Fourth, are they people who approach situations with a desire to conform to the rules, and focus on boundaries, guidelines, and correctness? Do they desire to be sure that constitution and bylaws requirements are met, correct procedures are followed, and budgets are met? Do they tend to embrace the Gospel of Matthew?

Which of these categories are most beneficial to understanding a congregation? Perhaps a prior question should be, How do you define *beneficial?* How about if we define it according to the contributions people make to the core spiritual strategic journey of the congregation that helps the congregation journey toward their full Kingdom potential?

With that understanding of beneficial, I would suggest the following seven categories of people in a congregation. They are *People of Pastoral Leadership, People of Passion, People of Position, People of Participation, People of Passivity, People of Perpetual Care,* and *People of Potential.* The first five form concentric circles moving outward from the center or core, represented by the first category, the *People of Pastoral Leadership.* The number of people in each of these circles includes or is a cumulative total of the circles within it. The *People of Perpetual Care* and the *People of Potential* are specialty circles. See below for a diagram of the concentric circles of people.

Concentric Circles of People Groups in a Congregation

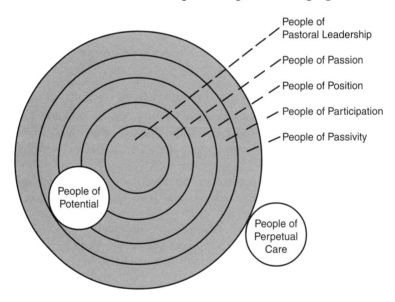

PEOPLE OF PASTORAL LEADERSHIP

The *People of Pastoral Leadership* are the senior pastor, other ordained clergy, and primary program staff who form the pastoral leadership community of your congregation. They are the initiating leaders who comprise the core circle of leadership. They have the primary responsibility to cast God's vision for the congregation and to focus on its fulfillment. How they do their casting and focusing will be an issue of significant concern throughout this book.

The *People of Pastoral Leadership* represent approximately 1 percent of the average number of active attending adults. Since the average North American congregation, according to multiple denominational research projects, has no more than 70 to 85 people in average weekly worship attendance, this typically is only the pastor of the congregation. In a mega congregation of 1,000 or more in average weekly worship attendance, of which 700 or more would be adults, this could easily be six to eight people who function in a pastoral, ministerial, ordained, or primary program leadership role.

Their contributions to the core spiritual journey of the congregation include, (1) a priestly role that focuses on the triune God and each person's spiritual encounters, growth, and ongoing discernment, (2) a prophetic role that calls the congregation to mission and movement, and (3) an initiating leadership role that fuels this movement within the congregation and throughout the congregation's context through unceasingly casting vision.

The *People of Pastoral Leadership* form the center or core circle of the congregation, not from a controlling perspective, but from an initiation perspective. They are to provide initiating leadership for the spiritual strategic journey of the congregation. Success for their initiating leadership begins with their ability to empower the next two categories of people to join them in forming an *Enduring Visionary Leadership Community* for the congregation.

PEOPLE OF PASSION

The *People of Passion* are a minimum of 7 percent of the average number of active attending adults or *Quad A's* in your congregation.[1] This circle includes the *People of Pastoral Leadership* circle, as each succeeding circle is cumulative and includes the circles closer to the center. This means that this circle represents the one percent *People of Pastoral Leadership*, plus an additional 6 percent who are the *People of Passion.*

This additional 6 percent have an obvious and contagious positive, spiritual passion about the future of the congregation. Their passion is obvious to others in the congregation, and they are respected for their passion and willingness to act on their convictions out of a sincere devotion to God and to the congregation.

They are the inspirational leadership of the spiritual strategic journey of your congregation. As such, they have no boundaries around their concept of the transformational work of God in individuals and in the entire congregational community. They long for the congregation to pursue and perfect their full Kingdom potential. They think and act not inside a box, but outside, if not beyond, the box.

They contribute greatly to the core spiritual journey of the congregation. They come alongside the *People of Pastoral Leadership* in casting vision. They express deep passion for the work of God within the congregation and its context. They embody urgency and deep commitment to the spiritual work of the congregation in the context God has placed them. In addition, they have a critical role in nurturing *People of Position* in the congregation to be captivated by God's vision for the congregation.

In a smaller membership congregation of no more than 80 to 85 in average weekly worship attendance, the *People of Passion* may be no more than four to six people. In a congregation of 1000 or more in average weekly worship attendance, the *People of Passion* will be at least 70 people.

PEOPLE OF POSITION

The *People of Position* are a minimum of 21 percent of the average number of active attending adults or *Quad A's* in your congregation.[2] This circle includes the 1 percent *People of Pastoral Leadership*, plus the 6 percent *People of Passion*, and another 14 percent, or a tripling of the size of the previous circle of influence.

In a smaller membership congregation the *People of Position* represent no more than 12 to 18 people. This number of people may be too small to deal with the issues needing to be addressed in a spiritual strategic journey. Thus, the numerology of transition and change may work against smaller membership congregations. Mega congregations may have at least 150 people in this category. This number begins to be so large that it may appear to be unmanageable. These size issues for the *People of Position* will be dealt with later.

People of Position hold one or more formal and informal leadership positions in the life of the congregation. They are often visible leaders in the congregation and typically have been members of the congregation longer than the average member. They are generally stakeholders in the congregation and feel a deep sense of ownership, accountability, and responsibility for the past and present of the congregation. It is somewhat difficult for them to project the values of the past and present into the future. The *People of Passion* can be effective in influencing the openness of *People of Position* to transition and change, but doing so is an art rather than a science.

The *People of Passion* and the *People of Position* are not mutually exclusive categories, in that people with formal and informal positions in the life of the congregation may also have great passion for the past, present, and future of the congregation. Many people with formal and informal positions in your congregation may already have been covered by the *People of Passion* category because they possess inner passion that is equipped to embrace the future of the congregation.

Enduring Visionary Leadership Community

Let's pause and look at the first three people groups–the *People of Pastoral Leadership, Passion,* and *Position*–and absorb the significance of their collective influence. The three together form the *Enduring Visionary Leadership Community* for the spiritual strategic journey of your congregation.[3] They function as the guiding coalition for the emerging future of your congregation. They are called on to work in a collaborative manner that will be highlighted in chapter 6.

If the *Enduring Visionary Leadership Community* becomes organized around God's emerging future for your congregation, your congregation will likely travel effectively in that direction. They clearly represent the necessary leadership of the congregation. It does not take a majority of your active congregation. It only requires the right 21 percent.

Just any collection of 21 percent is not specific enough. It must be the people who are perceived to be the *People of Pastoral Leadership, Passion,* and *Position.* In the popular image of getting the wrong people off the bus and the right people on the bus, the emphasis should be on the positive side of inviting the right people to be captivated by an exhilarating journey on the bus that is headed in the direction of the full Kingdom potential of your congregation.

Does this mean that with the right people serving as the *Enduring Visionary Leadership Community* no one will oppose the new direction of the congregation? No, opposition to the spiritual strategic journey may arise, but it is unlikely to derail the journey.

The *Enduring Visionary Leadership Community* contributes important elements to the core spiritual journey of the congregation. They provide empowerment, influence, and resources for the fulfillment of the congregation's spiritual strategic journey. Their specific contributions are to manage the resources of the congregation–involving people, finances, facilities, and the governance systems–in such a way that visionary leadership is empowered to help the congregation soar with its gifts, strengths, and preferences.

Minimum and Maximum Sizes for the Enduring Visionary Leadership Community

The percentages for the various categories of people presented thus far apply best to a certain size category of congregation. Probably a congregation of around 135 in weekly worship attendance is the typical size congregation for whom these numbers begin to fit best. They probably apply to congregations of up to 600 to 750 in average weekly worship attendance. But what about congregations that are larger, and the vast number, perhaps two-thirds of all North American congregations, who have less than 135 in weekly attendance?

Let's look at three different size congregations, beginning with the congregation with 135 in average weekly worship attendance. In this size congregation, and with a good age group balance, probably around 100 of the attendees are adults and 35 are preschoolers, children, or teenagers.

People of Pastoral Leadership make up 1 percent of the *Quad A's*, which is in this case one senior pastor. The *People of Passion* are 7 percent, or seven people. Twenty-one percent or 21 people compose the *People of Position.* These are the minimum numbers needed for a healthy congregation to have the basic leadership groups for a spiritual strategic journey. Again, these numbers and percentages will generally work for congregations with up to 600 to 750 in weekly attendance.

Smaller membership congregations with less than 135 in weekly attendance may achieve the percentages necessary to meet the requirements for the leadership categories, but they do not have the critical mass of leaders to handle the complexity of a spiritual strategic journey without modifications. Newer congregations that are growing through various size stages represent the one exception to this rule. They may have a current attendance of less than 135, but that is temporary. Thus they can handle a spiritual strategic journey with less than the minimum numbers.

Older congregations that were once larger than 135 in average attendance have difficulty handling the complexity of their culture and organizational structure without meeting the minimum numbers for the categories of people. Coaching a significant number of these congregations has shown that they always struggle with having the broad base of passion and the leadership capacity to turnaround or transform their situation. Unfortunately, struggle is very predictable in many congregations.

What about congregations larger than 600 to 750 in average attendance? For them the size categories begin to make a shift, and a new category emerges between the *People of Pastoral Leadership* and the *People of Passion.* This is a circle or category of people known as the *Discernment Community.* Typically this is three percent of the *Quad A's* who are made up of *People of Passion* and *People of Position.* They join the pastoral leadership in discovering the transition passages and change pathways for the spiritual strategic journey of the congregation.

For example, in a congregation of 1350 in average attendance, around 1000 would be *Quad A's.* Of this number 200 to 225 would be *People of Position,* 70 to 75 *People of Passion,* and ten people are *People of Pastoral Leadership.* The *Discernment Community* would be around 30 people including the *People of Pastoral Leadership.*

COACHING BREAK

✔ Gaze out the window for a minute. Ponder the situation of your congregation. What images come to mind?

✔ The *People of Pastoral Leadership,* the *People of Passion,* and the *People of Position* make up the leadership of your congregation. How do you feel about the strength and character of this *Enduring Visionary Leadership Community*? Do they have what if takes to move your congregation forward in response to God's leadership?

PEOPLE OF PARTICIPATION

The *People of Participation* are the next 42 percent of the average number of active, attending adults or *Quad A's.* These additional people represent the followership of the congregation who are aligned with the leadership. Frequently they are able to identify multiple people among the *People of Position* whom they trust to be providing positive, spiritual leadership for the congregation.

They desire to be part of a congregation that provides spiritual meaning and social stability. They look to leaders of the congregation to provide inspiration and programs, ministries, and activities that help them achieve this. Often they feel a sense of passionate urgency about the spiritual strategic journey of the congregation, and mild spiritual engagement, but cannot be counted on to provide leadership or to fully understand the necessity for the full spiritual strategic process.

In the core spiritual journey of the congregation the *People of Participation* are the willing workers. They respond to the call to mission, to be the people of salt and light in the congregation's context, and to be the people who ask for leadership to help them figure out how to continually grow in the grace and knowledge of God. In making these contributions they are steady and committed. They are generally positive and fulfilled as long as the leaders with whom they identify are positive and fulfilled in their involvement with the congregation.

PEOPLE OF PASSIVITY

The *People of Passivity* or *Pew Potatoes* are the remainder of the people in the average number in attendance in the congregation. These people attend less frequently than the average leader or follower, give less money, and are more likely to be involved primarily or only in corporate worship in the congregation.

Their current spiritual condition borders on being passive or casual. At one or more times in their lives they may have been actively involved and in significant leadership positions in one or more congregations. They are actually at a stage of life where they are making very little contribution to the core spiritual journey of the congregation. At the same time, they are people of worth and value created in the image of God to live and to love.

They have no proactive role in the spiritual strategic journey of the congregation. They are not a factor that must be considered. They will primarily hang around the outskirts of the congregation, not really aware of the particulars of the journey of their congregation. As long as the worship services and any other aspects of the congregation in which they participate are going reasonably well, they are satisfied.

PEOPLE OF PERPETUAL CARE

The *People of Perpetual Care* are the people whose names are on the role of the congregation but who do not actively participate in the congregation. Their attendance is noticed around Christmas and Easter, at weddings and funerals, and on special occasions in their lives or in the life of the church. You may also see them when out-of-town family members who are more active in their church are in town visiting.

People of Perpetual Care tend not to hold any church-elected leadership positions, give little or no money to the church, and do not typically make their presence known in the business affairs of the congregation except in the most severe crisis situations. But they want all the rites and pastoral presence at baptisms, weddings, funerals, and in times of life-threatening illness.

Rather than contributing to the core spiritual journey of the congregation, they tend to drain energy from the congregation. Their unanticipated requests for spiritual services often come at inconvenient times, with a sense of deep urgency, and a guilt motivation focused on the *People of Pastoral Leadership.* They expect *People of Pastoral Leadership* to provide them with what they want, when they want it. In the midst of these occasions are often great opportunities for the voice of God to be heard and the presence of God to be felt.

PEOPLE OF POTENTIAL

A *wild card* group of people in a congregation is the *People of Potential.* They do not represent a concentric circle, but are a swarming of people found among the *People of Participation, People of Position,* and *People of Passion.* They are people who have a great potential to contribute to the core leadership of the congregation, but they have not figured out how to connect, where to land, or why they ought to become more involved.

They are searchers. They are searching for place and meaning. Often their swarming is invisible or unseen by the *Enduring Visionary Leadership Community.* Perhaps their ability to practice faithfulness to their spiritual journey within the fellowship of your congregation has been discounted or marginalized.

The *Enduring Visionary Leadership Community* should watch for subtle changes in the behavior of these people, for such changes represent an open door of transition. These subtle changes can include an increase in attendance, an increase in financial support for the congregation and its ministry, and the asking of questions about the future of the congregation and how they can get involved.

Just as for years church consultants and coaches have talked about the subtle signs people show when they are becoming inactive or getting ready to drop out or leave a congregation, there are also signs that people are getting ready to get more involved in the congregation. While they are making little or no current contributions to the core spiritual journey of the congregation, often these people represent candidates for the next round of *People of Passion* or *People of Position.* Discover them avidly. Nurture them lovingly.

Who Are the People of Potential?

People of Potential can be young adults who are professionals or entrepreneurs who have a lot of ideas and creative energy to contribute. They are adults who recently became parents and see the value of deeper investment of time and efforts in church life as a model for their children. New Christians with a lot of passion about their faith can have tremendous potential in a congregation if properly involved in a discipleship process.

New people who have connected with the congregation may have sharp insights into the effectiveness of the congregation. These insights have not been tainted by the past to present culture of the congregation. "Empty nest" adults who are looking for new places in which to invest their time may be tremendous *People of Potential.* A similar situation is true for recent retirees, particularly if these people have taken early retirement and have generous resources to fund their retirement. People who have had a new spiritual encounter or experience may be looking for places to invest their new passion and fulfill its meaning in their lives.

The Relationship between the People Groups and Readiness for Transition and Change

Some years ago I heard the country comedian Jerry Clower talk about decision-making in his small town Mississippi church that was governed by congregational polity. He indicated that his pastor was a strong spiritual person who would sit in the pastor's study at the church building, read his Bible, pray earnestly to God, and discern the will of God for the church.

Then the pastor would share his discernment with the congregation. The result was that if more than 50 percent of the congregation agreed with his discernment, then the congregation would take the needed actions. If less than 50 percent of the congregation was convinced the pastor was right, then no action would be taken.

Congregations are governed in various ways. Yet many people would say that a majority of a congregation must be in favor of a new sense of direction before the congregation will embrace it. To an extent this is true. Whether a congregation votes on major decisions, a board handles them, or the pastor declares them, it is doubtful that much that is lasting will happen unless the full heart, soul, mind, and strength of the congregation is behind a new or renewed direction.

A strong relationship exists between the people groups described in this chapter and the readiness of a congregation for transition, change, and transformation. The key concept to take away from this chapter is that the *Enduring Visionary Leadership Community,* composed of the right 21 percent of the congregation, can effectively steer or navigate the spiritual strategic journey of the congregation. It does not take 50 percent of the congregation. It takes the right 21 percent.

I actually find this to be a freeing concept for many congregational leaders who are trying to figure out how they can get the majority of what sometimes seems like a mob to be in agreement on the future direction of the congregation. To discover that it only takes 21 percent of the congregation who are the *Pastoral, Passion,* and *Position* leaders of the congregation makes the transition, change, and transformation journey seem possible.

To follow up on the concept of readiness from chapter 2, when the *Enduring Visionary Leadership Community* is well formed and mature, then the congregation is ready to launch a successful spiritual strategic journey that may transform the congregation and empower it in the direction of its full Kingdom potential.

COACHING INSIGHTS

■ If you were to place the active attending adults in your congregation into these various categories, how many would be in each? Would you achieve the benchmark of having at least 7 percent in the *People of Passion* category? If not, what are the steps you could take to discover, discern, and develop a deeper level of passion in people about the present to future ministry of your congregation?

■ How about the total of 21 percent in the *People of Position* category that includes everyone in the first three circles? What can you do to create a process of sharing and discernment among the 21 percent that will bring them together as a true *Enduring Visionary Leadership Community* for the spiritual strategic journey of your congregation?

■ Who are the *People of Potential* in your congregation? What can you do to cultivate these people? As a pastoral leader, what can you do to rebalance your ministry time commitment to spend more time cultivating *People of Passion* and *People of Potential* and less time with *People of Passivity* and *People of Perpetual Care?*

PERSONAL REFLECTIONS

YOUR REFLECTIONS: What are your reflections on the material presented in this chapter?

_____

_____

_____

_____

_____

YOUR ACTIONS: What actions do you need to take about your life, ministry, and/or congregation based on the material presented in this chapter?

_____

_____

_____

_____

_____

YOUR ACCOUNTABILITY: How and by whom do you want to be held accountable for taking these actions?

_____

_____

_____

_____

_____

CHAPTER FOUR

Identifying Congregational Issues for a Spiritual Strategic Journey

EXECUTIVE SUMMARY

The purpose of this chapter is to introduce and dialogue about the ten congregational issues for generative dialogue for a spiritual strategic journey. These ten issues are visionary leadership, relationship experiences, programmatic emphases, accountable management, contextual relevance, people of pastoral leadership, people of passion, people of position, church growth, and communication and conflict. Generative dialogue around these ten issues is seen as a key component for congregational assessment and learning.

What are the ten most critical issues facing your congregation if it is going to engage in a meaningful spiritual strategic journey and reach its full Kingdom potential? Is reaching your annual budget one of the issues? Is another attracting more teenagers into the church? or being out of debt? or having many successful programs?

Could keeping the people over sixty-five years old happy while at the same time reaching new members who are less than thirty-five years old be one of these critical issues? Perhaps another is having the right pastor, one who can preach like Peter, pray like Paul, encourage like Barnabas, write like Luke, and cook like Martha. Or maybe a key critical issue involves having the right staff, people who can do all these things. Could having the most beautiful and largest church building in the area be critical?

Around fifteen years ago I started to reevaluate my approach to congregations. As I did, I began to figure out the crucial issues that congregations needed to address to successfully engage in a spiritual strategic journey. Addressing the issues would empower the journey.

Each congregation does not have to address these issues in exactly the same way, but they do need to address them in their context, using their collective spiritual giftedness, life skills, and personality preferences. None of the ten issues I will introduce to you in this chapter have to be carried out in a specific way by a congregation. They simply need to be addressed in a spiritual and strategic way so that the congregation can be empowered forward on its journey.

Some of my work began to look a little too much like one of the church health lists that were beginning to become popular during the mid-1990s. I realized they were significantly different, but could I effectively explain the difference? The critical difference is that church health lists are content-oriented lists that seek to suggest the form and substance of each issue. As such their long-term goal is to reimage congregations in the image of the content, form, or substance of the items on the church health list.

This is tragic, as the real focus of working with congregations is to enable them to be reimaged in God's image for them. To do this it is necessary to develop statements that are process-oriented rather than content-oriented. Process-oriented items and lists suggest areas with which congregations need to dialogue for discovery, discernment, and development of new strategic actions.

For example, I have seen church health lists that suggest that "healthy churches are reproducing churches that start new congregations." That is a great statement in many ways, and one with which I personally agree based on my subjective image of a great church. However, this statement assumes that all congregations are blessed with the gifts, skills, and desire to start new congregations. This is obviously untrue. Many congregations have no vision for church planting. Because I have a personal prejudice in favor of church planting being the most effective means of evangelism, I might wish this to be true. But, it is not.

It would be appropriate to have a statement on a church health list. The statement would read something like, "healthy churches are churches that have discerned how God is calling them to fulfill the Great Commission, rather than hoarding the gospel message, and are seeking to expand and extend the Kingdom of God with a 'GlobaLocal' perspective." Such a statement would fit all healthy congregations and allow for a unique expression of their category of health in each congregation.

A second key difference between my list and the traditional church health list is that church health lists place significant importance on the rating given to each item on their lists by the church member completing the church health inventory. Often church health lists suggest that congregation leadership should use the assessment to focus on strengthening the weak areas to enable the congregation to be healthier.

Such an approach is the exact opposite from the one that should be pursued. I love the statement I have heard consultant, writer, speaker, and educator Kennon Callahan say many times. He indicates that focus on all the weak areas of a congregation can bring it right up to neutral in its functioning. It is not possible to improve the effectiveness of the service of a congregation by improving all its weak areas. Effective improvement only comes about by discerning the strengths of a congregation and building on these. The strengths of a congregation will form the basis of its future, not its weaknesses.

Congregational Issues for Generative Dialogue for a Spiritual Strategic Journey

I call my list of ten issues *Congregational Issues for Generative Dialogue for a Spiritual Strategic Journey*. The two key words in this title are *dialogue* and *generative*. The issues are for dialogue because it is the dialogue within the leadership of a congregation that gives meaning and adds value to each issue, and not where each issue scored on a one-to-ten rating scale. Dialogue and consensus among congregational leaders is essential to a broad-based ownership of the issues critical to the future of congregational ministry.

The issues are called generative because the dialogue around them should ideally generate a new level or depth of understanding of each issue and its application to each congregation. Dialogue is desired rather than a score.

The following ten issues may be the subject of generative dialogue in congregations as they seek to determine their readiness for transition and change that leads to transformation while traveling along a spiritual strategic journey toward reaching their full Kingdom potential. As you read the core statements, think about your congregation. Rate where your congregation is now in regard to these statements along a scale of one to ten with ten being high. If your congregation excels in the subject area of the statement and reflects at a high level of the spirit and content of the statement, then it would rate an eight, nine, or ten. If your congregation proves to be very weak in the subject area and does not reflect the spirit and content of the statement, then it would rate a one, two, or three. It can actually rate anywhere on the scale that you feel fits your congregation.

Be sure to focus on where your congregation as a whole is right now from your personal perspective. Do not try to figure out where it once was, where it will be in three to five years, or where it ought to be. Do not try to figure out what others in your congregation might say. Focus strictly on what you feel about your congregation. Do not look at only your part of the congregation or at the perspective of your best friends. Look at your congregation as a whole. Look at your congregation today.

Generative Dialogue Issue One–Visionary Leadership

Statement: Our congregation has a strong, clear, and passionate sense of our identity involving mission and purpose *(who we are)*, our core values *(what we believe or highly value)*, our vision *(where we are heading)*, and our spiritual strategic journey as a congregation *(how we are getting there)*.

Dialogue: Does your congregation have a clear, passionate sense of who it is, what it believes or highly values, where it is headed, and how it is getting there? Is there obvious *Vision Plus Intentionality* within your congregation?

Vision is not a "fifteen-word-or-less" statement crafted by a committee in a smoke-filled back room, approved by a congregation or its board, printed on the worship folder, and recited on cue in worship services and other gatherings of the congregation. That is a vision statement. Any similarity between a vision statement and vision is purely accidental.

Vision is a movement of God that is memorable, and not a statement of humankind that is memorized. Congregational leadership casts and casts vision until the congregation is captivated by it. Vision is not something you catch. It is something by which you are caught.

Vision is not so much written as it is experienced. Vision must be sensed and experienced within a congregation rather than read or heard. When considering how vision comes to us, it may be helpful to consider how our New Testament came to us. It was first experienced. Then it was reflected upon and shared orally. After a number of years it began to be written down for consistent, accurate sharing of the drama of redemption with everyone who desired to know. Vision is experienced. We reflect on it and share it orally with our full heart, soul, mind, and strength. Ultimately, we write it down to have a consistent historic and dynamic sharing of vision with the existing and emerging congregation.

Generative Dialogue Issue Two—Relationship Experiences

Statement: Our congregation is doing well at attracting people to a Christ-centric faith journey *(evangelism)* and at helping people who are connected with our congregation to be on an intentional and maturing Christ-centric faith journey *(discipleship development)*. Among the results of the faith journey of people in our congregation is a deepening spirituality, the development of numerous new leaders, and a willingness by many people to get actively involved in congregational leadership positions and in places of ministry service within and beyond the congregation *(lay mobilization)*.

Dialogue: *Relationship Experiences* is best seen as the disciple-making process in congregations. It is about turning irreligious people into fully devoted followers of Christ. It is about relating people to God, to one another, and to the context in which their community of faith serves. It deals with connecting people to *Christ, Congregation, Community, Calling,* and *Commission.*

Connecting people with *Christ* involves the evangelism focus on pre-Christians who need and desire a faith-based encounter with Jesus the Christ, the Son of the living God. The *Christ* factor involves encounters and experiences with unchurched persons who claim a Christian spiritual journey, but are not regularly part of a Christ-centric, faith-based community. Further, it involves encounters and experiences with dechurched persons who have been turned off by church and left it.

Congregation is connecting people with a Christ-centric, faith-based community. This may involve ongoing participation with a local congregation, and even joining a congregation and accepting membership in a new or renewed commitment. This involves the subject areas of new membership recruitment and the initial assimilation of people into a local congregation, but not always in that order.

Community is more fully connecting people with a congregation, thus completing assimilation, or the process of assimilating new members into the full fellowship and care ministry components of the congregation. This is the point at which the congregation with which people have chosen to connect truly becomes home.

It is essential in a disciple-making process for people to engage in spiritual development and leadership development. This is the essence of *Calling*. People connect with their spiritual giftedness, life skills, and personality preferences to continually prepare themselves for Christlike service.

Lay mobilization is a key outcome or desired end result of a disciple-making process. Mobilizing people, connects them with the *Commission*. The implication is that people are connected with the Great Commission as they discern, discover, develop, and act on their personal ministry *Calling*.

Relationship Experiences is the real thing. It is the style of disciple-making for the congregation. It is the flavoring or identity of the congregation, while *Visionary Leadership* is the fuel or driving force for the congregation.

Generative Dialogue Issue Three–Programmatic Emphases

Statement: Our congregation has outstanding programs, ministries, and activities for which we are well known throughout our congregation and our geographic community or the target groups we serve. Our programs, ministries, and activities seem to be growing in numbers and quality. Our programs are meeting real, identified, spiritual, social, and emotional needs of people.

Dialogue: Programs, ministries, and activities are the visible expression and framework through which we anticipate the best possible relationship experiences can occur with God, with one another, and with the context in which your congregation serves. Programs are a means to the desired end results and not the end results themselves. Success in program, ministries, and activities does not necessarily mean success in the church.

Programs are the functional attempts to provide programs, ministries, services, activities, and training for people connected to the congregation by membership, fellowship, or through relationship processes. Programs require planning, scheduling, budgeting, leadership recruitment, materials and equipment resources, implementation, and evaluation.

We can hold the evidence of programs in our hands. It may be a calendar, budget, strategic or program plan, curriculum, enrollment and attendance reports, or evaluation sheets. We determine to do certain programs in a congregation, plan for them, provide resources for them, prepare for them, conduct them, evaluate them, and then often do them all over again.

Programs, ministries, services, activities, and training include, but are not limited to, worship, music, education and training, and weekday and community ministries. Programs are focused on bringing new external resources into the congregation. They are task-oriented. Specific, concrete projects that the congregation engages in, such as building programs, are examples of projects that fit the broader category of programs.

How Do *Relationship Experiences* and *Programmatic Emphases* Differ?

The end result differentiates programs and relationships. If the desired result is the ministry, activity, service, or training itself, then these elements act like programs. Programs carried out in this manner can become the desired end result or goal themselves. The success of the programs becomes the measurement of success for the congregation.

However, programs operated with a dynamic, flexible, process orientation might be relationship experiences. The desired end result or goal is changed spiritual behavior that should result from the program or activity. The measurement of success is the development of the individual believer or disciple or even of the pre-Christian.

Programs are task-oriented and provide stability for a congregation. Relationship experiences are people-oriented and empower flexibility within a congregation. Programs are things that congregations do or carry out. Relationship activities are things felt or experienced. For example, many congregations conduct Sunday school classes or worship experiences. If in the midst of these classes new insight to the Scriptures is discovered or if God is truly experienced as Lord in worship, then relationships occurs. These activities remain programs if the focus of Sunday school and worship is the habit, pattern, or doing of what is culturally acceptable in a particular congregation.

A crucial issue is whether or not the events and experiences in your congregation are programmatic emphases, or are they relationship experiences. Let's use your primary worship experience as an example. If people leave worship services in your congregation talking primarily about having been to an event or met an obligation, liking or disliking it, feeling like they may come again next Sunday if they are in town and want to attend worship, then worship services in your congregation for these people are a programmatic emphasis.

If people leave worship services in your congregation talking primarily about how great the experience was, how they felt the presence of God, how they were moved by the music and message, then worship services in your congregation for these people are relationship experiences.

Long-term congregational vitality and effectiveness is dependent on the ability to focus on creating and nurturing relationship experiences rather than program events. Does that mean that congregations should eliminate their program events? No! Program events are a necessary and crucial part of the organizing principles of congregations. Every congregation needs a strategy, structure, and system of program events.

What it means is that congregations must have program events and relationship experiences in proper alignment with one another. The purpose of program events should be to enable genuine relationship experiences to take place in the lives of individuals, in groups within the congregation, and in the congregation as a whole.

When congregations focus on the vision of God that is shared within the fellowship of a local congregation, then the emphasis given to program events moves to an emphasis on people. Therefore, program events that are dynamic, flexible, and fuel the relationship experiences will also fuel the future direction of the congregation.

When congregations focus on management, the emphasis on relationship experiences moves to an emphasis on maintaining program events. Congregations who focus on maintaining program events will have difficulty sustaining a broad-based ownership of God's vision for the congregation.

Generative Dialogue Issue Four–Accountable Management

Statement: Our congregation has excellent, flexible management systems *(teams, committees, councils, boards, leadership communities)* that empower the future direction of our congregation rather than seeking to control the future direction. Decision-making is open and responsive to congregational input. Finances are healthy and increasing each year. The management systems are supportive of the visionary leadership efforts by the pastor, staff, and congregational leadership.

Dialogue: Management is the administration of the various resources of the congregation, the formal and informal governance and decision-making structure of the congregation, the formal and informal traditions and culture of the congregation, and the readiness of the congregation for change and growth.

Management also relates to how congregations handle their day-to-day operations. This includes the operational planning process and how this is implemented to bring about growth and change in the congregation. This factor provides a basis for deciding how the people, financial, facilities, and equipment and materials resources of the congregation are utilized.

Finally, management deals with the efficiency of a congregation. Once a congregation attains the stage of "Maturity" on the congregational life cycle, its progress tends to be fueled by management rather than vision. Over a number of years, these management principles become increasingly controlling. Ultimately management becomes dysfunctional and management principles begin to break down.

What Are the Key Elements of Management?

Resources: The resources of a congregation are people and things. People include the pastor, staff, and lay leadership. Thus management will relate to the process of calling a pastor or other staff ministers. The infrastructure that mobilizes laity is addressed here. Lay mobilization as a movement is part of relationships.

Things include the finances, the facilities, the equipment, and various materials. These things are not intended to be in a lead role in the life of a congregation. They are intended to be resources that help the congregation fulfill its vision by empowering relationships. Many congregations have this reversed.

Governance: Governance relates to the administration and decision-making structure of the congregation. This includes the formal committees, councils, and boards, as well as the process for making decisions.

Governance and decision-making are intended to help guide or navigate the congregational processes, and to continually develop ownership within the congregation. Some congregations mistake governance and decision-making as the manner by which they are to control the congregation.

Tradition and Culture: Management may seem like an odd place for tradition and culture. In reality they are commodities that congregations deposit like financial assets in a bank. Their tendency is to maintain more than it is to empower. Some congregations add elements of tradition and culture to the list of core values of the congregation and overload core values with things that are really negotiable.

Readiness for Transition and Change: When management is handled in a flexible, supportive way, it helps congregations to be prepared for the new innovation or the new sense of God's movement. When management is used to control, it shuts down the readiness for change and transition in favor of maintaining the tradition and culture of the congregation. This is because change, even when for the better, is seen as loss.

Operations: Operations describes the day-to-day activities and functions of the congregation. Operations should be first of all effective, and then efficient, in support of the future of the congregation. Efficiency often dominates effectiveness.

One easy way to remember what Accountable Management refers to is to remember the words *Bodies, Bucks, Boards,* and *Buildings. Bodies* refer to the people who are called or appointed, employed, or who volunteer in the life of the congregation. *Bucks* refer to the finances of the congregation. Informal and formal decision-making processes are the *Boards. Buildings* apply to both facilities and capital equipment.

COACHING BREAK

✔ Gaze out the window for a minute. Ponder the situation of your congregation. What images come to mind?

✔ If you only know four things about your congregation, these first four issues we have just discussed are the most important. If your congregation is clear about vision, relationships, programs, and management, then it will be well aligned for effective ministry. Where is your congregation regarding these four issues?

Generative Dialogue Issue Five—Contextual Relevance

Statement: Our congregation is demographically similar to its geographic community or the target groups that it has served over the years. Little or no gap is developing between the persons attending our congregation and the geographic community or the target groups we have sought to serve over the past ten years. We are demographically reflective of the people we seek to serve in gender, age, race/ethnicity, socioeconomics, and lifestyle.

Dialogue: It is extremely important for congregations to know with whom their Christ-centric, faith-based community can best connect, given the community's gifts and skills and personal preferences. It is also important for them to be able to clearly evaluate whether or not they are being effective in reaching the people they say they are trying to reach.

It is not important whether or not a congregation is reaching a certain geographic community or parish, or if they are reaching certain target groups of people. It is just important that they are clear on who they are trying to reach, and that they are effective in reaching them. If they are, then they have contextual relevance. If they are not, then they do not.

It is essential that congregations seek to impact their context. Both geographic communities and target groups of people need to be transformed by God's empowerment displayed by compassionate followers of Jesus Christ. Contextual transformation involves making a revolutionary, Christlike difference in the place where your congregation lives, or among the people with whom your congregation dwells. To be relevant to your context, you must be part of God's empowerment to make it more loving and just.

Generative Dialogue Issue Six—People of Pastoral Leadership

Statement: Our pastor has a genuine commitment to transition and change for our congregation that may lead to transformation and the achievement of the full Kingdom potential of our congregation. In addition, our pastor is highly respected by our congregation, and they will proactively support our pastor's initiating leadership and vision casting as part of a spiritual, strategic journey toward reaching their full Kingdom potential.

Dialogue: The *People of Pastoral Leadership* are the senior pastor, other ordained clergy, and primary program staff who form the pastoral leadership community of your congregation. They are the initiating leaders who comprise the core group of leadership and have the primary responsibility for casting and focusing on the fulfillment of God's vision for the congregation. This is fully discussed in chapter 3.

Generative Dialogue Issue Seven—People of Passion

Statement: I can name at least seven people or 7 percent—whichever is higher—of the average number of active, attending adults in our congregation present on a typical weekend for worship who have a positive and passionate sense of urgency for transition and change that may lead to transformation and the achievement of the full Kingdom potential of our congregation. They also have the spiritual, leadership, and strategic knowledge and maturity to appropriately initiate and champion transition and change within our congregation.

Dialogue: The *People of Passion* are a minimum of 7 percent of the average number of active attending adults, or *Quad A's,* in your congregation including the 1 percent *People of Pastoral Leadership*. This is fully discussed in chapter 3.

Generative Dialogue Issue Eight–People of Position

Statement: Our key lay leaders have a genuine commitment to transition and change for our congregation that may lead to transformation and the achievement of the full Kingdom potential of our congregation. While not always the people of greatest passion about the future of the congregation, by position and power they are competent and committed to lead us to fulfill our full Kingdom potential. In addition, our congregation highly respects them and will proactively support their leadership in a spiritual, strategic journey toward reaching our full Kingdom potential.

Dialogue: The *People of Position* are a minimum of 21 percent of the average number of active attending adults or *Quad A's* in your congregation including the 1 percent *People of Pastoral Leadership* and the 6 additional percent *People of Passion*. So, the *People of Position* represent another 14 percent, creating a tripling of the size of the previous influence group, the *People of Passion*. This is also fully discussed in chapter 3.

Generative Dialogue Issue Nine–Church Growth

Statement: Our congregation has grown in active membership and weekly worship attendance during the past five to ten years by a minimum of 10 to 15 percent. *(Or, compared to the change over the past five to ten years in population or size of the geographic community or the target groups we serve, our congregation has sustained or achieved an attendance that could be legitimately called growing compared to our geographic community or target groups.)*

Dialogue: Growing congregations are increasing in participation at a sufficient pace that they are changing their size and characteristics within a five-to-ten-year period. To do this, they must grow by at least 10 to 15 percent during these five to ten years. This growth must occur in at least two aspects of the congregation. Active membership and weekly worship attendance are two indicators that speak loudly to the size reality of a congregation.

Growing by less than 10 to 15 percent within a five-to-ten-year period does not really change the size dynamics of a congregation. If the growth emphasis slackens, it is likely the congregation will revert back to their previous size patterns. Often people claim growth for a congregation by attendance increases of just a few people, or by membership increasing by one or two people. This is not growth. This is simply statistical anomalies that could more relate to how, when, and by whom people were counted on a particular Sunday rather than true growth.

Often growth cannot be defined without clearly understanding what is going on in the geographical context and the demographic characteristics of the people the congregation has been serving. If the geographical context of a congregation is growing at a decadal rate of 20 percent, and the congregation has been growing at a rate less than half that, then the congregation may actually be considered declining in relationship to the context in which it serves.

If the target group or groups of people the congregation serves have been diminishing in number over the past decade and the congregation has actually been stable in size, then perhaps the congregation could be considered growing. So growth is relative.

Even more confusing is the idea of how growth is counted. Almost all approaches to growth count individual people. One New Testament model that ought to be applied is that of the household. When the participation and membership of congregations is counted according to households, then it becomes possible for a congregation to decrease in the number of individual people participating and increase in the number of households present at the same time. This particularly happens in congregations where the number of one or two person households increases due to the aging of the congregation, or success in reaching single adult households.

Generative Dialogue Issue Ten–Communication and Conflict

Statement: Our congregation has clear, open, healthy communication channels that allow the congregation to identify and deal with any issues that might disrupt the sense of fellowship and unity, and perhaps produce unhealthy conflict. Our congregation works hard at creating and nurturing healthy relationships as a Christ-centric faith community and uses its diversity to build a deep, qualitative sense of being on a common journey. We know how to disagree with one another without being disagreeable in a way that can destroy our relationship with God and with one another.

Dialogue: For congregations to be on a healthy spiritual strategic journey, it is necessary not only for the spiritual maturity of the congregation to be above average, but also for the emotional maturity of the congregation to be above average. It is necessary for the congregation to have a healthy sense of being a Christ-centric, faith-based community that communicates openly and honestly with one another. The community must be able to dialogue about difficult and complex issues without losing their collective cool.

Many people with whom these generative dialogue issues have been shared thought they were doing well on these issues until they got to the last sentence. The idea that people can disagree without being disagreeable is a difficult concept to embrace, even in the church. Healthy communication channels must be written, heard, and seen. They must be regular, with many different spokespersons. They must have feedback loops that allow people to respond to what they are hearing and thus complete the communication process. When a church anticipates transition and change, communication must increase in intensity, and the time allocated for feedback must increase. Communication must be characterized by the words *discovery, discernment,* and *dialogue* much more than the words *debate, declaration,* and *demand.* The inevitability of some conflict existing any time transition, changes, and transformation are taking place must be accepted. But healthy processes that do not create either/or situations, but focus rather on both/and situations must predominate.

The Meaning of the Congregational Issues for Generative Dialogue for a Spiritual Strategic Journey

It has been my experience over the past decade that congregations who successfully engage in generative dialogue around these ten congregation issues often are able to move forward in a spiritual strategic journey process by affirming their strengths and building on them. These congregations seek to engage in discovery, discernment, and dialogue around these ten issues and find positive ways to apply the meaning of these issues to the journey of their congregation.

Congregations often use these ten issues as an open-ended assessment process out of which they can begin learning the things they need to know to actualize their journey. They often focus on the first four factors that deal with vision, relationships, programs, and management as one cluster. A second cluster they work with are six, seven, and eight, which relate to the three crucial people leadership groups within their congregation. Then they fill in with work on contextual relevance, growth, and communication and conflict.

Unexpected Discovery

Up to this point I have focused on the generative dialogue that springs forth from the presentation of these congregational issues. Although I have asked readers to rate their congregations on each factor on a scale from one to ten, I have not interpreted the meaning of these numbers. That has been intentional.

The numbers are primarily for the purpose of creating a beginning point for dialogue. If one person in a congregation believes *Visionary Leadership* should be rated a four and another person believes it should be rated as an eight, then there is a beginning point for dialogue. However, is it possible to suggest that the numbers have more meaning than as an entry point for dialogue? Yes! However, the meaning I discovered was unintended.

I discovered that the average total score of all persons in a congregation completing the *Congregational Issues for Generative Dialogue for a Spiritual Strategic Journey* is a predictor of the readiness of the congregation for a successful spiritual strategic journey. Initially I experienced that if a congregation had an average overall score that was less than 40 for all ten issues combined, then it did not have the readiness and vitality to successfully engage in a spiritual strategic journey.

I had the opportunity to observe this in various denominations in various parts of North America as I worked with clusters of congregations on their spiritual strategic journeys. In every case in which a congregation in the cluster had an average score of less than 40, they lagged behind in the process and were often unable to both grasp and actualize the concepts in that congregation.

Another interesting discovery was that whenever a congregation had an average score of 80 or more, they also exhibited signs of excellence and of already being on an effective spiritual strategic journey. They primarily needed continual coaching, learning, and affirmation that they were on the best possible journey and were making progress toward reaching their full Kingdom potential.

In recent years I have been able to further discern various categories of readiness and effectiveness using this scale. At this point, however, the research is not scientific, but experiential based on the congregations encountered in various settings.

These more recent understandings are covered in chapter 2 and are illustrated by the categories of congregations known as *Perfecting Congregations, Pursuing Congregations, Preparing Congregations, Providing Congregations,* and *Presiding Congregations.* The key difference is that for a congregation to experience a spiritual strategic journey that is a long-term solution rather than a short-term fix, they must have an average score of around 55 or above.

Any lower score would generally call for the congregation to work longer and more deeply on creating readiness for transition, change, and transformation. This, of course, would be progress for these congregations, and should be seen as a positive step forward. These congregations would want to focus more on the information in chapters 2, 6, and 7.

COACHING INSIGHTS

■ What is the average score among the leadership of your congregation on the *Congregational Issues for Generative Dialogue for a Spiritual Strategic Journey?* What are the implications of this average score? What do you believe your next positive steps ought to be in response to this score?

■ Out of the dialogue around these ten issues, what are the things that can be affirmed about the life and ministry of your congregation? What are the signs of health and strength in the life and ministry of your congregation?

■ As the same time, what are the greatest challenges facing your congregation with which you must deal to engage in a healthy spiritual strategic journey? How can these challenges be addressed by the things you can affirm about your congregation so that you focus on affirmation and building on that affirmation?

■ What are the three issues that are the strongest among your congregation today? Are they the people issues of *Pastoral Leadership*, *Passion*, and *Position*? If not, where are these issues in the life of the congregation, since it is more important that we transition people than it is that we change things?

■ Is your congregation driven more by Vision and Relationships than it is by Programs and Management? What are the implications for who is driving your journey as a congregation?

■ This last question is the key question for the next chapter. Take a few minutes to reflect on this chapter and then move on.

PERSONAL REFLECTIONS

YOUR REFLECTIONS: What are your reflections on the material presented in this chapter?

_____

_____

_____

_____

_____

YOUR ACTIONS: What actions do you need to take about your life, ministry, and/or congregation based on the material presented in this chapter?

_____

_____

_____

_____

_____

YOUR ACCOUNTABILITY: How and by whom do you want to be held accountable for taking these actions?

_____

_____

_____

_____

_____

Congregational Issues for Generative Dialogue for a Spiritual Strategic Journey

The following ten issues may be the subject of generative dialogue in congregations as they seek to determine their readiness for transition and change that leads to transformation while traveling along a spiritual strategic journey toward reaching their full Kingdom potential.

(Please provide your personal rating of your congregation on a scale of 1–10 on each of the following statements. An answer as low as 1 would mean that your congregation is not reflective of the statement. An answer as high as 10 would mean that your congregation is highly reflective of the statement. Answers in between these two extremes would suggest the relative agreement or disagreement you have with each statement when you think about your congregation.)

1. _____ VISIONARY LEADERSHIP: Our congregation has a strong, clear, and passionate sense of our identity involving mission and purpose *(who we are)*, our core values *(what we believe or highly value)*, our vision *(where we are headed)*, and our spiritual strategic journey as a congregation *(how we are getting there)*.

2. _____ RELATIONSHIP EXPERIENCES: Our congregation is doing well at attracting people to a Christ-centric faith journey *(evangelism)*, and at helping people who are connected with our congregation to be on an intentional and maturing Christ-centric faith journey *(discipleship development)*. Among the results of the faith journey of people in our congregation is a deepening spirituality, the development of numerous new leaders, and a willingness by many people to get actively involved in congregational leadership positions and in places of ministry service within and beyond the congregation *(lay mobilization)*.

3. _____ PROGRAMMATIC EMPHASES: Our congregation has outstanding programs, ministries, and activities for which we are well known throughout our congregation and our geographic community or the target groups we serve. Our programs, ministries, and activities seem to be growing in numbers and quality. Our programs are meeting real, identified, spiritual, social, and emotional needs of people.

4. _____ ACCOUNTABLE MANAGEMENT: Our congregation has excellent, flexible management systems *(teams, committees, councils, boards, leadership communities)* that empower the future direction of our congregation rather than seeking to control the future direction. Decision-making is open and responsive to congregational input.

Finances are healthy and increasing each year. The management systems are supportive of the visionary leadership efforts by the pastor, staff, and congregational leadership.

5. _____ **CONTEXTUAL RELEVANCE:** Our congregation is demographically similar to its geographic community or the target groups that it has served over the years. Little or no gap is developing between the persons attending our congregation and the geographic community or the target groups we have sought to serve over the past ten years. We are demographically reflective of the people we seek to serve in gender, age, race/ethnicity, socioeconomics, and lifestyle.

6. _____ **PEOPLE OF PASTORAL LEADERSHIP:** Our pastor has a genuine commitment to transition and change for our congregation that may lead to transformation and the achievement of the full Kingdom potential of our congregation. In addition, our pastor is highly respected by our congregation, and they will proactively support our pastor's initiating leadership and vision casting as part of a spiritual, strategic journey toward reaching their full Kingdom potential.

7. _____ **PEOPLE OF PASSION:** I can name at least seven people or 7 percent—whichever is higher—of the average number of active, attending adults in our congregation present on a typical weekend for worship who have a positive and passionate sense of urgency for transition and change that may lead to transformation and the achievement of the full Kingdom potential of our congregation. They also have the spiritual, leadership, and strategic knowledge and maturity to appropriately initiate and champion transition and change within our congregation.

8. _____ **PEOPLE OF POSITION:** Our key lay leaders have a genuine commitment to transition and change for our congregation that may lead to transformation and the achievement of the full Kingdom potential of our congregation. While not always the people of greatest passion about the future of the congregation, by position and power they are competent and committed to lead us to fulfill our full Kingdom potential. In addition, our congregation highly respects them and will proactively support their leadership in a spiritual, strategic journey toward reaching our full Kingdom potential.

9. _____ **CHURCH GROWTH:** Our congregation has grown in membership and weekly worship attendance during the past five to

ten years by a minimum of 10 to 15 percent. *(Or, compared to the change over the past five to ten years in population or size of the geographic community or the target groups we serve, our congregation has sustained or achieved an attendance that could be legitimately called growing compared to our geographic community or target groups.)*

10. _____ COMMUNICATION AND CONFLICT: Our congregation has clear, open, healthy communication channels that allow the congregation to identify and deal with any issues that might disrupt the sense of fellowship and unity, and perhaps produce unhealthy conflict. Our congregation works hard at creating and nurturing healthy relationships as a Christ-centric faith community and uses its diversity to build a deep, qualitative sense of being on a common journey. We know how to disagree with one another without being disagreeable in a way that can destroy our relationship with God and one another.

_____ **Total Number of Points**

CHAPTER FIVE

Recognizing the Life Cycle and Stages of Your Congregation's Development

EXECUTIVE SUMMARY

The purpose of this chapter is to share the life cycle and stages of congregational development as an assessment, learning, and intervention model for a spiritual strategic journey. The focus is on helping congregations identify where they are on the life cycle as a beginning point for launching their spiritual strategic journey. The life cycle chart is organized around the first four congregational issues introduced in the previous chapter. These are visionary leadership, relationship experiences, programmatic emphases, and accountable management. Suggestions are made for the next steps for a congregation once they figure out the stage of the life cycle in which they find themselves.

What are the categories you use to describe your congregation? What frameworks or assessment tools do you use? Is the best category size, age, location, growth status, worship style, denominational affiliation, facilities, disciple-making processes, pastoral leadership, programs for children, ethnicity, status in the community, or the primary age groups of the attendees?

Try the fuel and flavor of the organizing principles of congregations and the stages of development of congregations in a life cycle analysis. For numerous years, the concept of congregations as spiritual organisms with life cycles has existed. Life cycles are one of many assessment categories that may include many of the categories mentioned above.

Over the years, I have found the life cycle to be one of the best learning tools for congregational leaders. Properly understood, the life cycle provides an excellent assessment for a congregation and allows it to know its starting point, and the issues it must address, to be able to spiral forward to the next cycle in its spiritual strategic journey. To think strategically and act effectively outside the box and beyond the box, it is important to know the location of your starting point.

While a great deal of scientific theory and application lies behind the life cycle, I prefer to present it to congregational leaders as a story of congregations that must be experienced. I have been amazed over the years how often the perception of congregational leaders as to their location on the life cycle mirrors the statistics and scientific assessment as to their location.

What this has meant is that I do not use the statistical and scientific models any more. If a congregational leadership group is presented with a report that says where they are on the life cycle, they are likely to question it. When the same group hears a presentation of the life cycle and stages of congregational development and is asked to suggest where they are on the life cycle, they not only believe it, but they are incredibly accurate. So, it has face validity for them, and they are motivated to action based on it.

Four Organizing Principles That Form the DNA of the Life Cycle

A major element in understanding the life cycle of a congregation is to understand the pattern of the organizing principles that form the DNA and make up the various stages of congregational life. This life cycle is principle driven. The organizing principles are the same as the first four congregational issues for generative dialogue presented in the last chapter. For your review, here is a recap.

Vision: The current understanding of God's spiritual strategic direction for a local congregation that is cast by the leadership and owned by the membership.

Relationships: The relational processes by which persons are brought to faith in God through Jesus Christ; become connected to a local New Testament church; are assimilated into the fellowship, life, and care ministry of the church; have opportunities for spiritual growth and leadership development; and utilize their gifts and skills through Kingdom involvement.

Programs: The functional attempts to provide ministries, services, activities, and training for people connected to the congregation by membership, attendance, fellowship, or through relationship processes.

Management: The administration of the resources of the congregation, the decision-making structure of the congregation, the formal and informal culture of the congregation, and the openness of the congregation to change and grow.

Look at these four organizing principles as one approach to the assessment of a congregation. To empower our observation, reference 2 Corinthians 5:7, which admonishes us to walk by faith rather than by sight.

Congregations that focus more passion on Vision and Relationships are growing younger and more proactive every day. Younger does not necessarily mean the age demographics of the congregation are growing younger, but that may be a by-product. It means that, as a representation of the body of Christ, they appear younger or more vital. They are proactive in their actions and regularly seize the opportunities God is placing before them.

Congregations that focus more passion on Programs and Management are growing older and more passive every day. As a representation of the body of Christ they daily appear older and less vital. They are passive in their actions, and regularly seek to maintain past gains, an effort that leads to less satisfying results.

My intuition and experience tells me that upwards of 80 percent of the thousands of congregations I have encountered place more emphasis on Programs and Management than they do on Vision and Relationships. The 20 percent who focus more on Vision and Relationships probably account for the vast majority of Kingdom growth throughout North America.

Imagine a Car

Imagine a car as a metaphor for a congregation. Place Vision, Relationships, Programs, and Management in this vehicle in the seat best suited for each to symbolize a faithful, effective, and innovative journey for a congregation.

Who would drive? Vision, of course. Vision would be driving and fueling the forward progress of the vehicle. Who would navigate? Relationships would navigate and flavor the quality of the journey.

Who would be in the back seat behind Relationships? Programs would sit behind Relationships in a supporting role. It would provide the programs, ministries, and activities through which the best possible relationships could happen with God, with one another, and with the context the congregation serves.

So, Management would be in the back seat behind Vision? Yes. It would provide the administrative infrastructure that allows Vision to engage in *"FaithSoaring"* in response to God's leadership.

What happens when Vision gets tired and needs to take a nap in the back seat? Who drives? The answer begins with Scripture. A loose translation of the first part of Proverbs 29:18 says that where there is no vision the people perish. Or, where there is no vision the people cast off all restraint. Or, where there is no vision, the people run around in circles without any clear sense of direction and focus. Further, where there is no vision and Moses the leader stays too long on the mountain, then the people demand that Aaron the manager build them an idol image of God they can see and touch.

Where there is no Vision, Management drives! At first Management does an excellent job of driving. The longer Management drives and the longer Vision sleeps, the more likely the congregation will engage in activities that cause it to age and become more passive and less vital. The long-term result of this pattern is death.

Because of the view I have presented on Programs and Management, would it not be better to just leave them home and not take them on the journey? No. Programs and Management are an essential part of the journey. Alignment is the key. Each organizing principle must play out its appropriate role in its best seat in the vehicle for the journey to be excellent, transformational, and to approach the full Kingdom potential of the congregation.

Stages of Congregational Development

Every congregation has a life cycle into which the four organizing principles fit. Think of this life cycle as the journey of the congregation in the vehicle. Looking at congregations according to their life cycles assists in developing the ability to see, understand, and pursue opportunities and choices available to a congregation at a particular stage of development. This life cycle begins with Birth, followed by a period of growth, the achievement of Adulthood and Maturity, a period of aging, and then Death or Redevelopment.

Throughout their life congregations go through the life cycle multiple times. They develop following Birth, until one day they are on the aging side of the life cycle. At this point they have the opportunity to spiral forward to a new, partial life cycle. No matter how old a congregation is, still an obvious place exists on the life cycle that the congregation as an organism can identify as their current development stage location.

The oldest congregations I have shared the life cycle pattern with are more than 300 years old. They easily saw themselves on the life cycle. I remember in one congregation the leadership group laughed and said that it was probably cycle number forty for them.

The life cycle also relates to congregations in various political and social cultures. Some years ago, during my first trip to Eastern Europe, I was presenting the life cycle to a group of congregational leaders. At one point they challenged me. The issue was that I had told them this was my first trip to Eastern Europe. Their challenge was that I could not be telling the truth because as I explained the life cycle they knew I had already been in their churches and knew what they were going through.

The life cycle of a congregation includes ten stages of development. (See the Life Cycle chart on page 96.) The ten stages of development are: Birth, Infancy, Childhood, Adolescence, Adulthood, Maturity, Empty Nest, Retirement, Old Age, and Death. These ten stages relate to the five primary phases of the life cycle. These phases are, Phase One: Early Growth; Phase Two: Late Growth; Phase Three: Prime/Plateau; Phase Four: Early Aging; and Phase Five: Late Aging.

PHASE ONE: EARLY GROWTH

This phase involves the life cycle stages of Birth and Infancy and is preceded by a Gestation period.

Gestation: Gestation involves the time frame during which a church planting effort is getting ready to launch into life through the Birth of a new congregation. Gestation is a period of a couple of months to a couple of years before the Birth of a congregation, when the idea of a new congregation is being developed through prayer, planning, and preparation that emanates from a strong, positive sense of spiritual passion. Phase One is the time during which a congregation develops deep roots and early growth around the issues of *Vision* and *Relationships.* They walk by faith rather than by sight.

Birth: Birth is that period when *Vision* is dominant, and *relationships, programs,* and *management* are not. *Vision* is the fuel or energy that drives a new congregation forward.

Congregations at Birth are living out the mission, purpose, core values, and vision that God has given them for a new congregation that ought to be present in a certain place or among a specific target group of people. Leadership is expressed through Vision and assists in fueling the forward progress of the congregation. This leadership is God's leadership, which empowers congregational leaders to seize the day. The period of Birth only lasts about six months to two years. It is characterized by a passion to fulfill the spiritual strategic vision of the congregation.

During the Birth stage congregations must deal with various issues.

First, is our *Vision* generational? Is it intended to provide leadership and focus for us for the first twenty or more years of the congregation?

Second, what evangelism and congregational growth philosophy are we following? What methods do we need to use to bring into a Christ-centric, faith-based journey and community the people to whom God has called us?

Third, how can we be missionary from the first day, while being the product of missions? How do we develop a servant mentality within the congregation while simultaneously being served by our sponsorship or parenthood?

Fourth, what leadership and ministry styles are lay and pastoral leaders expressing? Will they be able to make the shift to different leadership styles as the congregation develops through the growing stages of the life cycle?

Fifth, will the founding pastor have to leave to allow a pastor with a different set of gifts and skills to take us to the next stage? Will the congregation be stunted in its growth and development because the pastor does not adapt spiritual gifts and life skills and does not move on in favor of a pastor who does have the necessary gifts and skills?

Sixth, will the lay leadership make the same or similar adjustments as the pastor, or will they also need to turnover? How will this leadership style crisis affect the congregation's ability to grow and develop in a healthy manner? How will it impact the congregation's ability to successfully navigate the passage to the Infancy stage?

Infancy: Infancy is that period when *Vision* and *Relationships* are dominant, but *programs* and *management* are not. The period of Infancy lasts three to five years. Congregations in Infancy are continuing to live out the *Vision* that God has given them for a congregation that ought to be present in a certain place or among a specific target group of people. *Vision* is the fuel or energy that will drive the congregation forward throughout the growth side of the life cycle. Discipleship patterns are expressed through the *Relationships* factor and assist in flavoring the congregation. These patterns hardwire the congregation's qualitative and quantitative growth patterns.

During the Infancy stage congregations must deal with various issues. First, are our *Relationships* intentional? What evangelism and congregational growth philosophy are we following? Do we know whom we, as a faith community, are gifted to reach for membership, and to make a focus of our outreach and missions efforts? Do we have regular, organized patterns of *Relationships*?

Second, do we have a clear understanding of our values and belief systems, or our spiritual identity? Have we adequately grounded our members, regular attendees, and prospects in the doctrines and disciplines of our congregation and–as appropriate–our denominational family? The effort to clarify identity at times causes some people who have been a part of the congregation to seek another congregation because they do not agree with the emerging belief system, or the identity of the congregation as it was being clarified.

Third, do we actively work to assimilate people into the fellowship and care ministry life of the congregation? Do we go beyond being friendly to helping new people to develop lasting friendships within the congregational family?

Fourth, what is our style of worship? Do we use a traditional pattern, a contemporary pattern, or a blended style of worship? What is the place of preaching and teaching in worship? What is the place of music and liturgy?

Fifth, what are our tactics for lay mobilization? How do we involve people in ministry and missions activities? Do we help people become fully devoted followers of Christ?

PHASE TWO: LATE GROWTH

This phase involves the life cycle stages of Childhood and Adolescence. Phase Two is the time during which a congregation develops and grows its *Programs*. They begin to walk by sight rather than by faith. This causes confusion in Adolescence.

Childhood: Childhood is that period when *Vision* and *Programs* are dominant, but *relationships* and *management* are not. The period of Childhood lasts five to six years. The Childhood stage of a congregation is characterized by an urgency to build programs, ministries, and activities similar to a full-service congregation. Energy and resources that were dedicated to an intentional disciple-making system during Infancy are now dedicated to program development.

During the Childhood stage significant emphasis is given to broadening the scale and deepening the scope of the programs, ministries, and activities for the chosen high-priority target groups. In a family/household-oriented congregation, this can result in major emphasis on programs, ministries, and activities for children less than eighteen years of age.

Several resource issues arise during Childhood.

First, what programs, ministries, and activities do we have budget and special gifts dollars to support? What can we fund through undesignated gifts? What will require designated gifts? And for what will we have to charge a fee?

Second, how should we focus our staff resources? Many congregations at this juncture have a pastor, secretary, and music director. Some will also have added a youth director. Several of these may not be full-time, if any are. Many may be volunteer. A key question will be what staff responsibilities to add next.

Third, facilities will be an issue. Few congregations can accurately predict exactly what type of facilities they will need for future programming. Facilities may need to be renovated, program groups moved around within the facilities, new facilities added, and new parking added.

Adolescence: Adolescence is that period when *Vision, Relationships,* and *Programs* are dominant, but *management* is not. The period of Adolescence lasts six to eight years. The Adolescence stage of a congregation is characterized by a passion to fulfill the strategic spiritual vision of the congregation. Because fulfillment of this *Vision* may be in sight, the congregation presses for a higher quality and quantity of ministry.

Agendas addressed during Adolescence may include the following:

1. Staff and leadership
2. Buildings and equipment
3. Formalizing management systems
4. Dealing with competing priorities expressed by laity
5. Congregational emotions and awkwardness
6. Raising the quality of programs
7. Deepening personal spirituality and community relationships
8. Consideration of jumping the curve to a second life cycle rather than continuing into Adulthood in this life cycle
9. Doing significant and meaningful missions work and ministry projects

10. Working harder on assimilating new people who connect with the congregation

Competition is evident in the Adolescent congregation. Two visions of the future seem to be dominant in the congregation. People who affiliated with the congregation during Birth or Infancy hold one *Vision.* This is a *Vision* of a strong worshiping community with intimate fellowship and care, and meaningful, corporate spirituality. People who affiliated with the congregation during Childhood and Adolescence hold the other *Vision.* The programs, ministries, and activities of the congregation that met specific needs of the family or household attracted them. Their *Vision* is one of a full service, family-focused congregation with opportunities for meaningful, individual spirituality.

PHASE THREE: PRIME/PLATEAU

This phase involves the life cycle stages of Adulthood and Maturity. Phase Three is the time during which a congregation reaches its prime. In Adulthood they have a balance of walking by faith and by sight. This balance begins to weaken in Maturity.

Adulthood: Adulthood is that period when *Vision, Relationships, Programs,* and *Management* share dominance. The period of Adulthood lasts three to five years. Adulthood is characterized by a congregation that is in its prime. It is relaxed. It is successful. It has a positive spirit. It is focused. It is clear about its *Vision,* and its *Vision* shares broad ownership in the congregation. It is positive about its future. It feels that it can accomplish anything to which it sets its mind, as long as it matches the will of God for the congregation.

A crucial characteristic is that the congregation may not be aware that this may be as good as it gets. It may not know that this is Adulthood. Having never been there, if this is the first life cycle of the congregation, they do not recognize Adulthood.

Often the high morale of the congregation parallels the strong sense of mission, purpose, core values, and vision. The congregation feels that it is contributing significantly to the work of the Kingdom. High levels of satisfaction are expressed related to the role and function of the staff.

Maturity: Maturity is that period when *Relationships, Programs,* and *Management* are dominant. *Vision* is no longer dominant. *Management* is controlling the direction of the congregation. A congregation that is past its prime characterizes Maturity. It is more passive than active. It is still successful in many areas. For the most part it has a positive spirit. The quality of what happens in Maturity is the highest of any stage in the life cycle. In fact, a crescendo of quality programs, ministries, and activities occurs during this stage.

It is no longer focused. It is no longer clear about its *vision.* The success culture of the congregation keeps it moving forward. It is blind to the fact that it no longer has an empowering *vision* that is fueling it forward. The feeling is that what the congregation is currently doing is working. There is no felt need to change. Besides, the finances of the congregation have never been better. In selected portions of the congregation the morale of the members and regular attendees is beginning to decline. At the same time the congregation feels that it is contributing significantly to the work of the Kingdom.

Phase Four: Early Aging

This phase involves the life cycle stages of Empty Nest and Retirement. Phase Four is the time during which a congregation diminishes, first in *programs* and then in *relationships.* They begin to hardwire a pattern into their congregational life of walking by sight more than by faith.

Empty Nest: Empty Nest is that period when *Relationships* and *Management* are dominant. *Vision* and *programs* are no longer dominant. *Management* is controlling the direction of the congregation. Empty Nest has three phases: Nostalgia, Disappointment, and Anger.

The Nostalgia phase is when a congregation hopes that tomorrow will bring a return of yesterday. Most of the stories told in the congregation are stories of remembrance. The Disappointment phase is when the congregation realizes that neither the quality nor the quantity of what the congregation is doing is what it once was. The result is that in the Disappointment phase some congregational leaders push the *commitment button* and urge people to be more committed to the work of the congregation.

The next phase is when a congregation seeks to focus blame on the things and persons who are keeping them from being what they once were and what they desire to be. The Anger phase can end up being a time of great conflict in the life of many congregations. The stress on pastoral leadership and lay leadership can be tremendous. The congregation in Empty Nest may telescope its time focus to the age group it wants to target with the most efforts. Congregations who want to target teenagers want to focus on yesterday. Those who want to target senior adults want to focus on today. Congregations who want to target adults ages twenty-five to forty-five and their children want to focus on tomorrow.

Retirement: Retirement is that period when *Programs* and *Management* are dominant. *Vision* and *relationships* are no longer dominant. *Management* is controlling the direction of the congregation. Many long-term members and attendees decided at the end of Empty Nest that this is no longer a good place to invite people to come and be members and attendees. Existing members and attendees may feel that new people will be disappointed in the congregation. Or new people may want to change the congregation, and if it does not work, then the congregation may be weaker than it is already. Simultaneously they want the congregation to be alive and vital long enough to help them with various life passages, including their own deaths.

The stakeholders in the congregation who are sixty years of age or more have been professing Christians for forty years or more and have been members for twenty years or more. They give permission for the newer, younger members and attendees to try new programmatic directions. At times this takes the form of an appeal made to a prospective pastor. The pastor search committee urges the new pastor to come lead them into a new era of transformation.

Transitions, changes, and new ideas are said to be welcomed and supported. About 18 to 24 months into the transitions and changes initiated by a pastor or newer, younger lay leaders, the stakeholders may realize that things are not working the way they thought they would. If so, they seek to stop the change efforts, and–if necessary–get rid of or discourage the leaders of the transitions and changes.

Phase Five: Late Aging

This phase involves the life cycle stages of Old Age and Death. Phase Five is the time during which a congregation institutionalizes its *Management* and loses sight of *vision* and *relationships.* They walk by sight only.

Old Age: Old Age is that period when *Management* is the only one of the four organizing principles that is dominant. *Vision, relationships,* and *programs* are no longer dominant. *Management* is the only thing left to control the direction of the congregation. Old Age is that stage of a congregation's life cycle when it is functioning on fumes rather than being fueled by *Vision.* The habit or pattern of gathering for worship and fellowship is the primary factor keeping the congregation going.

The congregation is now at subsistence level. It is a preaching station or a chaplaincy ministry. Death is not necessarily nearby, but proactive meaningful congregation life that is generating new energy is gone. Death is not necessarily imminent or inevitable for Old Age congregations. It is not imminent in that Old Age congregations generally have the ability and resources to survive long past any viable, proactive ministry life.

Death: Death is that period when none of the four organizing principles is dominant. *Vision, relationships,* and *programs* are no longer even present. *Management* is the only organizing principle left, and its role is brief and confined. At Death a congregation ceases to exist as a community of worship, discipleship, and fellowship.

The desire is gone to meet regularly to worship God, to engage in spiritual growth activities, and to actively organize for fellowship and mutual support. Probably all three of these need to exist in some regular form for congregational life to be viable. What dies when these three are not present is the congregational movement. During the latter stages of congregational life many members and regular attendees probably deepened their inability to divide their faith in Christ from the cultural practices of a specific congregation in a specific location.

Death is not inevitable for any congregation. The life cycle and stages of development are not deterministic; that is, if a congregation has a Birth, it is not inevitable that it will have a Death. Having said that Death is not inevitable, congregations who are aging, are dysfunctional, and who wait until Late Aging to seek a turnaround are unlikely to experience a positive, successful future. They may not avoid Death.

COACHING BREAK

✔ Gaze out the window for a minute. Ponder the situation of your congregation. What images come to mind?

✔ At which stage of the life cycle is your congregation as a whole today? Parts of your congregation may be at various stages, but if you step back and look at your congregation as a whole, where does it appear to be? Once you know the answer to that question, then you can determine your next steps.

Observations Concerning the Pattern of the Life Cycle

Several observations need to be made concerning the pattern of the life cycle.

First, the four organizing principles are present with varying degrees of strength and dominance at each stage of the life cycle. For example, at Birth *Vision* is dominating. *Relationships, programs,* and *management* are present, but are not fully expressed or dominant. When an organizing principle is being expressed in a fully developed and dominant form, its corresponding letter is capitalized in the diagram on page 96, When not fully developed and dominant, the letter representing that principle is in lower case.

Second, the life cycle is not strictly defined in terms of time. Each stage is more of a developmental progression than it is a natural result of a certain amount of time having passed. The stages from Birth through Adulthood tend to take about a generation of time, or twenty-two to twenty-seven years. Defining time beyond that portion of the life cycle is difficult and not crucial to the process.

Third, progression through the various stages from Birth to Death is not inevitable. Development of a congregation can be halted, or a congregation may redevelop rather than decline to Death. Congregations will actually go through numerous partial life cycles where they spiral forward to a new Infancy, Childhood, Adolescence, or Adulthood and then live out this new partial life cycle over the next seven to nine years.

Fourth, another crucial concept is contained in the question: Now that I know where my congregation is on the life cycle, how do I provide positive, spiritually based change leadership?

Observations about Life on the Growth Side of the Life Cycle: Developing Congregations

First, for a congregation to keep developing, it needs to focus on the organizing principle formula of the next stage of development. For example, following five to six years in Childhood, a congregation should focus heavily on relationships to move it beyond the program, ministry, and activity development stage of their life to the energy of Adolescence.

Second, congregations can become dysfunctional and stop developing. Some congregations will then stagnate and move into a holding pattern that resembles Retirement or Old Age. Others will experience Death within a generation. The arrested development of congregations is something that often happens during the Childhood stage. This is particularly true of congregations that did not have a strong, passionate, positive vision as a part of their founding. Obvious examples of congregations in which this occurs are congregations that split out from other congregations and seek in the new congregations to recreate the past they believe they lost.

Arrested development also happens when new congregations are a franchise of another congregation and seek to emulate their parent or partner rather than developing a unique vision and patterns of relationships and programs that fit what God has called them to be and do.

Third, *vision* and *relationships* fuel congregations on the growth side. *Programs* and *management* sustain congregations on the aging side.

Fourth, no more than 20 to 25 percent of congregations are on the growth side of the life cycle.

Fifth, the transition, change, and transformation style utilized is different for different stages of the life cycle. This means that a project approach will work at one stage, a program approach at a second, and a process approach at another.

Sixth, congregational leaders need different leadership styles for different stages of the life cycle. Assessment of the leadership style of ministerial and lay leaders is crucial to determining the change and growth process that will be successful.

Seventh, the issues to be addressed are different for different stages of the life cycle. Some of these are age-related issues; spiritual issues; transition, change, and transformation issues; program issues; relationships issues; management issues; and vision issues.

Observations about Life on the Aging Side of the Life Cycle: Redeveloping Congregations

First, the vast majority of congregations who seek to initiate a new spiritual strategic journey are on the aging side of the life cycle. The percentage of congregations on the aging side is between 75 and 80 percent.

Second, because of their position on the aging side of the life cycle, congregations are being sustained by their *management* rather than fueled by their *vision*.

Third, the transition, change, and transformation strategies are different for different aging stages. What works at one stage does not necessarily work at another stage. The prescription for transition and change or the intervention strategy will be different.

Fourth, the length of time it takes to produce lasting change is different for different stages of the life cycle. Generally, the more aging the congregation, the longer it takes to produce lasting change. The key element will be whether a fix or a solution can be achieved in a given congregation.

Fifth, some people feel there should be no aging side to the life cycle because congregations should redevelop with a new vision, a new life cycle, or an explosive curve of new, positive transition, change, and growth. This is the ideal. The ideal will happen less than 20 percent of the time, perhaps less than 10 percent of the time. What about the other 80 or more percent?

Sixth, the Death of a congregation is not inevitable and often not desirable. The life cycle and stages of development are not deterministic. Congregations can and often do redevelop and spiral forward to a new partial life cycle that may last a minimum of seven to nine years.

Seventh, having said Death is not inevitable, we must quickly add that aging congregations are often dysfunctional. If they wait until Phase Five: Late Aging to seek a turnaround, they are unlikely to experience a positive, successful future. They may not avoid Death.

Using the Life Cycle as an Intervention Tool

The intervention question is, Now that I know where my congregation is on the life cycle, how do I provide positive, spiritually based transformational leadership? Can I go back to the growth side of the life cycle?

Oh no! Wait! Please don't use that four-letter word! Do you know what it was? It was the word *back*. Please never talk to a congregation about going back. To do so invites people to talk about going back to the way things were. We must talk about going forward to the new thing God is doing in our midst, the new journey toward which God is pulling us.

Any effort focused on going back to the way things were will be driven by management rather than vision. The opportunity to be captivated by the new vision God has for your congregation is a terrible open door to waste. Please treat this opportunity with great care, wonderful joy, and spiritual passion.

The following section is about how to redevelop a congregation on the aging side once an appropriate assessment is completed. It deals with 75 to 80 percent of all congregations.

An Intervention Framework

Every stage has a redevelopment formula, a process theme, a destination, strategies, a time frame, and a desired end result that will characterize its redevelopment or *FaithSoaring.*

Redevelopment Formula: Each stage has a characteristic formula. For example, the formula for Maturity is *vRPM.* This means that *vision* is no longer dominant, but *relationships, programs,* and *management* are.

Each stage also has a redevelopment formula. This is the formula of dominance to utilize to redevelop the congregation. In the case of Maturity the formula is VRPm. This means to emphasize *vision, relationships,* and *programs,* and de-emphasize *management.*

Process Theme: A different process theme or style of redevelopment exists for each stage. Maturity calls for Revisioning. Empty Nest calls for Revitalization. Retirement calls for Renewal. Old Age calls for Reinventing. Death calls for Resurrection.

Rate of Change: The rate of change can be continuous, discontinuous, or radical in relationship to the past.

Destination: The destination refers to the place in that next cycle of congregational life toward which a congregation is seeking to redevelop. Some stages have more than one probable destination.

Strategies: The strategies are the particular order in which the organizing principles are addressed to move forward to the new destination. Different stages and destinations impact the strategies that are appropriate and effective.

Time Frame: The time frame is the amount of time the change pathways and transition passages last before true transformation to a new life cycle has occurred.

Desired End Result: The desired end result of each intervention is generally the same. A seven-to-nine-year period of redeveloped life is generally the best for which congregations can aspire.

Intervention at the Various Aging Stages

Maturity: Maturity is that stage of a congregation's life cycle when it is functioning well, with some sense of efficiency and effectiveness. However, it is no longer clear concerning its focus and sense of strategic spiritual direction. Signs of malaise exist. Members cannot articulate the vision anymore. They no longer are certain as to who they are and where they are heading in the future.

The formula for Maturity is *vRPM.* The redevelopment formula is *VRPm.* The process theme is Revisioning, which is a process of developing a new sense of vision and strategic spiritual direction. The destination for the Revisioning effort is Adulthood. The strategy is to diminish the *Management* practices of the congregation that control rather than empower. Second, reaffirm or create new *Vision.* A congregation should then reengineer the *Management* systems to empower the new sense of *Vision* and strategic spiritual direction. The time frame for this type of redevelopment is 6 to 18 months. The new partial life cycle should be able to last for seven to nine years.

Empty Nest: Empty Nest is that stage of a congregation's life cycle when it is at first nostalgic and later angry about the loss of the past. Ultimately, the congregation will look for something or someone to blame for the situation in which they find themselves. The formula for Empty Nest is *vRpM.* The redevelopment formula is *vRPm.* The process theme is Revitalization. Revitalization involves revitalizing or creating new *Programs* that lead to reaffirmed or new Relationships. Revitalization allows for a reaffirmed or new *Vision* to emerge. The destination for Revitalization is Adulthood if change that is continuous with the past is attempted. If change that is discontinuous is attempted, then the destination is Adolescence. The strategy is to diminish *Management.* Revitalization or creation of new *Programs* follows this. Then efforts are made at affirming or creating new *Relationships.* When these efforts are developing well, then it is time to ask questions about a reaffirmed or new *Vision.* Finally, the *Management* systems need to be reengineered. The time frame for this redevelopment is 18 to 36 months. The desired end result is a revitalized congregation with a partial life cycle of seven to nine years.

Retirement: Retirement is the stage in a congregation's life when despair and hope are both present. Hope rests in new opportunities. Despair is evident in how long it has been since the prime of the congregation.

The formula for Retirement is *vrPM.* The redevelopment formula is *vRpm.* The process theme is Renewal. Renewal involves renewing *Relationships* in a congregation followed by revitalizing the *Programs* structure of the congregation. The destination for the Renewal effort is Adolescence if change that is discontinuous with the past is attempted. If change that is radical in regard to the past is attempted, then the destination is Childhood. The strategy is to diminish the *Management* systems. Then renew or create new *Relationships* feelings. When this is going well, then renew or create new *Programs.* When acceptance of a new direction is occurring, then reaffirm or cast a new *Vision.* Finally, the *Management* systems are reengineered. This time frame is three to five years. The desired end result is for the renewed period to last seven to nine years and to form a new partial life cycle.

Old Age: Old Age is that stage in a congregation's life when it reaches subsistence level. It is functioning as a preaching station or chaplaincy ministry for the remaining members and their families and a friendship network. The habit or tradition of meeting as a congregation fuels the congregation's life long after a vital, flexible spiritual community is viable.

The formula for Old Age is *vrpM.* The redevelopment formula is *vrPm.* The process theme is Reinventing. Reinventing involves a major redesign of the congregation to have a viable, vital, empowered future. The destination for the Reinventing is Childhood if changes are made that are discontinuous. If radical changes are attempted, then the destination is Infancy. The strategy is to diminish *Management.*

Creating new programs and ministries can stabilize the *Programs* structure. Then cast and seek ownership for a new *Vision.* Out of this, seek to develop new *Relationships.* Then the *Management* systems are reengineered. The time frame is three to five years, but with stability reached within six to eighteen months. The desired end result is a period that may last seven to nine years and forms a new partial life cycle.

Death: At death, the congregation ceases to exist as an active community of vision, worship, discipleship, and fellowship. The formula of Death is *m.* The formula of redevelopment is *Vrpm.* The process theme is Resurrection. Resurrection involves the creation of a new, transformed congregational life that bears little or no resemblance to the life that went before it.

The destination for Resurrection is Infancy if change that is radical is attempted. If a complete Rechurching effort takes place, then Birth is the destination. The strategy is to seek to discover if there is a *Vision* for a new congregation. Then a new pattern of *Relationships* is developed. The time frame is six to eighteen months. The desired end result is a new life cycle whose growth side may last fifteen to eighteen years.

The following chart summarizes the eight transition passages and change pathways for redevelopment of congregations:

Implications of Redevelopment Strategies for Congregations

First, do something that is stage and size appropriate. General research and specific observation indicates that six out of ten congregations who are aging, plateaued, and declining choose to do little or nothing that is effective in response to their situation. The first step toward doing something that is stage and size appropriate is to thoroughly assess your situation to define current reality.

Second, create a sense of urgency. If your situation calls for transition and change actions, then share this information in a convincing spiritual and strategic manner with the congregation. Develop a guiding coalition or critical mass of people who are spiritually and strategically committed to helping the congregation reach its full potential in Kingdom service.

Congregational Redevelopment Transition Passages and Change Pathways

STAGE	PROCESS THEME	RATE OF TRANSITION AND CHANGE	TIME FRAME	DESTINATION
Maturity	Revisioning	Continuous	6–18 months	Adulthood
Empty Nest	Revitalization	Continuous	18–36 months	Adulthood
Empty Nest	Revitalization	Discontinuous	18–36 months	Adolescence
Retirement	Renewal	Discontinuous	3–5 years	Adolescence
Retirement	Renewal	Radical	3–5 years	Childhood
Old Age	Reinvent	Discontinuous	18–36 months	Childhood
Old Age	Reinvent	Radical	18–36 months	Infancy
Death	Resurrection	Radical	6–18 months	Infancy

Third, discover vision and take intentional actions. Engage in a strategic spiritual journey that seeks to discover and develop ownership around an empowering vision for Kingdom progress. Even before vision is clear, take intentional actions intended to help the congregation move forward in Kingdom service. Vision will focus these actions.

Reference Thoughts

Numerous sources have dealt with the life cycle as an assessment and learning or intervention tool for congregations. Here are three: Jere Allen and George Bullard, *Shaping a Future for the Church in the Changing Community,* Atlanta: Home Mission Board, SBC, 1981; Robert D. Dale, *To Dream Again,* Nashville: Broadman Press, 1981; Martin F. Saarinen, *The Life Cycle of a Congregation,* Washington: The Alban Institute, 1986.

Also www.SSJTutorial.org is a major interactive Web site that is based on the life cycle and stages of a congregation. This is part of the larger Web resource known as www.CongregationalResources.org, hosted by The Alban Institute and the Indianapolis Center for Congregations, and funded by the Lilly Endowment.

COACHING INSIGHTS

■ What are the strength and alignment of the four organizing principles of *Vision, Relationships, Programs,* and *Management* in your congregation? What is the positive contribution that each is making to your spiritual strategic journey? Who is driving the vehicle that symbolizes your congregation?

■ In which stage of life cycle development is your congregation? Is it on the growing side or the aging side of its life cycle? What are the implications of its stage? Do you know the next steps to take? What is the relationship of its stage to the need for readiness described in other chapters of this book?

■ Do you know the next steps to take? Do you know who you must have as an *Enduring Visionary Leadership Community* to successfully take the next steps? Who needs to take the initiative? When will they do it?

■ Has it occurred to you how your congregation might avoid aging past the Prime stage? What would it take to hardwire into your congregational culture the need to redevelop itself once each decade after the first time its redevelops forward from the aging side of the life cycle? Since redevelopment is not a permanent solution, but a seven-to-nine-year solution, this is a necessary and essential consideration.

PERSONAL REFLECTIONS

YOUR REFLECTIONS: What are your reflections on the material presented in this chapter?

_____

_____

_____

_____

_____

YOUR ACTIONS: What actions do you need to take about your life, ministry, and/or congregation based on the material presented in this chapter?

_____

_____

_____

_____

_____

YOUR ACCOUNTABILITY: How and by whom do you want to be held accountable for taking these actions?

_____

_____

_____

_____

_____

The Life Cycle and Stages of Congregational Development

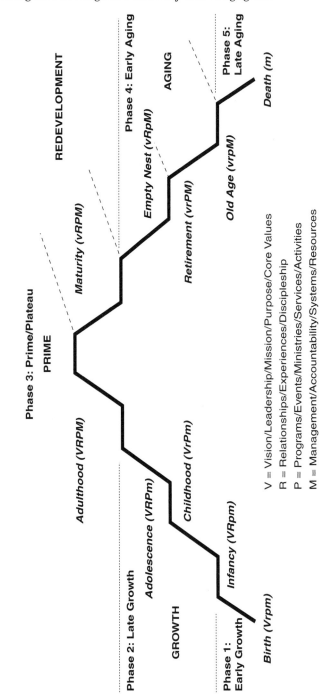

V = Vision/Leadership/Mission/Purpose/Core Values
R = Relationships/Experiences/Discipleship
P = Programs/Events/Ministries/Services/Activities
M = Management/Accountability/Systems/Resources

CHAPTER SIX

Taking a New Look at Transition, Change, and Transformation

EXECUTIVE SUMMARY

The purpose of this chapter is to talk about the relationship of transition, change, and transformation. The focus is on building models based upon transition first, rather than change first as the key element in creating a movement that will result in transformation. A key secondary focus is around diminishing the controlling aspects of management as an essential exercise to empower transition and change to achieve transformation. A final focus is on meeting the collaborative challenge among congregational leadership.

Long ago, in a land not so far way, in a time known as the twentieth century, if congregational leaders wanted to do something different or better, they would change something—with or without permission of the congregation or its board. Then they would figuratively hold on to the nearest utility pole with all their strength to try to withstand the wind that would blow by them at sixty to seventy-five miles per hour.

They called the wind transition. The wind represented the reaction to the change that was made, and the necessary transition in emotion, perspective, and behavior that was necessary to adjust to the change that had been made.

Because congregational leaders did not see any alternative to the force and pain of transition and because they liked the rush they felt when they won, they would repeat this cycle over and over again. The only trouble was that sometimes they did not win. Even when they won, they had to pay the consequences. These included marginalizing or alienating people from the fellowship of the congregation.

Like many of us, these congregational leaders forgot a major fact of human relationships. The first feeling that congregational participants not prepared for change experience is the emotion of loss. When change occurs, participants often feel they have lost something or had it taken away. Unfortunately, the first action many congregational participants take, in response to change they view as destructive, is to do or say nothing. They are in shock and cannot find their voice. When they regain their voice in a few days, weeks, or months and react to what they perceive to be a negative situation, their delayed opposition surprises and dismays congregational leaders.

The loss experienced in a congregation can be over something that was positive, negative, or dysfunctional. It really does not matter. The key point is that it is different and happened outside the realm of empowerment or control by the people feeling the loss.

Suppose your congregation includes a long-term usher. He has been greeting people and handing out worship folders at a certain door in the vestibule of the sanctuary for many years. He is now old and gruff. Perhaps he was always gruff. His gruff nature was particularly focused on new people he did not recognize as part of the congregational family. As part of a renewed effort in the congregation to become more guest friendly, a congregational leader convinces this usher to move to the parking team that helps people find available parking spaces in a now too-small parking area.

The first Sunday this former usher is no longer at his post, some congregational participants complain about his absence. They miss him. They were accustomed to seeing him at a certain door. When questioned, they acknowledge that he was hard to get along with and was not friendly. At the same time they say he represents something that is familiar about coming to worship, and they miss that. This represents good change, but questionable transition. The process followed to make the change did not provide support for the change.

Embrace Your Full Kingdom Potential, Skip Transformation, and Abandon Change

The change processes that once characterized congregations were left-brained rather than right-brained. They developed in the generation following World War II. February 9, 1964, represented a symbolic hinge point when the generation that followed World War II ended. North American demographics moved from the birth generation known as Baby Boomers to the birth generation known as Baby Busters. The appearance of the Beatles singing group on the Ed Sullivan show on Sunday night, February 9, 1964, symbolized this transition, birthing a new kind of music on America's favorite television show and thus introducing a new generation's taste to the public at large.

Change processes characteristic of much of the second half of the twentieth century do not have the ability to truly transform a congregation and help it reach its full Kingdom potential. Why? Change models focused on pushing. Transformation focuses on pulling. Change focused on clinicians and consultants. Transformation focuses on coaches and peer learning communities. Change focused on congregations responding to an outside expert. Transformation focuses on raising the capacity of the congregation to focus on their own challenges. Change fixed problems. Transformation focuses on affirming what is right and building on it.

But, as was indicated in chapter 1, even transformation can be seen as a destination. Congregations may well believe they can arrive at the place called transformation. Such is not the case! It is necessary to challenge congregations with the larger, more eternal concept of reaching their full Kingdom potential. To begin this approach, the starting point must be different.

First Steps for Transition, Change, and Transformation

The first step is to focus on the need for transition before change, rather than change followed by transition. Transition is about morale, people, and relationships. Change is about mission, tasks, and responsibilities. Change is left-brained and modern. Transition is right-brained and postmodern. Change is about a way of thinking and acting that is diminishing as the first steps in transformation. Transition is about the emerging first steps in transformation that will empower change to take place.

FOCUS ON TRANSITION BEFORE CHANGE

In reality many people in congregational life are very aware of the transition first approach to change. We see it every time a new senior pastor comes to a congregation. We talk about the new senior pastor having some currency to spend on making changes during his or her first six to eighteen months at this church. When six to eighteen months have passed, the honeymoon is over. When all the currency has been spent, the senior pastor must earn more currency before additional changes can be made.

What if we recognize this pattern as being typical of congregations and seek to use it to empower change, transformation, and a super journey toward reaching the full Kingdom potential of the congregation? OK! But how would it work?

The first steps revolve around raising the morale of the congregation. Work on deepening relationships with God, with one another, and with the context in which the congregation serves. This builds up a currency to spend on making changes. It also builds up a sense of expectation and anticipation that changes will be made, that something is going to improve in the congregation, that spiritual and strategic functioning of the congregation is going to escalate.

When the discernment and intuition of congregational leadership tells them the timing is right, then they embark on change pathways that bubble up in the midst of the new relationships. They do so with the currency or transition assets they need to address the change deficits that shout for new spiritual and strategic initiatives.

To a certain degree transition and change represent a seesaw or cyclical action that always begins with transition followed by change, followed by transition, followed by change, and so forth. Often both transition and change are occurring at the same time. New transition is being built for the next round of changes while current changes are being implemented. When carried out very artistically, the whole congregational system moves in the direction of transformation.

What happens when the congregational transition process gets stuck and changes are not made? Transition currency is like an open piece of chocolate candy in your pants pocket on a hot day. If not consumed quickly, it will melt, create a mess, and you will lose the value of the candy.

When a congregation gets stuck in transition, it will lose the new value and empowerment created through transition if it is not spent on change. If a congregation gets stuck in the euphoria of transition and loses sight of the need for change, at some point the expectation and anticipation of change will turn to anger. Then the congregation will lose all, if not more than all, of the good will and energy for the future that was created by transition activities.

The hoped for scenario is that, through a repeating cycle of transition and change, the congregation will make progress toward the destination of transformation. The only difficulty is that transformation is a moving target. At the same time the congregation is moving towards transformation, what it means to be transformed is moving away from the congregation.

TRANSFORMATION IS NOT THE DESTINATION

Thus, the congregation may or may not be drawing closer to what it means to be transformed. Worse yet, the congregation, once moving forward, may decide to slow down or stop its transformational journey. But what it means to be transformed is still in motion. This only increases once again the distance between the congregation and transformation.

Taking this analogy to another dimension, transformation is not the destination anyway. The destination is a continual spiritual strategic journey toward the full Kingdom potential of the congregation. In the spirit of "The Chronicles of Narnia," referred to in chapter 1, the full Kingdom potential of the congregation is further up and further in.

To approach a spiritual strategic journey that has its foresight focused on the full Kingdom potential of the congregation, congregations must embrace the hockey playing philosophy of Wayne Gretzky. Wayne was an outstanding, all-star Canadian hockey player. When asked how he always seemed to be in the middle of the action or play, Wayne indicated that rather than skating to where the puck is, he skated to where it was going to be.

Congregations who desire to reach their full Kingdom potential will continually embrace their understanding of their potential, skip transformation, and abandon change. Only then will they transcend the incremental transition and change factors that keep them basically the same year after year. They will not only think and act outside the box of current congregational ministry, but beyond the box to the new thing God in doing in them.

While all of this may sound great, let's ask the critical question: How can I do all this in my congregation when it is so controlled by people with a management mentality? These are often very good people with a deep commitment to the past and present of the congregation, but they do not see the need to embrace a transformational future, much less to let go of the past and engage in *FaithSoaring* based on the new thing God is doing.

Diminish the Controlling Aspects of Management

A crucial early step in the process of congregational redevelopment during Maturity, Empty Nest, Retirement, and Old Age is to diminish the controlling aspects of the management processes in the congregation. Management is the administration of the various resources of the congregation, the formal and informal governance and decision-making structure of the congregation, the formal and informal traditions and culture of the congregation, and the readiness of the congregation for change and growth.

Management also relates to how a congregation handles its day-to-day operations. This includes its operational planning process and how this is implemented to bring about growth and change in the congregation. This factor provides a basis for deciding how the people, financial, facilities, and equipment and materials resources of the congregation are utilized. Finally, management deals with the efficiency of a congregation.

Once a congregation attains the stage of Maturity on the life cycle, its progress tends to be fueled by Management rather than Vision. During Maturity, Empty Nest, and early Retirement these management principles become increasingly controlling. By late Retirement the management principles begin to break down.

The specific management groups differ according to the doctrine, polity, or discipline of a particular denominational tradition. However, management groups can at times be known by such names as elders, deacons, boards, council, finance, nominating, personnel, trustees, and other names.

How Management Becomes Controlling

When a congregation is born, flexibility and creativity are high; and controllability is low. As a congregation develops and establishes its patterns of relating, flexibility and creativity begin to decrease; and controllability begins to increase.

Management becomes controlling in a congregation by the end of the first generation of its existence, when vision becomes diminished. When this happens, management begins to fuel the forward progress on the congregation. Management steps into the vacuum created by the lack of an empowering and fueling vision. Management is empowering when it is in a support role, but controlling when it is in a lead role. In its lead and controlling role it keeps congregations from redeveloping because they prefer to manage the resources they have rather than taking risks to acquire new and different resources.

It is important for congregations to see that the role of management must diminish or unfreeze during a transition and change process that is being attempted on the aging side of the life cycle. The controlling aspects of management, which include the tendency to keep things as they have been, will need to diminish for a congregation to try new patterns or new energy from which a new vision can emerge.

CREATING AN URGENCY TO DIMINISH MANAGEMENT

At least three ways exist to create an urgency to diminish management. First is to define the reality of the controlling aspects of management. Second is to build broad-based ownership around the new understanding of God's vision that is emerging in the congregation. Third is to use a crisis as an opportunity to look at all the systems of the congregation and reorganize around those that empower rather than those that control.

To define the reality of the controlling aspects of management, take some measurements. One tendency of congregations is to, over time, add decision-making and policy-development groups to the mixture of the leadership and management of the congregation.

Take a measurement of the number of official management groups that existed in the congregation ten years ago. Compare that to the number that exist today. In the typical congregation this number grows over time. These official management groups become a larger percentage of the official groups of any kind in the congregation that require recruitment of leadership each year. Often the number of official management groups in a congregation will increase even when the membership, attendance, and the number of people otherwise connected with the congregation have plateaued or are declining.

A second tendency of congregations is to place on official management groups the same people for multiple terms of service. Over time this may result in management groups being made up of persons who are older than the average member of the congregation and who have longer tenure of membership than the average member. Measure the number of people who were in various management positions ten years ago, and are still in the same or similar management positions today.

This second tendency leads to decisions and policies that seek to sustain the past, with insufficient regard for the new things that God is doing in the congregation. Appropriate attachment to the heritage of the congregation is a good thing. Holding on to the past when doing so may keep a congregation from reaching its potential is a bad thing.

When this second tendency fully develops, some official or unofficial group within the congregation begins to act like an executive committee for the congregation and takes control of day-to-day decisions. Generally, the motives of this group are good. Their desire is to help the congregation succeed if it is a strong congregation, or survive if it is a weak congregation.

A third tendency of congregations is to add steps to the decision-making and policy-development procedures or process. Issues that used to go directly to the final decision-making group—council, board, or congregation—now must go through several steps of review. This is not to suggest that accountability is a negative thing, but to suggest that unnecessary review slows decision-making and discourages transition and change that might keep a congregation flexible and responsive to new opportunities.

Creating an urgency to diminish management may also result from strong, positive focus on the new God-given vision that is emerging within a congregation. A broad-based group of people may feel new passion for Kingdom concerns and realize that management practices may need to be set aside or relaxed for a while to allow a new Kingdom movement to develop within the congregation.

This is certainly the ideal way for flexibility to again replace controllability as the lead characteristic or mood within the congregation. It definitely avoids what may become unhealthy confrontations between leadership and management when the controlling aspects of management are addressed.

At times, a major crisis may threaten a congregation's future existence. This can cause the congregation to reinvent itself and its management structure. This may involve reengineering the management structure to make it leaner. Such action is generally a good by-product of a crisis. It may allow a congregation to make Kingdom progress quicker and more effectively.

TACTICS TO USE TO DIMINISH MANAGEMENT

Existing management groups can diminish their controlling tendencies by asking a different set of questions about management decisions and processes than might be their traditional pattern. Some of these new questions are as follow:

1. What decisions can we make that will empower the vision and help create relationship experiences in our congregation?

2. How can we make this decision in a way that will include more people in the life and ministry of the congregation and encourage their spiritual development as disciples?
3. How do we both honor the past and the present obligations of the congregation and display a genuine openness to new traditions that may need to be formed that will help us to be relevant in the twenty-first century?
4. Why do we need this additional step or area of accountability? Will it help the congregation be more flexible, or more controllable?
5. What seems impossible today, but, if it could happen, would transform the congregation's ability to serve in the midst of God's Kingdom?

Another tactic that can be used is to decrease the number of decision-making and policy-development groups in the life of the congregation. Retain only the management groups that are essential to maintaining organizational accountability and effectiveness. Reengineering the decision-making and policy-development process to take out unnecessary and redundant steps is another tactic. Ask which steps matter to people connected with the congregation, and which steps help the congregation to better fulfill its Kingdom vision.

An additional helpful tactic is to reduce the number of people it takes to fill the various decision-making and policy-development groups in the congregation. Some congregations are unbalanced to the point that more people are involved in management activities than are involved in ministry activities.

Misty and the Invisible Fence as an Image of Controlling Your Congregation

My next-door neighbor has a dog–a black lab named Misty. She is a beautiful dog who loves to play, but cannot run free. Our community has a leash law for dogs and cats. The way my neighbor deals with this challenge, and allows Misty some freedom, is to have an invisible electric fence around the perimeter of the yard. The electric fence controls the movements of Misty by containing her roaming within a defined, acceptable area.

Often when I am outside and Misty is in her outside domain, she will run toward me and then stop about six feet before the edge of her yard. She knows where the invisible fence is. She was shocked by it numerous times when she was being trained to know the limits of her domain. The invisible fence keeps Misty inside a certain area, unless the fence is turned off and the owners have her on a leash. When on a leash, she knows she will not be shocked. She is not afraid to journey outside her yard with her owners in tow.

I was thinking recently about Misty's situation, and comparing it to the situation of many congregations. Often congregations are controlled by an invisible electric fence. This fence defines the perimeter of the work of the congregational leadership. Their domain is clear. Their programs, ministries, and activities are confined to a certain area. Owners or stakeholders turn the electric fence on and off. They let the congregation experiment beyond the fence, but with a leash that can draw them back if they go too far away from the owners.

The process of transition and then change that characterizes the spiritual strategic journey of a congregation focuses on creating a desire for change or urgency to move beyond the invisible fence. It motivates congregational managers to turn off the electric fence to empower new adventures rather than controlling current patterns of ministry.

As the process of transition works, congregational leaders are given permission to venture beyond the typical domain controlled by the congregational managers. Empowerment is present to soar beyond the past into a future that is emerging. While this empowerment is not usually for radical changes, it is a real empowerment for moving outside the box, yard, or closed system of the congregation.

The difficulty is that often congregational leaders are still afraid to venture beyond their domain. They are afraid of getting shocked even though the electric fence is turned off. They are afraid the stakeholders will pull the choke chain when the leaders least expect it.

Therefore, even though the managers have given what may very well be a brief period of empowerment, the change efforts may still fail because leaders do not know how to act with newfound freedom or know whether to trust this new freedom.

When this happens, it may actually be the leaders of the congregation who are controlling its future rather than the managers. The leaders are afraid of success and change themselves. They are so bound by the traditional reaction of managers that they do not know how to soar with new empowerment.

WHO IS REALLY CONTROLLING YOUR CONGREGATION?

If a congregation engages in transition efforts that successfully create a new sense of expectation, urgency, and anticipation of change, but still cannot bring itself to change, who then is really controlling the congregation?

Diminishing the controlling aspects of management is an essential part of the transition and change process leading to transformation. Often congregations underestimate the amount of time and effort they must give to diminishing the controlling aspects of management so that they can move forward along their spiritual strategic journey.

In many situations in which I have been coaching a congregation along a spiritual strategic journey, I have realized that one of two things happened. Either we failed to engage in sufficient efforts at diminishing the controlling aspects of management, or for some reason the congregational leadership did not gain the confidence necessary to move forward beyond its controlling aspects (as symbolized by the electric fence).

WHAT ARE THE THINGS AND WHO ARE THE PEOPLE?

Recently I have used a new exercise to move the *People of Passion* and the *People of Position* in a congregation deeper into dialogue about the factors controlling them. Similar to many dialogue exercises I facilitate, this process is open-ended and revolves around posing two questions and calling on leaders to struggle with their meaning for their congregation.

The questions in this case are, *(1) What Are the Things, and (2) Who Are the People, Controlling Your Congregation Whose Influence Must Be Diminished Before We Can Move Forward?* I invite a leadership community of the congregation to spend at least one session of several hours wrestling with these questions for their congregation.

Then I stick in a twist. I ask them to begin the dialogue by talking about the ways in which they personally are controlling the congregation and keeping it from moving beyond its current patterns of ministry. At first they are surprised that I want them to begin with themselves. They were ready to pounce on certain situations and people.

What I want them to do is acknowledge their own co-dependence on the way things have been in their congregation, on their belief that managers will stop change so that they do not have to move outside their own comfort zone as leaders, and on their own fear of the new and transformational. Too many leaders are actually afraid for their congregation to grow, change, and move into areas of ministry for which they will have to provide leadership for which they feel unprepared.

Every time I have used this exercise, leaders have successfully been able to talk about how they themselves are actually controlling the future of their congregation by their unwillingness and even fear to act in response to God's vision for their congregation.

When they do get around to talking about other things and people who are controlling their congregation, they often realize it is their own anticipation of the controlling actions of others that keep them from leading the congregation forward. It is not controlling people of the past who are keeping the congregation from moving forward.

For example, one congregational leadership community quickly identified their feelings concerning an affluent member of their congregation who gives liberally to their congregation when things are going the way he wants. He uses his money to hold the congregation hostage to his perspective on what the congregation ought to be doing.

This leadership community acknowledged in their dialogue that it is not this person and his money that is holding the congregation hostage. Rather the unwillingness of the leaders to cast a clear vision and stick with it in spite of any opposition this controlling manager may pose is keeping the congregation from being a true Christlike community in word and deed.

Confronting the Antagonist in Our Heart

My most dramatic experience helping a congregation with this phenomenon involved this type of controlling manager or antagonist. Several times per year he would take over some formal or informal gathering by shouting at people and claiming that he rather than they was truly committed to the future integrity of the congregation. A few families each year dropped out of active participation in the congregation following such an incident.

At a planning retreat with their congregation, I knew that this individual would probably react badly and publicly to a proposal for the congregation to relocate. When the proposal came, he stood to his feet, started shouting, and sought to take over the meeting. I strongly confronted him. This resulted in him and his wife leaving the meeting and the remaining participants and me debriefing this situation for the next hour.

Many people present acknowledged they had always refused to confront this controlling manager because he was partially right in his accusations of them. None of them truly felt they were as committed to the congregation as was this individual. However, they knew they were at a crossroads in the life of the congregation and must act on their collective courage to change the congregation's situation.

A month later the congregation voted by more than one hundred to six to relocate. They relocated within the year to a place for which they had a clear focus, purpose, and vision. Within two years they had more than tripled in size, and now fifteen years later continue a positive, passionate ministry in their new location.

The antagonist? He and his wife, and the two other couples who voted with them against the relocation, moved on to another congregation where they have been quiet supportive members. Truly everyone was released from his or her psychological, theological, and geographic captivity. The antagonist was in their heart. The electric fence no longer could contain them.

If your congregation, like the one in this example, and congruent with the principles presented on diminishing the controlling aspects of your congregation, can break through the swamp lands of control, do you still have what it takes to engage the collaboration challenge?

COACHING BREAK

✔ Gaze out the window for a minute. Ponder the situation of your congregation. What images come to mind?

✔ Who is controlling your congregation? Are you? If so, what should you to do about it? The more we seek to control things around us, the more we end up squeezing vital life out of that which we claim to love the most.

Can Congregational Leadership Meet the Collaboration Challenge?

Recently as I was spending a weekend coaching a congregation, I became renewed in the convictions I am expressing in this book and have explicitly described in chapter 3. If the *Pastoral, Passionate,* and *Positional* leadership of a congregation can get their act together as spiritual and strategic leaders and agree concerning the future of their congregation, then it is likely the congregation will follow.

My renewal happened as I spoke to the leadership of the congregation one evening. I realized anew that leadership, by one or two of the core leadership groups, was not going to make a transformational difference in this congregation. I realized anew that as long as the *Pastoral, Passionate,* or *Positional* leadership felt that their specific viewpoint on the future of the congregation was the only valid viewpoint, the congregation would fail.

In the case of this congregation, I realized they have a tremendous opportunity to meet the collaboration challenge. They have taken the past several years to dramatically prepare for their current opportunity, so it has not been an easy challenge for which to develop the capacity. Now they are ready! But before they can accomplish anything on a spiritual journey, the three groups must collaborate and come to an agreement as to their proposed destination. Only then can they expect the congregation to follow them and to succeed in the journey.

CAN THIS HAPPEN IN YOUR CONGREGATION?

Can the *People of Pastoral Leadership,* the *People of Passion,* and the *People of Position* in your congregation meet the collaboration challenge? Can they cooperate deeply enough to lay aside their own images of the past, present, and future of their congregation? Can they agree about a future vision for their congregation that is God-inspired?

Can they focus with unity around a common goal? Can they be the unified leadership of the congregation focusing on helping the entire congregation to travel along their spiritual strategic journey toward reaching their full Kingdom potential?

If they cannot, then it is unlikely the congregation will ever reach it full Kingdom potential. They will miss the synergistic impact of a unified leadership group using their spiritual and strategic resources to their fullest extent in response to the leadership of God.

WHAT IS THE COLLABORATION CHALLENGE?

The collaboration challenge is the ability of these three categories of leadership—Pastoral, Passionate, and Positional—to work together as a diverse, yet unified, group of people with unique gifts, skills, and preferences toward the future, full Kingdom potential of their congregation. Simply asked, Can they focus their spiritual and strategic energies on a transformational future for their congregation?

Congregational collaboration is the art of working together on a spiritual strategic journey in a direction that represents the synergy of the various gifts, skills, and preferences of the congregational members and regular attendees. It is a journey forward to that which is unseen, toward which only God can effectively pull the congregation. It is a journey crafted in the image of God.

Collaboration as a historical concept also has the idea of collaborating with an enemy against your country, party, organization, or cause. Within a congregation, collaboration occurs when people with a diverse view of the past, present, and future of the congregation determine that it is a greater good, or the more loving Christlike thing to do, to work with all the categories of leadership to build the strongest possible spiritual and strategic future for the congregation.

This may not seem like a huge challenge, but it is. The inability of these three leadership categories to work together leads to mediocre or casual ministry in thousands of congregations. The successful ability of these three leadership categories to lead is essential to a congregation that engages in a ministry of success, significance, and possible surrender to the will of God.

The Pastoral and Passionate leadership cannot lead the successful transformation of the congregation without the Positional leadership. The Pastoral and Positional leadership cannot lead the successful transformation of a congregation without the Passionate leadership. The Passionate and Positional leadership cannot lead the successful transformation of the congregation without the Pastoral leadership. All these leadership categories have strengths to contribute to a transformational journey.

WHAT ARE BARRIERS TO MEETING THE COLLABORATIVE CHALLENGE?

To lead a congregation toward its Kingdom potential, you must understand and recognize the barriers that prevent collaborative leadership. Important barriers include:

First, culture and heritage are more important in the congregation, particularly among the Positional leadership, than is the obvious presence of Christ, and a commitment to *FaithSoaring*. The ability to walk by faith rather than by sight in the spirit of 2 Corinthians 5:7 is the essence of *FaithSoaring*.

Second, the Passionate leadership does not understand nor respect the culture and heritage of the congregation, but rather wants to reject anything that either happened before they came to the church or does not match their vision of the future of the church.

Third, the Pastoral leadership feels they need to be the sole initiator of vision in the congregation, and/or they cannot successfully share vision in a way that creates broad-based ownership in the congregation. Without empowerment around vision, full collaboration will be difficult.

Fourth, the Pastoral, Passionate, and Positional leadership focus primarily on their own personal goals. Pastoral leadership generally has goals surrounding fulfillment of their personal call to ministry. They are at times in search of a congregation that will allow them to fulfill their mission rather than helping the congregation they serve to fulfill God's mission. They especially see Positional leadership as blockers, but even at times they see the zealous nature of Passionate leadership as being another type of barrier.

Passionate leadership tends to focus on an adventure of significance. They are often overachievers who are impatient with the rate or pace of transition and change in their congregation. They particularly feel Positional leadership is reactionary, but also see Pastoral leadership as seeking to impose a rigid future direction that does not allow them the freedom of expression.

Positional leadership is often comfortable with their surroundings, and is in search of increased comfort and security. They believe they have worked hard over the years to help the church work efficiently, and they are unsure the best thing for their church is to allow the Pastoral leadership fulfillment needs and the Passionate leadership adventure needs to change the past-to-present patterns of their congregation.

What Are Signs That Your Congregation Has Met the Collaboration Challenge?

Congregations do meet the Collaboration Challenge. Certain signs show you that you have succeeded in this challenge. They include:

First, an obvious commitment by the Pastoral, Passionate, and Positional leadership to a unified future-oriented spiritual strategic journey for the congregation. This journey is not a compromise of various viewpoints, but a synergistic journey that will empower the congregational *FaithSoaring* well beyond what it could do if only the one perspective dominated.

Second, all three leadership categories are able to embrace a common understanding of the past, present, and future of the congregation. Traditionally, Positional leadership seems to have the strongest focus on the past, Passionate leadership on the present, and Pastoral leadership on the future. When the collaboration challenge is met, all three leadership categories show a healthy appreciation for all three time dimensions.

Third, the remainder of the active congregation is captivated by the sense of unity and direction being expressed by the 21 percent. This is not an elitist movement of the 21 percent but an empowerment movement that captivates the spiritual imagination of the entire active congregation.

Can the *People of Pastoral Leadership,* the *People of Passion,* and the *People of Position* in your congregation meet the collaboration challenge?

COACHING INSIGHTS

■ It is essential for your congregation to meet the collaboration challenge so that it can achieve *FaithSoaring* in its spiritual strategic journey. Here are some questions for the collaborative challenge in your congregation:

■ Who are the Pastoral, Passionate, and Positional leadership within your congregation? What are the gifts, strengths, and preferences they bring to the spiritual and strategic journey of your congregation? At what depth do they know one another? How familiar are they with one another's life stories? How familiar are they with one another's spiritual pilgrimages? What can you do to gain this depth of relationship among them?

■ What is their ability to see the past, present, and future of their congregation? What is the evidence they have a healthy ability to see all three time dimensions? Around what spiritual and strategic issues are they unified? What are the next significant issues about which they need to have dialogue in an attempt to achieve unity?

■ What are the issues yet to be resolved that impact the collaboration challenge? What steps do you need to take to address these issues?

■ It is necessary for the controlling aspects of management to be diminished before a congregation can make the necessary transitions and changes to achieve transformation as part of a spiritual strategic journey. Yet, control is not always where we expect to find it in a congregation.

■ How would you characterize the domain in which your congregation functions, the invisible fence that surrounds it, and the stakeholders who control the fence and hold the leash? To what extent are you as a leader controlling your congregation when the fence is turned off and the stakeholders give you permission to roam outside your typical domain?

■ As a congregational leader, are you afraid of change and success? Have you become so comfortable with the way things are that you might undermine new opportunities available to your congregation because you are afraid to seize them? What are the things and who are the people that control your congregation? Whose influence must be diminished before you can move forward? Begin answering these questions by listing the ways you control your own congregation.

PERSONAL REFLECTIONS

YOUR REFLECTIONS: What are your reflections on the material presented in this chapter?

_____

_____

_____

_____

_____

YOUR ACTIONS: What actions do you need to take about your life, ministry, and/or congregation based on the material presented in this chapter?

_____

_____

_____

_____

_____

YOUR ACCOUNTABILITY: How and by whom do you want to be held accountable for taking these actions?

_____

_____

_____

_____

_____

CHAPTER SEVEN

Spiritual Relationships and Discernment as an Essential Process

EXECUTIVE SUMMARY

The purpose of this chapter is to focus on building spiritual relationships and engaging in discernment as an essential process for achieving breakthrough transformation. The focus will be on the process of one hundred days of share and prayer triplets as a relationship and spiritual exercise to create movement. We will share various examples congregations have used in their spiritual strategic journey.

Many congregational leaders raise a common cry. They do not want to use systems and processes for transition, change, and transformation that actually originate from the business world and are just superimposed on the congregational setting. Their concern is substantially correct. Substantive differences exist that make it unreasonable to expect business models to work in congregations.

Businesses are organizations whose focus is primarily on tasks and profits. Congregations are organisms whose focus is primarily on relationships and faithfulness. For the most part businesses are secular institutions that approach people primarily as a resource for the fulfillment of business goals. On the other hand, congregations, for the most part, are sacred movements that approach people as persons of worth created in the image of God to live and to love.

With this is mind, it becomes obvious that spiritual relationships and discernment are essential processes in congregations but are at best optional processes in those businesses who desire to operate with a spiritual motif. A few companies I have encountered along the way, such as ServiceMaster™ and Chick-fil-A™, are businesses at which a spiritual motif is part of their core focus and not optional.

ServiceMaster™

At ServiceMaster™ the first organizational objective is "To honor God in all we do." The full text of the objective as reported on the corporate Web site at http://corporate.servicemaster.com is as follows:

> We believe that every person–regardless of personal beliefs or differences–has been created in the image and likeness of God. We seek to recognize the dignity, worth, and potential of each individual and believe that everyone has intrinsic worth and value. This objective challenges us to have commitment to truth and to deliver what we promise. It provides the basis for our belief in servant leadership. It is not an expression of a particular religious belief, or a basis for exclusion. Rather, it is a mandate for inclusion, and a constant reminder for us to do the right thing in the right way.

For years I have resonated with the objective and culture of ServiceMaster™, have always experienced the name as implying service that honors the Master, and knew that the word *Master* did not refer to the dominate executive by the name of William Pollard, but to the Triune God. You may not know the company name ServiceMaster™, but may have experienced them as TruGreen ChemLawn™, Terminix™, Merry Maids™, or American Home Shield™.

Chick-fil-A™

When I think of Chick-fil-A™, I immediately think of its founder. I met Truett Cathy three decades ago when his mother was staying in the same hotel where I was staying. Truett Cathy is the embodiment of Christian character in so many ways. He has grown Chick-fil-A™ into one of the largest privately owned restaurant chains in North America, while also serving a higher calling and not opening on Sundays so that a day of spiritual and physical rest is available for all the employees.

The official statement of corporate purpose on the Web site at www.chickfila.com is, "to glorify God by being a faithful steward of all that is entrusted to us and to have a positive influence on all who come in contact with Chick-fil-A™." A spiritual foundation is non-negotiable in everything they do.

Many more examples of a spiritual focus exist in various business organizations. That still does not mean businesses can approach the organic spiritual nature that best characterizes Christ-centric, faith-based congregations. Congregations continue to have a unique existence as organic spiritual communities and so need an approach to reaching their full Kingdom potential that begins, is permeated by, and ends with spiritual relationships and discernment.

There is a counterpoint. Businesses and congregations are both composed of people. All of these people are persons of worth created in the image of God to live and to love. Depending on your theological approach to humanity, the people in business organizations and congregations alike are all post–original-sin or sinfulness people.

As a result of this common nature, persons who are Christians are also human beings. Often they act more like human beings than like the Christ they serve. You put them all together in a congregation, and often that congregation acts more like a human institution than like the Christ it serves. Because this is true, individuals and congregations often act in ways that are predictable according to what we know from philosophy, sociology, and psychology about that way people act and interact.

The principles of organizational development, therefore, have a lot to say about how congregations develop, grow, decline, and reach–or fail to reach–their full Kingdom potential. At the same time, organizational development models cannot explain or inspire the captivating sense of movement present in congregations who are obviously in the center of God's will for their life and ministry. Spiritual relationships and discernment exhibit a DNA in Christ-centric, faith-based communities known as congregations. This Christ-centered DNA cannot otherwise be seen in organizations composed of human beings.

An Approach to Spiritual Relationships and Discernment

More than a dozen years ago, Ron Lewis, a congregational consulting friend, introduced me to the concept of spiritual preparation for congregational transition, change, and growth using a "100 days of prayer" process. I never really learned a lot about the details of his process, and I suspect he was not the first person in recent history to suggest this type of process; but for me it was a critical learning movement.

At that particular time I was spending a significant percentage of my consulting and coaching efforts working with congregations on issues of conflict. I quickly began to think of ways that such a process could be used as a tool for healing and reconciliation in congregations. In a short period I developed the concept of share and prayer triplets as an approach to healing and reconciliation.

It worked in many situations because it is difficult for people who share out loud their faith pilgrimage with two other persons and then pray out loud for one another over a period of more then three months to stay in conflict with each other. A spiritual synergy has the potential to happen when people draw close to one another in a spiritual relationship and discern what God is saying to them and their congregation.

Launching a Spiritual Strategic Journey with 100 Days of Share and Prayer Triplets

Building spiritual relationships and engaging in discernment activities that emerge out of prayer experiences are vital parts of the ministry of congregations. It is a major part of the fuel that provides energy and empowerment to congregations. However, prayer movements in congregations seldom happen without some forethought or intentional action.

WHAT IS "100 DAYS OF SHARE AND PRAYER TRIPLETS"?

It is a process by which several to numerous groups of three people each meet ten times over the period of 100 days for around 100 minutes to share, within their triplet, various aspects of their personal spiritual pilgrimage, to dialogue about the spiritual strategic journey of their congregation, and to pray aloud for one another and for their congregation.

The desired end results of this effort are several. The first is that the people in each triplet will grow closer to one another, become more committed to the journey of their congregation, and be more open to the movement of God through their congregation. The second is that an overall sense of movement will emerge in the congregation. They will see that God is up to something in their fellowship and that the congregation must respond to God's leading.

The third desired result is that people will develop a sense of passionate urgency and spiritual readiness for the new thing that God is doing in and through their congregation. The fourth is that people will have transitioned in their readiness to the point that they can name empowering changes that need to take place in their congregation and can demonstrate readiness to be embraced by those changes. While that is a lot to ask, it is possible for it all to begin occurring during the 100 days of share and prayer triplets.

WHY LAUNCH A SPIRITUAL STRATEGIC JOURNEY WITH 100 DAYS OF SHARE AND PRAYER TRIPLETS?

These 100 days provide individuals and congregations many great opportunities. We can outline some of the most important.

First, launching a spiritual strategic journey is a great opportunity to initiate a renewed emphasis on in-depth dialogue among congregational participants. At times it appears that people connected with congregations have lost the ability to communicate and dialogue at an in-depth level. Too much conversation is shallow and does not produce close and mature fellowship within faith communities.

When this is the situation, the congregation has little or no basis for spiritual relationships that allow us to hold one another accountable for growing in the grace and knowledge of our Lord and Savior Jesus Christ. True fellowship and community cannot exist in the congregation. People outside the congregation believe that when Christians stand around in a circle and sing "Kum ba Yah," they represent false community. And these outsiders are often correct!

When spiritual relationships in a congregation are shallow, it is easy for the smallest conflict event to become the occasion for major debate. In the midst of shallow relationships the congregation has no room for God's sense of vision for the congregation to captivate them. So no unifying purpose is obvious. Even diligent searching cannot find one.

Second, launching a spiritual strategic journey is a great time for congregations as faith communities to commit to and covenant with one another that the interpersonal conflicts and congregational fights that have characterized many congregations will not be allowed to characterize this congregation. Beginning a spiritual strategic journey with 100 days of share and prayer triplets is one way to symbolize this commitment.

Drawing close to one another for 100 days is not an event with a series of meetings to fulfill. For congregations it can be a new beginning. This length of time is long enough to begin to hardwire new patterns of relationships with God, with one another, and with the context in which we serve.

Thus, for the share and prayer triplets to be successful, persons involved in them must covenant to build new relationships with one another, just as God through Christ built a new relationship with us through death, burial, and resurrection.

Third, launching a spiritual strategic journey provides a new beginning for interpersonal relationships in congregations. With an increase in the diversity of many congregations, too many people connected with congregations do not know one another. They do not understand each other's cultural or doctrinal perspectives, do not comprehend the generational differences, and fail to realize the diversity of religious practices and backgrounds that people bring with them to worship each week.

A key organizing principle for the share and prayer triplets is that each triplet is composed of people who are not best friends. They should be composed of people from diverse corners of the congregation so that the myopia about congregational life that settles in when people only relate to friends they have known over the years can be broken.

Congregations need new members, if only because they can inject new energy and relationships into the life and ministry of the congregation. Share and prayer triplets are an opportunity to be intentional about the establishment of new relationships.

Fourth, launching a spiritual strategic journey provides a renewed opportunity to honor the Triune God. God is the focus of our worship. Jesus Christ is the head of the church. The Holy Spirit is our constant companion and guide. It is a fantastic idea to mark a new beginning by seeking to renew and strengthen our primary relationship with the Triune God.

Share and prayer triplets symbolize and are a real expression of the need to begin every new thing with prayerful relationships. The church exists to worship God, and to serve Him in the loving manner that He has served us through Christ.

Fifth, launching a spiritual strategic journey marks a new beginning. It is appropriate to anchor a new beginning with a spiritual process that involves a large percentage of the active people in your congregation.

Share and prayer triplets are not for the few or the elite. They are for everyone. The figurative Holy of Holies expands to include the entire congregation when the congregation approaches life with the Triune God through a demonstrable spiritual exercise that makes a public statement of commitment to God, and a private statement of doing so with humble accountability to a couple of fellow pilgrims.

Sixth, launching a spiritual strategic journey will bring significant changes and will require people to transition to new understandings. Some changes may threaten the spiritual or cultural comfort of people connected with congregations. Prayer is a way for people to deal spiritually and emotionally with the changes by which they are impacted and with the resulting sense of loss they are experiencing.

Too often we use expressions such as "prayer changes things" in a stale manner as we are trying to find the right words to show that we are spiritual. The reality *is* that "prayer changes things." If we take prayer seriously, then we will experience changes for which we can only be prepared if we are indeed praying that God will come quickly.

If we really pray with one another, new and different things may happen in our lives. We may be open to hearing the voice of God and knowing that voice immediately, rather than thinking it is the "Eli's" in our lives who are calling us. As long as we think it is "Eli" calling us, we do not have to answer with our full heart, soul, mind, and strength. If God calls, we must give our all.

Seventh, launching a spiritual strategic journey provides a great opportunity to begin new God-inspired kingdom initiatives. Share and prayer triplets are a great way to build person-to-person and household-to-household ownership of any new initiative.

When we launch a new spiritual strategic journey an implied, and to a degree a stated, agenda stands in our midst. This agenda claims that we are seeking to be open to the new thing God is preparing to do in our congregation. Often by the middle to the end of the 100 days of share and prayer triplets, people are being inspired to articulate feelings about new things God might be calling their congregation to do in ministry in the midst of His kingdom.

WHAT SHOULD BE YOUR EXPECTATIONS OF THE RESULTS?

The share and prayer triplet process should not be initiated simply as an event or project to fulfill or complete. It should be seen as a spiritual relationship and discernment exercise for which we need to develop high expectations, in the faith that God will show us over time that even these expectations are too small.

First, while 100 days of share and prayer triplets may not necessarily produce miracles in your congregation, the experience can sharpen the relational and spiritual sensitivity of many people connected with your congregation. For some congregational participants, the share and prayer triplet experience may be the first time, or the first time in a long time, that they have engaged in this intense and long of a spiritual exercise.

If they follow through with sincerity for the whole process, it can be highly significant for them. Some have reported that it is the best experience they have encountered in their relationship with their congregation.

Second, share and prayer triplets can build relationships between people who have not had the opportunity to get to know one another. People of different age generations, tenure in their connection with the congregation, denominational and church backgrounds, and theological perspectives can build understanding of the faith journeys of other people.

You should expect that the ability of the congregation to talk about diverse and controversial subjects may be increased through the share and prayer triplet process. One of the first benefits might be the ability of the congregation to talk about change actions without unnecessarily escalating conflict within the congregation.

Third, unfortunately many people in a congregation may never have learned how to pray for another person. This will provide an opportunity for them to experience the spiritual and emotional joy of praying unselfishly for others.

Intercessory prayer may seem like a no-brainer for you. For many people this is something they ask others to do and something they do not feel worthy to do. The share and prayer triplet participants should pray faithfully for one another and for others who come up in the dialogue.

The real breakthrough may come when participants ask the other participants in their triplet to pray for more than surface issues in their own lives. They may share a vulnerability that will enhance and deepen the spiritual depth of their triplet, and perhaps of the spiritual relationship and discernment of the congregation if this is a phenomenon that spreads throughout the congregation.

Fourth, God answers prayer. Your congregation and the people connected with it may benefit greatly from answered prayer. Hopefully they will see the power of prayer and use it more often—especially in a servant leadership way that benefits others.

We often pray without really expecting results. When results come, we are surprised. When multiple triplets in a congregation are praying and answers come, it has a synergistic impact on the spiritual relationship and discernment life of the congregation.

COACHING BREAK

✔ Gaze out the window for a minute. Ponder the situation of your congregation. What images come to mind?

✔ Think about open sharing and praying out loud in a triple relationship. Does that bring warmth to your heart or fear to your mind? Are you at all afraid to tell others who you are as a spiritual person? Have past experiences with this type of process been meaningful or shallow? What can you do to make this a meaningful process for you and your congregation?

How to Launch a Spiritual Strategic Journey with 100 Days of Share and Prayer Triplets

The concept of 100 days of share and prayer triplets is simple and straightforward. There is no magic about it. It simply takes motivation, organization, and commitment.

First, the congregational leadership challenges people to come together in triplets ten times for 100 minutes each time over a period of 100 days. These numbers are the goals for each triplet, and many will complete the process meeting all of the required times, for most of the minutes, within 100 to 120 days. In a sense it is not legalistic adherence of the numbers that matters, but faithful fulfillment of the intent of the time together.

Second, the triplets are asked to spend their time sharing their personal hopes, hurts, and dreams, and sharing their affirmations, challenges, and vision for their congregation. Many congregations who are engaging the spiritual strategic journey process suggested and implied by this book will focus on one of the ten *Congregational Issues for Generative Dialogue for a Spiritual Strategic Journey* each time they meet. (See chapter 4.)

Congregations often put together a prayer guide for use by the triplets. Samples of prayer guides can be seen on my Web log at www.BullardJournal.org, and at www.PursuingVitalMinistry.org.

Third, the triplets are asked to pray aloud for one another and for their congregation. While this seems like a simple request, it is amazing how often this is a barrier for some people. I remember a whimsical experience with a group of congregations in the Anglican tradition. When I got to this part of the explanation for the share and prayer triplets, I was informed that Anglicans do not pray out loud without a prayer book in their hand.

I suggested, "Try it. You'll like it." At the end of the 100 days, representatives from four of the seven congregations acknowledged that it was one of the most spiritually powerful experiences of their lives. Three of the congregations did a second round of triplets and doubled the number of people who had been involved in the first round.

Fourth, the triplets are asked to share with the congregation the progress they are making. Each triplet should submit prayer requests they desire to have other triplets or the entire congregation pray for. They should be careful to determine that sharing each request will not infringe on someone's privacy. Such sharing not only increases the effectiveness and power of prayer when more people are praying, but it also helps others become aware of the type of prayer needs present within the congregational community.

Fifth, the congregation supports and unites around the significance of the triplets through corporate worship and celebration. While observing the 100 days, the congregation should also focus its primary worship services around themes congruent with the share and prayer triplet process.

This may effectively involve the whole active congregation in the spiritual relationship and discernment process, whether or not they are personally involved in a triplet. To enhance these worship services, invite a person from a share and prayer triplet to briefly share in each worship experience. Ask them to emphasize what is going on in their triplet that exhibits a deepening spirituality.

FORMATION OF THE SHARE AND PRAYER TRIPLETS

The *People of Passion*, who are the seven percent that includes the *People of Pastoral Leadership*, should take the initiative to form the share and prayer triplets. Their goal should be to involve at least the next 14 percent of the *Quad A's* (see page 29) in the congregation who are the *People of Position*. The share and prayer triplet process becomes an exceptionally powerful way to build the essential bond between the *People of Pastoral Leadership, the People of Passion,* and the *People of Position* in a way that can create the *Enduring Visionary Leadership Community* in a powerful way.

This is a specific invitation from the *People of Passion* to individuals who are seen as the *People of Position* in the life of the congregation. The invitations should be to specifically named people, with each person of passion taking the names of two people perceived to be people of position and inviting them to come together to form a share and prayer triplet.

Those persons asked to form a triplet should use the following guidelines in inviting people to be a part of a triplet. First, they should not be members of their household, close friends, or close relatives. Second, they should be people of a different age group, length of time connected with the congregation, and perspective on the life and ministry of the congregation.

Third, they should be willing to enter into a *no-exit* relationship. This means that each person will agree to stay actively connected to the triplet for the 100 days, even though there may be some challenging moments as the triplets deal with significant and meaningful issues.

SHARING AND PRAYING IN THE TRIPLETS

Triplet participants should share their personal hopes, hurts, and dreams as well as their affirmations, challenges, and vision for their congregation. To initiate this they may need to engage in some trust-building activities though which they share their life stories and spiritual journeys with one another.

These trust-building activities could be initiated in a large group setting where all the triplets come together for the first time and receive orientation and coaching. The pastor, staff ministers, and members of the leadership team should lead this orientation and coaching. They might even model trust-building activities during the orientation session by demonstrating how this could happen during the meeting of a triplet.

Triplet participants should pray aloud for one another and for their congregation. Praying aloud is extremely important. This adds value to the ability of prayer to bless one another. Participants should lift one another up in prayer. The congregation and its health and Kingdom progress should be a subject of prayer. Triplets could keep a journal of the key issues for which they are praying on an ongoing basis. Such a journal should include any statement of covenant and confidentiality the triplet establishes.

SHARING WITH THE CONGREGATION

A consistent and regular method should be used for the triplet participants to share with the congregation the progress their triplet is making. One method is to ask a participant from a triplet to take three or four minutes in each congregational worship service to share the joy of what is happening in their triplet. The public example by various members of triplets over the 100 days is a great testimony to the process, spreads the spirit of the triplets to the larger congregation, and brings inspiration to other triplet groups.

A second way would be to have a triplet participant write a short article about the quality of sharing and praying in their triplet. The article could be placed in the church's newsletter, displayed on its Web site, or distributed by e-mail to interested persons. A third way would be for triplets to share prayer requests, particularly related to the congregation. They could place these requests on a churchwide prayer list posted in a common place in the church facilities and on the church's Web site. Then other triplets, the congregation in worship, various group settings, and individuals could refer to the list and pray for the concerns listed.

CONGREGATIONAL SUPPORT FOR THE TRIPLETS

The congregation should support and rally around the significance of the triplets through corporate worship and celebration. One way to do this is to have the worship themes tied to the suggested dialogue agenda for the triplets. This would reinforce what the triplets are talking about and connect other congregational members not in a triplet to the triplet movement .

Some pastors have actually used the ten *Congregational Issues for Generative Dialogue for a Spiritual Strategic Journey* as the subject of a sermon series while the triplet process is taking place. At least the liturgy and worship elements can certainly reflect a challenge for the congregation to seek to discern the future that God has for it.

At the end of the 100 days of prayer the congregation should conduct a corporate worship celebration. This provides occasion for the body as a whole to rejoice concerning answered prayer and new relationships, the congregation's renewed sense of community, and the anticipation of the new things God will do with their increased spiritual unity and what may be an emerging consensus around the congregational journey.

When to Launch a Spiritual Strategic Journey with 100 Days of Share and Prayer Triplets

I have found three appropriate times during the year to use 100 days of share and prayer triplets to launch a spiritual strategic journey. My favorite actually has nothing to do with the religious significance or the liturgical calendar, but best fits the season of the year. This is to launch the triplets around Memorial Day and complete them around Labor Day.

While summer may seem like an unusual time to engage in triplets, it can actually be a great time. It is increasingly difficult to do many large group things in congregations during summer months. It is relatively easy for three people to find ten times to get together over a fourteen-week period from Memorial Day to Labor Day. During a time that many congregations feel they are at a low point, new spiritual resources can actually be developed.

Then the Labor Day period is a wonderful time to combine a fellowship celebration and a spiritual celebration to bring the congregation together to rejoice over answered prayer. It then allows for a great programmatic response during the fall when the transition created through the triplets can be expressed in changes and new initiatives.

The other two times during the year when the triplets can have a significant impact are the 100 days leading up to Christmas Eve, and the 100 days leading up to Easter Sunday. Both of these seasons provide for a great motivational crescendo and spiritual celebration. Beautiful opportunities for discernment exist with deep theological significance that can celebrate the best the Christian life has to offer in a congregational community.

Another way to look at the timing of share and prayer triplets is to look at the seasons of congregational life. The focus of this book is to suggest that the triplets are of greatest value when launching a spiritual strategic journey. I have suggested them as a breakthrough tool during times of healing and reconciliation in the midst of unhealthy conflict.

Great value can be gained by the use of triplets during the interim period between pastors. Such a use can actually help a congregation gain spiritual strength during the interim period, rather than being in cultural and leadership hibernation. It is a proven fact that an intensive spiritual process often enhances the transition and change that takes place during a time of a major building project and capital fundraising. Share and prayer triplets can be tailor-made for these occasions.

As a follow-up to a lay renewal emphasis, as preparation for an evangelism or new member recruitment focus, and as an instrument for a deepening spiritual relationship in a disciple-making process, a share and prayer triplets process can be extremely valuable.

One lingering question may be, "Why 100 days?" Many of the most popular spiritual processes, and the liturgical season of Lent itself, focus on forty days. I thought about this for a long time and observed numerous congregations in the process until I had a new learning that answered this question for me. It takes around three months to fully change the behaviors and spiritual practices of congregational participants. Anything less could just be a process in which they engage for a season, rather than a process that could be life-changing for the congregation and the participants.

Don't Pray Unless You Are Prepared for Something to Happen

The 100 days of share and prayer triplets, when taken seriously by a congregation, are not just an exercise in keeping the congregation busy with spiritual exercises. This process can really make a difference in the life of a congregation. Often differences begin to emerge immediately when a congregation starts praying.

Several years ago I was serving as an interim preaching/teaching pastor for a congregation. Basically I spoke in the worship services on Sundays, and led a Bible study at a mid-week prayer gathering.

During that interim time, I led the congregation in some of the elements of a spiritual strategic journey as described in this book. One intentional exercise was the share and prayer triplets. While not connected to a full spiritual strategic journey process, and while participants were not chosen by the tightly knit process suggested in this chapter, the triplets did focus around prayer and preparation for the next pastor for the congregation.

The first week the triplets were to begin meeting, I arrived at the church late Wednesday afternoon to prepare for the evening Bible study. Just as I arrived, the church secretary indicated that one of the members was in the library waiting in hopes she would be able to talk with me. I went in to speak to the woman.

She wanted to know if it would be possible for the third member of her triplet to be a homebound person in the congregation. I was delighted to hear this suggestion, as ministry by congregations to homebound persons is a special interest of mine. I immediately affirmed her inspired thought.

She indicated that earlier that day as she was struggling with who should be the third person in her triplet, she was impressed during a time of personal prayer to ask a certain homebound person. She contacted the person she had already approached about connecting in a triplet, and that person readily agreed with the idea. They both knew they would have to go to the homebound person's house to have their triplet gatherings.

I asked Linda if I could share the story of her triplet during the prayer gathering that evening. She agreed. I gladly shared this wonderful story, not knowing that the real surprise and evidence of God's leading was yet to come.

After the prayer gathering, Elizabeth, the chairperson of the pastor search committee, approached me. Often we would talk about process issues related to her committee's vital work so it was not unusual for her to approach me. However, this time was different. She looked different. She actually looked like she was shaking.

She wanted to tell me about this first gathering of her share and prayer triplet that had taken place two days earlier. One of the prayer concerns that arose during that first session was that the congregation would find a way to reach out in a special way to homebound persons in the congregation. Wow! Two days before Linda was impressed in our daily devotion to reach out to a homebound person, Elizabeth's triplet was praying that this door would be opened.

Guess who were the two people I invited to share the testimony of the value of their share and prayer triplet with the congregation at worship the next Sunday? Don't pray unless you are prepared for something to happen.

COACHING INSIGHTS

■ Spiritual relationships and discernment are an essential process in the spiritual strategic journey of a congregation. They must be nurtured with great care.

■ To what extent do your congregational leaders understand the essential difference between a business planning model and a spiritual strategic model? What is their experience with each? Are there any spiritual discernment practices they need to experience before they are ready to lead the congregation in a spiritual strategic journey?

■ What small group and prayer emphases has your congregation used in its ministry over the past five to ten years? Which have been most effective? What made them effective? What were barriers to their effectiveness? How can any barriers be overcome?

■ Perhaps the clergy leaders and a small group of lay leaders in your congregation could experiment for thirty to forty days with the share and prayer triplet process, and out of that suggest ways that it might best work for your congregation. In the process they would also deepen relationships with one another and thus begin the process of building spiritual relationships and discernment.

■ When you consider the use of share and prayer triplets, what are your expectations of this process for your congregation? What are the history and pattern of the impact of prayer on the life and ministry of your congregation? Who are the people of the most genuine prayer and discernment in your congregation? How can you get them involved in this process?

■ What has been the impact of answered prayer on the life and ministry of your congregation? How does your congregation handle its awareness of the presence of God in worship, programs, ministries, and activities within the life of the congregation?

PERSONAL REFLECTIONS

YOUR REFLECTIONS: What are your reflections on the material presented in this chapter?

_____

_____

_____

_____

YOUR ACTIONS: What actions do you need to take about your life, ministry, and/or congregation based on the material presented in this chapter?

_____

_____

_____

_____

YOUR ACCOUNTABILITY: How and by whom do you want to be held accountable for taking these actions?

_____

_____

_____

_____

CHAPTER EIGHT

Future Storytelling for Your Congregation

EXECUTIVE SUMMARY

The purpose of this chapter is to explain the future storytelling process for congregations. The focus will be on the twelve steps of the future storytelling process that move from identifying choices, to developing scenarios, to drafting a future story, to sharing the story, to developing a future story fulfillment map. A story of exploration begins this chapter.

Several years ago I was leading a retreat of Christian leaders at a conference center in the midst of a beautiful range of mountains. One afternoon a group of us decided to climb the mountain that was right behind the conference center. There was a rough trail we could follow that represented the climb of others who had gone before us.

Before we began our journey, we looked around at the beauty and majesty of the range of mountains. We also noted that we could not see very far, or with great clarity, because we were only at the beginning. From the bottom of the mountains, we could only look up and see our immediate context. Then we climbed for a while.

Upon arriving at a place to take a rest, we looked around again at the range of mountains and realized that our view had dramatically changed. We commented about the different perspective that now presented itself to us, the enhanced beauty, and the ability to see farther and with more clarity than we had been able to see when we started the climb.

Then we continued our climb. We had similar revelations about our climb and the range of mountains at the next two rest stops. Finally, we reached the summit of our mountain. What a view! We could now see farther and with greater clarity than we could have imagined at the beginning of our climb. We wondered out loud if this was the same range of mountains we had viewed at the beginning of our journey. They looked so different.

We realized several things from our new vantage point. First, a whole new world that we could not see at the beginning of our journey was out there. Second, in spite of the fact the range of mountains looked like a totally different set of mountains than they did when we began the climb, they were the same mountains; and they did not move. We moved. We changed perspective.

Third, the mountain we climbed was not the highest mountain in the range. Many more mountains beckoned us to climb them and discover even greater perspectives that were further up and further in. Fourth, we can now look out, and not just up, and can begin to have an initial understanding of our mountain-climbing potential. At the same time, our full potential is still elusive to us.

Fifth, as we climb other mountains in the range of mountains, we will surely see farther and with even greater clarity. What adventures and challenges they will offer we cannot know until we journey toward them. In reality, it would appear our journey will never end, but the learnings, insights, revelations, and discoveries will continue to excite, inspire, and bring us fulfillment beyond what we had ever dreamed.

Implications for the Journey

What are the implications of this mountain climbing image for the journey of congregations toward their full kingdom potential? First, at the beginning of our spiritual strategic journey we cannot know the distance or length of our congregational journey. Nor can we see with clarity the vision God has for us. None of us knows our full Kingdom potential. We must live into it, but it will always be further up and further in.

Second, as we journey in the direction of our current under-standing of our full Kingdom potential, we will continually discover, discern, and develop new insights into our potential. We will continually be able to see farther and with more clarity. We will develop capacities that, at the beginning of the journey, we did not even know we would need.

Third, our understanding of our full Kingdom potential is not static. It is continually changing as we journey in the direction toward which God is pulling us. As we mature in our journey, we have a deeper understanding of our potential and our capacity for Kingdom service.

Why Should You Seek to Tell the Future Story of Your Congregation?

The spiritual strategic journey of a congregation is not pushed forward by a strategic or long-range plan. It is pulled forward by a continually clearer view of the full Kingdom potential toward which God is calling your congregation.

We cannot know in detailed specifics God's future for our congregation. We cannot state that future in words that will remain accurate for very long. Yet, we can imagine, project, and articulate that future based upon our current understanding of the full Kingdom potential of our congregation. We articulate the future by creating the future story of the congregation that is a narrative of the transitions, changes, and transformations God's vision will lead the congregation to make. We begin the story from the perspective of the congregation's reaching its full Kingdom potential, and then work backward to create the story.

Articulating the congregation's future story in this way will allow us to have a goal or destination in front of us toward which we are traveling. It will allow the Merlin factor that was presented in chapter 1 to create in us a sense of pull toward a destination we may have a hint about in the midst of our heart, soul, mind, and strength.

You should tell the future story of your congregation because it is much more likely to become a reality if you articulate it and focus your actions on seeking to achieve it. The key factor is continual openness to the new things God is seeking to say to your congregation as you journey toward the fulfillment of your story. The new things will often change the details of the story and at various hinge points can even transition and change our entire understanding of our full potential for Kingdom ministry.

Future Storytelling at First Church

One of the first times I was motivated to use a future storytelling process in a congregation happened when visiting a congregation for a different reason. The presenting issue from a large, county seat First Church was that they needed help in staff development, team-building, and evaluation. Upon arriving at the church, I was presented with a packet of materials I had requested. What I was particularly interested in seeing from this very large congregation was their ministry plan, the position descriptions for the ministers, an annual programs and ministries plan, and the performance appraisal instruments used to evaluate its staff ministry.

When I pulled everything out, I realized something was missing. I turned to the receptionist and asked her if a copy of the congregation's ministry plan had been mistakenly omitted from the packet. Her response was that the congregation did not have one. This response was not unusual, but it was disappointing.

I do not expect every congregation to have a written ministry plan, but I hope they have something that represents a clear sense of mission, vision, or key leverage strategies they are seeking to fulfill. I hope that an increasing number of congregations find themselves on an intentional spiritual, strategic journey that will take them toward a destination to which they feel God is leading them, whether they have this in writing are not.

It is a lot easier to develop staff, deepen their sense of working as a team, and evaluate them in an affirming and building manner when the congregation knows who it is, what it believes, where it is heading, how it is going to get there, and what constitutes faithful progress along their spiritual strategic journey. When these elements are not present, congregations are generally overmanaged and under-led. The congregation's board may act more like they are managing an institution than navigating a Christ-centric faith-based journey.

I was doing fine with what I was learning about the congregation until I discovered the congregation had a Facilities Leadership Team ready to recommend to the congregation an architect that would help them develop renovation and new construction plans that would cost them more than ten million dollars over the next three to five years.

This congregation does not know who it is, what it believes, where it is heading, how it is going to get there, and what constitutes faithful progress; but they are going to invest more than ten million dollars in new and renovated facilities? It did not know what its programs, ministries, and activities were likely to be in the year 2017, but it knew what its facilities were likely to look like in the year 2050. Any new or renovated facilities would still be in use five decades later.

Through a series of events that can only be described as God's divine intervention, I found myself within the next thirty days helping this congregation through a quick and concise process of future storytelling to visualize the destination of the congregation if it embraced its God-given spiritual strategic journey.

How Can You Tell the Future Story of Your Congregation?

While some may see it as an oversimplification, the key answer to this question is, "Just tell it!" Don't just sit there! Tell the story God is stirring up within you. My guess is that the raw material for the future story of your congregation is already present within your congregation as God is working to bring forth His vision for your congregation.

Imagine What God Is Calling You to Be

My basic approach to this process is not fancy or complicated. It involves a straightforward approach. It begins by imagining what God might be calling your congregation to be like ten to twelve years from now.

I am writing these words in the year 2005. Twelve years from now is the year 2017. October 31, 2017 is the 500th anniversary of the event that symbolizes the beginning of the Reformation. On October 31, 1517, Martin Luther is reported to have nailed his ninety-five theses to the door of the Wittenburg Church in Germany. With that in mind, ask this question: "If our congregation travels along its spiritual strategic journey toward its emerging understanding of its full Kingdom potential, what will be the story of the life and ministry of our congregation on October 31, 2017?"

Find Interests for Your Future Community

Another simple, straightforward way to approach this is to consider what might be going on in your congregation that would interest people outside your congregation ten to twelve years from now. What if the religious news editor for your local newspaper had heard about the life and ministry of your congregation, and the servant leadership characteristics of your congregation, and asked in the year 2017 to visit your congregation for the purpose of writing a feature story for the newspaper? What would that story say about the life and ministry of your congregation in 2017? What would it say about the things that had happened over the past ten to twelve years to achieve your excellent practice of ministry?

Let God Tell the Story through Congregational Leaders

In First Church, the how of this process emerged quite easily. In this particular congregation, the process followed was quick and concise because the time available to develop the story was brief.

The overall principle used was that I let God tell the story through the congregational leaders. I simply became a facilitator and scribe.

Involve the Proper People in Creating the Story

I began on a Wednesday afternoon with the pastor. He told me his story concerning the past, present, and future of the congregation. Thursday morning I met with the ministerial staff, including the pastor, and engaged them in a brainstorming session in response to a single question. The question was, *What will characterize the visionary leadership, relationship experiences, programmatic emphases, and accountable management of this congregation ten years from now if it is reaching its full God-given Kingdom potential?*

This question required some elaboration. The ministers came to understand what a Future Story talks about:

- about God's vision for the congregation
- about the relationship of the congregation to God and to one another
- about creating these relationships through an intentional disciple-making process
- about the visible programs, ministries, and activities of the congregation
- about the management systems that operate in a manner that makes managers accountable to the direction set by the visionary leadership of the congregation

From Thursday afternoon through Friday morning I met with several focus groups of lay leaders and asked them the same question. Friday afternoon, I studied my notes and composed three scenarios of the future of this congregation that could become their future story.

Friday night we had a dinner meeting with 100 lay leaders from the congregation. During the meeting, I talked with the participants about visionary leadership, relationships experiences, programmatic emphases, and accountable management. I showed how each of these fit into the life cycle and stages of congregational development. Then in small groups, the participants brainstormed ideas about how these factors were currently being played out in the life of the congregation and sought to identify the congregation's current stage on the life cycle.

Later that evening I revised the three scenarios based on the new input from the dinner meeting participants. This prepared me for an all-day Saturday workshop with the ministerial staff and around twenty-five to thirty lay leaders of the congregation. During this meeting, I presented, and then the participants debated, the three scenarios. After all viewpoints had been fully discussed, we then began to describe the characteristics of the future story of the congregation.

Develop Consensus and Craft the Story

Having reached a consensus on its characteristics, we drafted a future story for the congregation. Later sessions with the pastor, ministerial staff, and key lay leaders refined the story and led them to be embraced by the future story. We then presented the story back to the 100 people who had been present at the Friday night dinner meeting. Finally we presented it to the entire congregation for dialogue.

Once developed, refined, and celebrated, the future story became a navigational tool for the congregational spiritual strategic journey. The Facilities Leadership Team made a major change in the architectural direction in which they were heading. They even changed architects to get one who understood the ministry philosophy put forth in the future story.

The most significant changes they made related to their future approach to worship services. Their original thought had been to construct a 2,000–seat worship center. However, their future story indicated a strong feeling among a broad-based group of congregational leaders that God was leading them to be a congregation with multiple worshiping communities. They would probably not need one large worship center, but three places of different sizes and styles where worship could take place.

Remember that the original presenting issue for this consultant was how they do staff development, teambuilding, and evaluation. The future story even brought great insight and clarity to the staff leadership arena. It allowed each of these issues to be dealt with in a positive and empowering manner.

Reasons for Using a Storytelling Approach

I decided to use a storytelling approach in this congregation for numerous reasons.

First, it would allow the congregation to quickly come to consensus concerning the major themes surrounding relationships experiences and programmatic emphases that might characterize it ten years from now.

Second, it was not a detailed, mechanistic planning model that would restrict the spiritual thinking and intuition of the congregation. It would not shut out the new things God might do in their midst that did not exactly fit their plan.

Third, storytelling is more characteristic of a movement approach to the spiritual strategic journey of a congregation.

Fourth, a movement approach is more conducive to a postmodern era that will focus on chaos, community, character, and commitment to that which is genuine and authentic about a Christ-centric faith-based journey.

Fifth, traditional strategic planning–as it has been practiced–seems to push a congregation forward to a more desirable future. A storytelling approach seeks to pull the congregation forward to the future God is unfolding.

Sixth, the story of a congregation is dynamic and changes as new understandings of God's leadership emerge in the congregation and are articulated by its leadership.

Seventh, if the process followed involves lay leadership ownership that is regularly reinforced and if the story evolves as new spiritual and strategic understandings emerge, then the congregation never has to vote on its future by voting on its story. The story simply begins to play out. It becomes a self-fulfilling prophecy as visionary leadership navigates the spiritual strategic journey.

COACHING BREAK

✔ Gaze out the window for a minute. Ponder the situation of your congregation. What images come to mind?

✔ Have you ever engaged in personal, spiritual storytelling? What is your past story of your personal spiritual pilgrimage? your present story? your future story?

Twelve Steps in the Congregational Future Storytelling Process

For several years I have experimented with a twelve-step process for congregational future storytelling. For initial clarity, let me state the twelve steps, and then go back through them in some detail.

First, identify the three choices or scenarios your congregation would like to pursue.

Second, brainstorm characteristics each choice or scenario might exhibit ten to twelve years from now.

Third, write three brief scenarios based on your choices and brainstorming of characteristics.

Fourth, choose one scenario to pursue more deeply, and on which to base your future storytelling process.

Fifth, write the first draft of your future story.

Sixth, develop and implement a plan for sharing your story and building ownership within your congregation.

Seventh, share your draft with other congregations for affirmations, challenges, and suggestions.

Eighth, rewrite your future story based on feedback and new insights from your congregation and other congregations.

Ninth, develop and implement a plan for sharing your story and building ownership within your congregation.

Tenth, brainstorm fulfillment actions for living into the story.

Eleventh, develop *Future Story Fulfillment Map* (see chart on page 151) for living into the story.

Twelfth, live into your story and reaffirm it through some celebration experience every 120 days. Update it as the journey becomes clearer and you can see farther.

Step One: Identify Three Choices or Scenarios

The process of writing the future story of a congregation should be initiated by the *People of Pastoral Leadership* and become a primary focus of the work of the *Enduring Visionary Leadership Community*. Throughout the process various periods of dialogue with the active congregation should take place. A key part of the early steps is the development of three choices or scenarios for the future of the congregation.

Why three? Making only one choice is often myopic, leads to a closed or group think mentality, and fails to show openness to the new thing God might be doing in the congregation. Two is always a bad number of choices to consider as it creates a dichotomous situation in which people position themselves around one or the other of the choices and create an either/or situation that contributes to competition in the life of the congregation. This mirroring of the traditional political election situation is never a healthy model to bring into a congregation.

Three choices allow a congregation to include in the choices the major directional thoughts of the future of the congregation held by the majority of the active participants. It also allows the congregation to include in its choices one or two ideas that may have been considered in the recent past, but were discounted because there was a powerful directional choice already held by the leadership of the congregation.

Three allows for true dialogue rather than debate. It lowers the amount of "them and us" talk in the congregation. It may create a situation where God's sense of focus for the congregation can break through and be heard throughout the congregation. God's full Kingdom potential for a congregation may be at a point beyond the congregation's current vision, farther up and in enough that it is not easily seen or felt without the congregation doing something that opens themselves up to the new thing God is doing in their midst. Identify possible futures for your congregation toward which God might be drawing you. Focus on three choices or scenarios your congregation would like to pursue concerning its emerging future.

At least three different approaches to, or types of, choices or scenarios exist. One focuses around the rate or pace of transition and change. A second focuses on organizational and ministry choices or scenarios for the congregation as a whole. The third focuses on customized choices or scenarios developed by the congregation out of the vision for and circumstances under which they are doing ministry.

1. RATES OR PACES OF TRANSITION AND CHANGE

The three rates or paces of transition and change, as one approach to choices or scenarios, are *incremental, significant,* and *radical.* This approach is generally used by a congregation that feels it is substantially certain about its future direction, but desires to project what that future might be like based on different rates or paces of transition and change.

Incremental transition and change means doing the same or similar things in the same or similar ways, focused on the same or similar target groups of people using the same or similar leadership. Using transition and change in worship styles as an example, incremental transition and change in worship would involve making small changes in the style or structure of an element of worship on a regular basis. The changes are small, incremental ones so that few if any attendees feel stressed because of the changes. This makes the transition of worship styles easy to attain.

While regular worship attendees may not feel the changes, a person who has been away from the church, such as a college student, and returns to the church following a year away, immediately recognizes that worship has changed significantly. A person who has been attending the church throughout the year may recognize that changes have taken place, but generally has found them pleasing, as he or she has been given time to react to the changes.

Significant transition and change involves doing different things in different ways, focused on different target groups of people using different leadership. Sticking with the worship image, this would involve starting a new worship service in a congregation with a different structure and style that focuses on new target groups of people and primarily uses different worship leaders than those who lead the other worship services of the congregation. The congregation now has a choice of two or more worship services of differing structure and style that they can attend.

Radical transition and change takes place when the congregation figuratively turns the page and starts with a clean or new page in designing the programs, ministries, and activities of the congregation. The way this would work with the worship image is that a new worship service of a different structure and style would replace existing worship service(s). The new service would primarily focus on the next target groups of people the congregation feels it can reach. Members and attendees must move forward to the new worship service or not attend worship.

2. Choices for Congregations

A second approach focuses on a set list of organizational and ministry choices or scenarios for the congregation as a whole, from which they can choose three. Here are a baker's dozen of organizational choices that will be explained in greater detail in chapter 9. Choice one is to stay the course and remain substantially the same. Choice two is to merge with other congregations. Choice three is to relocate to a more promising location. Choice four is to become a multiple communities congregation.

Choice five is to become a multigenerational congregation. Choice six is to be a neighborhood or community-focused congregation. Choice seven is to become a multiple site congregation. Choice eight is to become a metropolitan regional congregation. Choice nine is to be a social service or special purpose congregation.

Choice ten is to become a multiple worshiping communities congregation. Choice eleven is to become multiple congregations within a congregation. Choice twelve is to become a multicultural congregation. Choice thirteen is to become a congregational multiplication movement.

3. Customized Choices

A third approach is for congregations to come up with customized choices or scenarios. These may draw from the other two approaches, but will be unique to this congregation. These are choices or scenarios developed by a local congregation out of their own spiritual strategic journey. Congregations often use this type of choices or scenarios approach when they have clear thoughts about the future choices they face and want to investigate these thoughts or choices more deeply. At times these customized choices arise from combining some of the ideas in the structure choices or scenarios and then including some differentiation of the rate or pace within these.

Whichever of the three approaches a congregation chooses, ideas should be developed through dialogue, surveys, or feedback from the congregation, perhaps in the share and prayer triplets, in gatherings of the 21 percent, or in town hall meetings. The three possible or probable choices or scenarios for the congregation set the agenda for any and all of these meetings. The *Enduring Visionary Leadership Community* will have to meet several times to create the scenarios and to incorporate input from the various meetings.

Step Two: Brainstorm Future Characteristics of Each Choice or Scenario

Brainstorm characteristics of each choice or scenario as they may express themselves ten to twelve years from now if the congregation faithfully moves forward toward its full Kingdom potential. Brainstorm characteristics that fit any of the three choices or scenarios. Assign characteristics from any preliminary brainstorming to the choice or scenario they best seem to fit.

While this step should primarily be implemented by the *Enduring Visionary Leadership Community*, this is also a great place to involve at least the 63 percent of *People of Participation* in the congregation. The brainstormed characteristics simply need to be listed and not prioritized. However, when the brainstorming is substantially complete, the characteristics may be prioritized by the *Enduring Visionary Leadership Community* to provide guidance for the scenario writing groups formed in the next step of this process.

For review, using the three choices or scenarios as a framework, the *Enduring Visionary Leadership Community* develops ideas through dialogue, surveys, or feedback from the active congregation for the three possible or probable choices or scenarios for the congregation. This may take two sessions. One would be for obtaining input from the active congregation. The other would be for the *Enduring Visionary*

Leadership Community to dialogue, prioritize, and assign the ideas that are developed to the appropriate choice or scenario.

Step Three: Write Three Brief Future Scenarios

Divide the *Enduring Visionary Leadership Community* into three teams to write the scenarios for the future of your congregation. As much as possible, let members choose the team they wish to join. Each team is to take one of the three scenario choices and write a brief future scenario of 500 to 750 words. They should use the brainstorming as the raw material, and write in narrative form three 500-to-750-word scenarios. Then develop a method, including written, oral, and visual forms, to present each scenario to at least the *Enduring Visionary Leadership Community.*

The groups working on each scenario should be made up of people representing all three of the following types. First are people who are very passionate that *this* is the scenario on which they must write if they are to be faithful to their view of the future of the congregation. Second are people who are opposed to this scenario, but are willing to open themselves up to looking at the promise or hope inherent in this scenario. Third are people who are undecided, but are willing to give of themselves to this process with great enthusiasm.

The three teams should be given around three to four weeks to develop their scenario and the method they will use to present it to the other two teams. Or it is possible to plan a scenario-writing day for a Saturday, or a Sunday afternoon and evening, and accomplish in one day what might otherwise take up to one month. Some preparation work would need to be done before this writing day.

Step Four: Pursue One Scenario More Deeply

Choose one scenario to pursue more deeply. You will base your future storytelling process on this choice. Begin by having each scenario-writing team present their scenario to the full *Enduring Visionary Leadership Community.* Have thorough dialogue concerning each scenario. Then choose one of the scenarios as the one around which to write the future story for the congregation. In doing this, you will probably identify ideas from all three scenarios that seem to fit the one scenario around which the future story will be written.

Step Five: Write the First Draft of Your Future Story

Choose a writing team out of the *Enduring Visionary Leadership Community* to develop a full draft of the future story of the congregation. These drafts are often 1500 to 2500 words in length, written in a narrative form, and speaking as if they were written ten to twelve years from now, based on the future journey of the congregation and the future characteristics of the congregation.

The writing team should have seven or fewer members. One or two of these should be seen as good storywriters. Some congregations recruit someone from outside the congregation to provide writing services for the story. This may be an actual news reporter, a writer of fiction, a storyteller, or a playwright.

This writing team should be given three to four weeks to accomplish their task. They may also fulfill their assignment during a story-writing overnight retreat. In either case they should develop the story, prepare to present it in written, oral, and visual forms, and then present it to the *Enduring Visionary Leadership Community* for dialogue, affirmation, challenge, and refinement.

Step Six: Develop and Implement a Plan for Sharing with Your Congregation

Develop and implement a plan for sharing your story and building ownership within your congregation. Once the *Enduring Visionary Leadership Community* has reviewed and refined the story, then prepare to share this draft with the active congregation. It should be a goal to share the story in some manner with up to 63 percent of the average number of active, attending adults, or the *People of Participation.*

Sharing the story should involve some open means for dialogue and feedback from the congregation. Their response is important. Their insights into what God may be doing in the congregation will probably prove to be very meaningful. Such a process may also discover places of stress for the participants in the congregation where the story is outside their comfort zone.

Step Seven: Share Your Story with Other Congregations

Share your future story draft with the *People of Passion* from other congregations for affirmation, challenge, and suggestions. Often these may be congregations with whom you have some type of relationship. A spiritual strategic journey process that will be highlighted in chapters 11 and 12 involves the *People of Passion* from three to seven congregations meeting periodically over the course of a year to share reflections on each of their own spiritual strategic journeys, and to get feedback from sister congregations.

The sharing of stories should be done face-to-face with the *People of Passion* from other congregations, in a manner similar to how you did it in your own congregation. The ideal time for it to be done is when each congregation has developed a draft of their story that can be shared with others. At times this step comes before the previous step. One of my most enjoyable experiences was observing three congregations sharing their stories with one another. They each gave feedback that improved not only the stories, but also the presentation of the stories to their respective congregations.

Step Eight: Rewrite the Future Story

Rewrite your future story based on feedback and new insights from your congregation and other congregations. After you have written and presented your story, you will know better how to write in a manner that captivates the imagination of your congregation, speaks prophetically to the work of your congregation, and sees farther into the future than you had at first been able to see.

At this juncture you are trying to polish the story to the point that it communicates the passion and spiritual vitality the *Enduring Visionary Leadership Community* feels. You are not seeking to polish the story too finely because the story will always be dynamic and in the process of becoming as you see more clearly the leadership of God while you travel in the direction of God's current leading.

Step Nine: Share Your Plan and Build Ownership for Your Story

Develop and implement a plan for sharing your story and building ownership within your congregation. Determine how you can share the new version of the story with at least the 63 percent *People of Participation* within the congregation. This will be the story with which you will move forward. It is important that a broad base of ownership for the story exists throughout the congregation.

Ownership is the key concept, rather than formal approval being the key concept. It is enormously important that neither the congregation nor its board vote on approving the future story. That's right; formal approval should not be sought. Why?

When congregations vote on their long-range or strategic plans, thus giving them formal status, they tend to canonize these plans. Then two things happen. First, they seek to follow the plans like they are the law of the Medes and the Persians. One or more people or teams in the congregation emerge who perceive their role to be one of making sure that the congregation follows the plans to the exact letter. Often when the exact letter of a plan is followed, the spirit of the plan is lost.

Within months or a year the congregation or the *Enduring Visionary Leadership Community* often recognize that the plans are irrelevant to what is actually going on in the congregation. If your congregation is making progress along its spiritual strategic journey, then a static plan can become irrelevant very quickly.

The future story of your congregation is intended to represent the current understanding of the spiritual strategic direction of your congregation as it is being pulled forward by God, who knows your perfect future. As the story of the mountain climbing at the beginning of this chapter illustrates, as you journey toward the summit, you regularly come to new understandings about your journey and your ability to see the future toward which you are traveling. Your future story must remain a dynamic, ever-changing narrative that seeks to remain relevant to the current congregational understanding of the future story toward which God is pulling your congregation.

Step Ten: Brainstorm Fulfillment Actions for Your Story

Brainstorm fulfillment actions for living into the future story of your congregation. At this step, the difference between a long-range or strategic plan that pushes your congregation forward to the future and a pull approach involving a future story that moves you begins to become clear.

The push approach moves by an arithmetic pattern. A congregation seeks to identify those actions it can take that will help it make progress over the next several years based on the straight-line trends of the past to present. Each succeeding year needs to show progress over the year before. Success is measured by effective implementation of strategies that show growth in quality and quantity each year.

A geometric pattern propels the pull approach. The *Enduring Visionary Leadership Community* can project implementation actions with the full Kingdom potential of the congregation in mind. The challenging future story will imply seemingly impossible goals. These projections should propel the congregation forward in developing the new capacities needed to reach these dreamworld goals. Rather than asking if the congregation can make some progress each year, the strategic implementation actions focus around how much progress your congregation must make each year to achieve the future characteristics of the congregation laid out in the future story.

In this step it is necessary to brainstorm those actions that must be taken over the next several years for the congregation to live into the future story with faithfulness, effectiveness, and innovation. At this point it is important to identity the key, empowering actions that will make the critical difference in the congregation's ability to serve in ways that will propel it toward its full Kingdom potential. That does not mean identifying every specific implementation action implied by your future story. It means identifying those that will have the greatest Kingdom impact and focusing on them. Many other issues that need to be addressed in the story will likely be dealt with along the journey. They will arise simply as the overflow of the positive actions that are taking place.

Step Eleven: Develop Future Story Fulfillment Map

Develop a *Future Story Fulfillment Map* for living into the story. This should be a map of the high priority fulfillment actions for living into your congregation's story. Keep it active and up-to-date for a rolling three to five years into the future. (See *Future Story Fulfillment Map* on page 151.)

At the end of this chapter you will see a relatively familiar planning chart called the *Future Story Fulfillment Map.* It is not so much the type of form used, but what goes on the form that will differentiate this from a routine planning form. These unique contents will allow it to emerge as a map for the journey, similar to the way Internet-based mapping programs provide driving directions that lead us exactly to where we wish to travel.

Column One: Fulfillment Actions. Let's work our way through the *Future Story Fulfillment Map.* The first column is called *Fulfillment Actions,* and may contain up to twenty-one actions. In this column you should list the actions from the brainstorming in the previous step. List them in three priority sections. The top seven actions are *Highest Priority* actions. The next seven are *Higher Priority* actions. And the third seven are *High Priority* actions. Any identified actions beyond these twenty-one should be held in reserve for possible focus another day.

Column Two: Story Fulfillment. The second column is called *Story Fulfillment.* It asks the critical question about each fulfillment action: What part of the story does this action help us fulfill? You must be able to connect every fulfillment action to a specific place in the narrative at which it provides strategic support. Some leaders in a congregation at this juncture will seek to interject their favorite program, ministry, or activity as a necessary fulfillment action. If they are successful, they will disrupt the effectiveness of the spiritual strategic journey.

Columns Three to Five: Time Urgency. The next three columns deal with time urgency. The first of these focuses on specific actions or steps that must take place during the next three to six months for each fulfillment action to be realized. The second column is for actions during the period of six to eighteen months, when many short-term steps must take place. The third column is for the steps that will take three to five years to be realized. Not all fulfillment actions will have time implications that fit all three categories, but some will.

Column Six: Accountability. The final column focuses on accountability. It is important to know who will be held accountable for each of the up to twenty-one fulfillment actions. Almost all of the fulfillment actions should point to a lay leadership team or community in the congregation rather than to a staff person. The congregation, with initiation and leadership from the *People of Pastoral Leadership*, must take responsibility for living into their future story. Overall accountability rests with the *Enduring Visionary Leadership Community*.

Step Twelve: Live, Celebrate, and Update Your Story

Live into your story, reaffirm it through some celebration experience every 120 days, and update it as the journey becomes clearer and you can see farther. Now the fun part begins. Actually it has already begun. It has always been my experience that a congregation begins to experience fulfillment of the intended actions for its spiritual strategic journey even while the preparation for the journey is still going on. Action does not wait until the whistle sounds for the beginning of the journey.

Every 120 days, or about three times per year, plan a gathering of the *Enduring Visionary Leadership Community* to celebrate places where the future story is being fulfilled. Invite to these celebrations anyone directly impacted by the fulfillment of a portion of the future story. Invite them to engage in *Vision Fulfillment Storytelling*. This is the telling of the stories concerning experiences in which the future story of the congregation has had an impact on the life and ministry of the congregation. These stories should also be shared with the entire congregation so members can be impacted by the experiences of story fulfillment. Sharing these stories should take place through telling the stories, writing and distributing the stories, and showing the evidence of the impact of the stories.

As a result of the fulfillment of some portion of the story, that part of the story will need to be rewritten or otherwise updated to keep it relevant to the new things God is doing in and through the congregation. God is actively at work. As a result of the fulfillment of portions of the future story, your congregation can now see the next mountain and its summit. It needs to project the story farther into the future with more depth. The future story of your congregation will continually be rewritten. It is dynamic. It is never finished.

Future Storytelling Resources

Not many resources exist on how to visualize the future story of a congregation. A book from the business world that can act as a jumping-off point is *The Dream Society: How the Coming Shift from Information to Imagination Will Transform Our Business* by Rolf Jensen (McGraw-Hill, 1999). Another book that provides inspiration for future storytelling for congregations is Leonard Sweet's *Post-Modern Pilgrims: First-Century Passion for the 21ˢᵗ Century World* (Nashville: Broadman & Holman, 2000).

COACHING INSIGHTS

■ Describe the mountains you must climb in your congregation's spiritual strategic journey. Does the mountain climbing image work for you? If not, what image do you find helpful? What are the implications of the mountain climbing image, or your image, for your congregation's journey toward its full Kingdom potential?

■ Why should you seek to tell the future story of your congregation? What benefits do you see for the life and ministry of your congregation from telling its future story? What are the barriers to telling your story?

■ Do you need to consider developing a relationship with a personal ministry coach to move you from thought to action? If you get stuck at this stage in the journey, then a coach is something you ought to consider.

■ What parts of the twelve steps make the most sense to you? What parts do not? How are you going to resolve your uncertainty about the steps? Take action today on resolving this uncertainty.

■ By this point, are you clear who makes up the *Enduring Visionary Leadership Community* in your congregation? What do you need to do to further clarify the makeup of this community? What are the next steps for this community in forming and telling the future story of your congregation?

PERSONAL REFLECTIONS

YOUR REFLECTIONS: What are your reflections on the material presented in this chapter?

_____

_____

_____

_____

_____

YOUR ACTIONS: What actions do you need to take about your life, ministry, and/or congregation based on the material presented in this chapter?

_____

_____

_____

_____

_____

YOUR ACCOUNTABILITY: How and by whom do you want to be held accountable for taking these actions?

_____

_____

_____

_____

_____

Living into Our Future Story: Future Story Fulfillment Map

Fulfillment Actions	Story Fulfillment	Immediate Steps	Steps within the Next 6 to 18 Months	Steps within the Next 3 to 5 Years	Who Will Be Accountable for These?
(To live into our future story, these are the actions we need to take.)	(What part of the story does this help us fulfill?)	(These actions need to be taken as soon as possible.)	(These short-term actions need to take place soon.)	(These actions may require various stages of action to fulfill.)	(Who should be held accountable for taking these actions?)
HIGHEST PRIORITY ACTIONS 1. 2. 3. 4. 5. 6. 7.					
HIGHER PRIORITY ACTIONS 1. 2. 3. 4. 5. 6. 7.					
HIGH PRIORITY ACTIONS 1. 2. 3. 4. 5. 6. 7.					

CHAPTER NINE

Choices for Congregations

EXECUTIVE SUMMARY

The purpose of this chapter is to share summaries of the thirteen choices congregations frequently consider as they write the future story of their ministry and organizational future. For each choice the following questions are answered: What is the essence of this choice? Who ought to consider this choice? What are strategic transition and change issues to address? What are essential resources to have available to embrace this choice?

Congregations have many choices to make. None is as significant as the choice they make concerning the holistic ministry and organizational direction of the congregation. Presented here are a baker's dozen of possible choices for congregations to consider as they think about scenarios for their future as part of telling their future story as presented in chapter 8.

These choices have been developed over a number of years. Admittedly these thirteen have certain types of congregations in mind and do not necessarily address all types of situations. The urban congregation is addressed more than the rural congregation. The congregation that is at least ten to twelve years old is addressed more than those that are younger. Modern congregations are addressed more than postmodern congregations.

These thirteen choices are considered pump primers, as in the priming of a well pump to get water flowing. By this I mean that this is not an exhaustive list, but a list to get the *Enduring Visionary Leadership Community* of a congregation to think outside their current box about innovative ideas concerning their future.

While these thirteen choices have appeared in several places in other forms, probably the most popular place to find them before this book came out has been at www.SSJTutorial.org, a Web-based tutorial written by this author as part of the overall Congregational Resources Web site of The Alban Institute and the Indianapolis Center for Congregations.

Choice One–Stay the Course and Remain Substantially the Same

What Is the Essence of This Choice?

Choose to continue substantially the same spiritual strategic journey the congregation is experiencing. This choice calls for only incremental transition and change by the congregation. The congregational leadership sees the current direction as desirable or as the only choice around which the congregation expresses any passion.

Who Ought to Consider This Choice?

Make this choice in five situations:

- You feel the current direction is the best direction for the congregation at this time.
- No other choice has appeal to the congregation.
- You cannot develop sufficient passion for a different choice.
- You feel the current direction is the most faithful direction.
- Other choices would require the congregation to sacrifice core values it holds dearly and deeply.

Sometimes you follow this path but do not choose it. Often a congregation cannot obtain consensus on a different direction so they must continue in substantially the current direction. They continue this until the congregation develops greater passion or urgency for a different choice or until circumstances in the congregation or its context require a different choice.

Congregations may do this even when they are aware that continuing in substantially the current direction–if that direction is the diminishing of the vitality of the congregation–may result in the eventual death of the congregation. While long-term survival of the congregation may be an issue for some, death is a potential reality the congregation is willing to face.

What Are Strategic Transition and Change Issues to Address?

To stay the course and continue substantially the same spiritual strategic journey does not mean to do nothing. It is still important for the congregation to create a visualization of the future story of the congregation both in the short-term of six to eighteen months and in the long-term of ten to twelve years. However, it is likely the congregation primarily looks at the short-term and spends most of its energy solving problems or addressing urgent challenges.

Typically, moving toward more diversity in participants, membership, and leadership is not a transition and change issue these congregations address. Rather, they seek additional harmony and homogeneity. A scenario of what this future might look like in ten to twelve years, and ultimately a future story, should be developed.

What Are Essential Resources to Have Available to Embrace This Choice?

Readiness, including a sense of passion or urgency, to continue embracing the current spiritual strategic journey of the congregation is an essential resource. Case studies to observe and from which to learn must be sought. It is essential to discover and dialogue with congregations who made this choice at least five years ago. What was its impact on them?

Congregational leaders must know the strategic actions this choice calls for. Many strategic actions will be tactical and incremental in nature. The congregation must identify a context or target team that is demographically congruent with the membership of the congregation so that they have new people to attract to their journey as a congregation. The congregation must remember how to attract new people to their spiritual strategic journey as a congregation and to a Christ-centric, faith-based journey as an individual.

They must understand how to do evangelism, new member recruitment, and new member assimilation. And they must develop a healthy practice of engaging in these activities. A vision must still be incorporated into a future story of the congregation's life even if it remains the same. This highlights an essential resource, which is hope. The congregation's leadership must radiate a positive sense of hope concerning the future.

A critical mass of leadership must be present. That requires a minimum of 21 adult leaders who can provide the passion, spirituality, leadership, and strategic knowledge necessary to lead this congregation forward. Without this minimum number for a leadership community, the congregation may not have the people resources necessary for a fulfilling journey. Programs, ministries, and activities consistent with the past and present of the congregation must be present or developed. Coaching from a Christian leadership coach should be sought. This person may also move into a consulting and training role when requested by the congregation to help it deal with essential opportunities and challenges.

Choice Two–Merge with Other Congregations
What Is the Essence of This Choice?

Choose to merge with other congregations. Here you have two choices. One type of merger results in a new congregation, and another in a congregation of congregations.

In a new congregation a single, integrative Christ-centric, faith-based community is developed and implemented at one or more locations. The congregation develops a unified constitutional, corporate, worship, discipleship, fellowship, and ministry system.

In a congregation of congregations multiple congregations exist at one or more locations in a covenant relationship. These separate congregations maintain some identity distinctiveness in their denominational, constitutional, corporate, worship, and fellowship systems.

Who Ought to Consider This Choice?

Congregations should consider this choice under the following conditions:
- They have only part of the resources needed for the next steps in their journey and thus need a close, meaningful relationship with another set of resources as represented by the membership of another congregation or two.
- They have hope and vision but lack the minimum number of adult leaders to make the changes and transitions necessary to transform.
- Their context or target teams have so radically changed that to minister effectively in their current context they must bring cross-cultural or intergenerational leadership and resources to their ministry.
- They have a healthy focus on their ministry, but their context, facilities, or leadership no longer matches their ministry.

What Are Strategic Transition and Change Issues to Address?

The merger of two congregations has within it the desire to resist diversity and to create more harmony. Too many times, however, this desired result does not happen. Often two congregations merge because of the weakness of one or both congregations. Such mergers may lead to inevitable conflict through "them and us" attitudes that may develop. Merger may lead to the culture and core values of one congregation dominating, minimizing, and even eliminating the culture and core values of the other congregation. Within three to five years the merger of two congregations out of weakness may result in a congregation no larger than the size of the larger of the two at the time of merger.

The merger of three or more congregations is much better than the merger of two congregations. It creates enough strength that the merged congregation may be able to soar with quality and quantity. It minimizes "them and us" attitudes that can characterize the merger of two congregations. It allows for the development of a new sense of mission, purpose, core values, and vision, and for a unique, transforming spiritual, strategic journey. The merger of three or more congregations is more complex, but will lead to greater potential.

What Are Essential Resources to Have Available to Embrace This Choice?

Readiness, including a sense of urgency, is essential. A commitment must exist to create a new genuine congregational culture that is much more than simply adapting various parts of the culture of each merging congregation. The new culture must involve collaborative efforts to build a new sense of community and culture. Discover and dialogue with congregations who made this choice at least five years ago.

The new congregation must develop a clear vision of what the merged congregation will look like five to ten years after the merger. Then the leadership of each congregation involved in the merger must claim ownership of and passionate commitment to the new vision. A minimum critical mass of leadership must emerge. This leadership must look beyond the current merger into the future to see the next stages of the congregation's spiritual strategic journey. At least 21 percent of the average number of active attending adults in each congregation participating in the merger must be highly passionate about the merger and fully committed to spiritual, strategic, and leadership actions. These leaders must take faithful, effective, and innovative actions.

A commitment to and involvement in relevant actions should produce results. Within ten years after the merger, at least fifty percent of the active members of the congregation should be people who were never part of the either of the congregations who merged. Coaching from a Christian leadership coach should be sought. Leadership, finances, and facilities are critical resources for the institutional aspects of the merger.

Choice Three–Relocate to a More Promising Location
What Is the Essence of This Choice?

The essence of this choice is to relocate the meeting place of a congregation to a place that repositions the congregation for more effective growth and ministry. Generally this refers to congregations who are at least a generation old and whose location has become a liability rather than an asset. However, it can also apply to younger congregations who did not adequately project their natural growth potential or were not able to afford a right-sized location during their birth and infancy as a congregation.

A location that becomes a liability is one that is too small to accommodate the size and diversity of the congregation's programs, ministries, or activities. Without room to expand in the available space and being unable to make any of various schedule alternatives work, a congregation may find that relocation is the best choice.

Why not transition to being a congregation that worships at multiple sites? This is certainly a viable choice in many situations and ought to be considered before relocation is attempted. However, the size of the primary congregation's location may be too small or undesirable, and so relocation is a good choice.

Who Ought to Consider This Choice?

Effective relocations emerge from the strength of the spiritual strategic journey of the congregation and represent a natural next step. Congregations should consider this choice under certain conditions:

- The full Kingdom potential is greater than their current location can accommodate.
- The long-term cost of renovating aging facilities or retrofitting them for a new generation of ministry is greater than the cost of relocating.
- The need for parking cannot be met.

Four or five decades ago the typical household might only have one car to a family of four or five people. Now it is not unusual to find that a household of three people has three cars at church. Past history indicates that a parking space would be needed for every 2.5 people attending a congregational worship service. Now that figure is almost always less than two people per car, and in some cases is as low as 1.5. Therefore, 40 percent more parking spaces might be needed to accommodate the same number of people as were coming to the church several decades ago.

Relocation is a bad choice for weak congregations. It is seldom effective in these cases without reinventing the congregation. Reasons for relocation out of weakness include the following:

- The members of the congregation no longer live around the facilities.
- The demographics of the congregation's context have changed racially, ethnically, socioeconomically, in lifestyle, or in population density. The congregational attendance is declining, and they want to move to an area where they can grow.

What Are Strategic Transition and Change Issues to Address?

Relocation can empower diversity. In its new facilities the congregation should create a minimum of three different types of places where worship can occur. Each worship place should be targeted to reach one of the following, depending on the community and the congregation:

- a different age group
- a racial or ethnic group
- a special purpose group
- a socioeconomic group
- seekers of a Christ-centric faith experience
- persons seeking a spiritual experience that they do not know how to define

In a new location a congregation might start out with a multicultural vision in mind and seek to develop a program, ministry, and activities strategy that affirms multiple cultures. It will also be important to develop a multicultural staff.

The construction of new facilities, or the renovation of existing facilities in the new location, should focus around a large gathering space or commons. This becomes the crossroads of the congregation, where the diversity of people who make up the congregation can meet, greet, connect, and build community. Future congregational unity will not develop by everyone being in a single worship service, but by people having a common place where they can intersect and build deep and meaningful relationships.

What Are Essential Resources to Have Available to Embrace This Choice?

Readiness for a spiritual strategic journey that actually involves picking up and going to a new place God will show the congregation is an essential resource. This is not just a real estate relocation! It is a transfer of the mission, purpose, and vision of the congregation to a new launching point. Discover and dialogue with congregations who made this choice at least ten years ago and learn from them.

A vision must be incorporated into a future story of the congregation's potential in the new location. This must be a clear vision of a positive future to which people are urged to commit. Such a clear vision owned by the leadership and people stands opposed to a fantasy of what the congregation might be able to do in the new location. A congregation that relocates can too easily fall into the trap of thinking, "If we build it, they will come."

Congregational leadership must make the commitment to journey to the new location. It could be that the Sunday morning travel time will increase significantly for some leaders. If too many leaders determine that this is a good time to move in another direction for a church community, then relocation can leave the congregation with inadequate leadership. Leaders and potential leaders living outside the new context must make long-term commitments to invest their spiritual, leadership, strategic, and financial resources in the congregation.

Faithful, effective, and innovative actions should take place that can meet the inevitable challenge of higher quality programs, ministries, and activities at the new site. Coaching from a Christian leadership coach should be sought because of all the transitions that are invisible behind the highly visible changes brought about by relocation.

Choice Four–Multiple Communities Congregation
What Is the Essence of This Choice?

Choose to become a congregation that focuses both on people who reside within one to three miles of the congregational facilities, and on people who reside farther away. Seek to build an integrative congregation that does worship, programs, ministries, and activities together around a common spiritual vision and fellowship bond.

Who Ought to Consider This Choice?

Congregations should consider this choice when they have been neighborhood or community congregations and can still reach new people from the neighborhood or overall community, but now also have people who drive to the facilities from outside the primary ministry area.

Their context presents unique opportunities for mission and ministry that captivate the spiritual imagination and energies of people who reside in that context, people who once lived there, and people who want to be part of the ministry of the congregation in light of the unique opportunities.

They are located in urban areas of transition from which former residents have moved, and into which are moving new residents of a different set of racial, ethnic, socioeconomic, and lifestyle characteristics.

What Are Strategic Transition and Change Issues to Address?

The greatest risk of this choice is that the congregation may lose a percentage of its current membership. People who reside farther than five miles away may use this as an opportunity to connect with a congregation closer to their residence. They may drop out of regular or irregular church attendance. They may leave when the worship, programs, ministries, and activities of their congregation no longer speak to their needs. They may leave when the needs and urging of their children motivates them to seek out a congregation with friends who are culturally closer to the culture of their children under 18 years of age.

Often these congregations will depend on the financial and management leadership of those households who reside more than five miles away to sustain the organizational vitality of the congregation.

What Are Essential Resources to Have Available to Embrace This Choice?

Readiness, including a sense of urgency, is essential. Discover and dialogue with congregations who embraced this choice at least five years ago. You must be captivated by a vision and incorporate it into a future story of the congregation's potential. This must be a clear vision of a positive future to which people are urged to commit. You cannot depend simply on a survival plan to keep the congregation from dying. To fulfill the vision and realize your congregation's full

Kingdom potential, you must have a minimum critical mass of leadership remaining even after some people have decided to leave. Leadership that is bicultural should be considered. Such leadership can get deep in scope in the context of the congregation and also minister effectively to people who drive into the context to worship, learn, fellowship, and minister. People outside the context must make long-term commitments to invest their spiritual, leadership, strategic, and financial resources in the congregation.

The entire leadership from all groups must agree that every leadership team must have persons from both communities genuinely and significantly involved in their activities. Faithful, effective, and innovative actions should take place. Coaching from a Christian leadership coach should be sought.

Choice Five–Multigenerational Congregation
What Is the Essence of This Choice?

The essence of this choice is to have a congregation that embraces various generations by offering programs, ministries, and activities through worship, discipleship, and fellowship that address the unique needs of various generations.

For the purpose of these congregations, generations may be defined in at least two different ways.

First, one perspective sees five distinguishable generations of people born in the period from about 1910 through 2000, with a sixth generation just now being born since the turn of the millennium. The trailing edge of current living generations are in their nineties, and the leading edge are preschoolers. The worship, discipleship, and fellowship needs of these generations are extremely different. What was going on in the world and in the church when each generation developed their Christ-centric faith patterns was very different.

Therefore, the various differences in perspectives represented within one congregation with numerous generations present can be overwhelming. Sociological research teaches us that a congregation with three distinguishable generations present can stretch with relative ease to meet the worship, discipleship, and fellowship needs of these three generations.

However, as congregations age and find themselves embracing a fourth or fifth generation of people, the diversity required to have authentic ministry to each generation is more than many congregations can handle. A fourth generation adds significant tension to the day-to-day life of the congregation. A fifth generation may add regular open conflict, and even a split in the congregation that can involve a significant group of people–generally the younger generation or two–leaving the congregation.

A second way to look at generations is to study new immigrant groups in a given country. The first generation primarily speaks the language of the country or culture from which they emigrated. The second generation is bilingual, and the third generation primarily speaks the language of the new country.

In these situations churches built by and ministering to the first generation may find conflict with the second or third generation. Such conflict arises from the inability to speak authentically to the worship, discipleship, and fellowship needs of the second and third generation. Therefore, congregations that are both multigenerational and multicultural are difficult faith communities to sustain.

Who Ought to Consider This Choice?

Congregations with the opportunity to reach multiple generations of people ought to consider methods for programs, ministries, and activities that will positively address the needs of the various generations. This means that multiple worshiping communities, a diverse small group system, and a variety of intergenerational fellowship experiences will be important in these situations.

What Are Strategic Transition and Change Issues to Address?

Multiple generations empower diversity and bring forth a diversity of programs, ministries, and activities. Congregations who figure out how to benefit from the cacophony of sounds and qualities that emerge from generational diversity will be faith communities of great beauty and joy.

Harmony can be achieved through two different types of spiritual and fellowship gatherings. The first type is intergenerational in nature. These congregations need regular gatherings intended to build relationships between the various generations. Face-to-face worship experiences should have representatives from all generations leading in worship and sharing elements of their worship style. Such worship or fellowship experiences that gather the various generations together must happen monthly. About three times each year the scope of these experiences should be extended to include every active participant in the congregation.

The second type of gathering is an inter-tenure fellowship experience that involves people who have been participating in the congregation for different lengths of time. New people may be clueless as to the dynamics of an intergenerational congregation unless they are intentionally brought into the fold through fellowship, assimilation, and orientation activities. In many congregational situations inter-tenure issues are even more difficult to bring harmony around than are intergenerational issues.

What Are Essential Resources to Have Available to Embrace This Choice?

Readiness to embrace diversity of structure and style is an essential aptitude for the leadership and participants in these congregations. Numerous congregations embrace this choice in some way, so it should be easy to discover and dialogue with congregations who have intentionally been engaging in this choice for five to seven years or more. Multiple relationship transitions characterize this choice, and must be understood by congregational leadership.

Knowledge of the differing characteristics of various birth generations and how they worship, fellowship, grow spiritually, and engage in mission must be obtained. Leadership must understand that structure and style in worship and in other areas does not necessarily change the substance of the Gospel message.

Congregational leadership must be from a diversity of birth generations or immigrant generations. They must understand how to do evangelism, new member recruitment, and new member assimilation across generational lines. A vision for a multigenerational congregation must be a partner with the core values of the congrega-tion. Coaching from a Christian leadership coach should be sought to deal with the fuzzy areas that will be present as the congregation seeks to reach various generations.

Choice Six–Neighborhood or Community-Focused Congregation

What Is the Essence of This Choice?

Choose to become a congregation that intentionally focuses on the programs, ministries, and activities that meet real needs, in real time, of real people who reside in the neighborhood (within one mile) or larger community (within two to three miles) near the location of the congregation.

Who Ought to Consider This Choice?

Congregations should make this choice if the following are true:

- Members have a strong, deep, and abiding commitment to their location to such an extent that if they were not ministering in their context they would feel a sense of loss.

- Members have a positive ability to reach people within their neighborhood or community for worship, learning, fellowship, and ministry.

What Are Strategic Change and Transition Issues to Address?

This choice involves a strong risk. Over a period of time, you may lose the support and participation of people who drive into the congregational location from the suburbs:

- They may connect with a congregation closer to their residence.
- They may drop out of regular or irregular church attendance.
- They may leave when the worship, programs, ministries, and activities of their congregation no longer speak to their needs.
- They may leave when the needs–and even the urging–of their children under 18 years old motivate them to seek out a congregation with friends who are culturally closer to the culture of their children.

This is similar to the multiple communities congregation except this choice does not intentionally seek to maintain worship, programs, ministries, and activities for people who reside farther away than five miles. This choice may appeal to members with a Christian missionary stance. These people may live farther away than five miles but be willing to lower their personal desires in favor of ministering to the people who comprise the current context around the congregation.

What Are Essential Resources to Have Available to Embrace This Choice?

A missionary passion for the geographic context and its spiritual, social, educational, government, and physical characteristics must captivate the congregation. Dialogue with congregations who made this choice at least five years ago is a great resource to have. Also, dialogue with other congregations who are intentionally focusing on the same or similar neighborhood or community will inform your congregation's journey.

Deep and thorough knowledge of the people and structures of the context in which your congregation is going to be immersed will be vital to structuring the programs, ministries, and activities that will be effective. Within your congregation, vision should shine brightly on the context and should excite the congregational leadership about the Kingdom possibilities of focusing on their neighborhood or community.

The congregation should have a realistic understanding of present leaders who will stay or leave once the focus is so deeply on the neighborhood or community. It should also know how to raise up a new generation of leaders who are indigenous to the context. This is a place where insightful coaching from a Christian leadership coach will be a great asset.

COACHING BREAK

✔ Gaze out the window for a minute. Ponder the situation of your congregation. What images come to mind?

✔ Which of these choices presented to this point seem to make the most sense for your congregation? Would you know how to lead a congregation to relocate or to merge with one or more other congregations?

✔ To this point, the choices are fairly classic and were common thirty to forty years ago. The next seven are somewhat more complicated, and, while not altogether new, have been taken to a new dimension over the past couple of decades.

Choice Seven–Multiple Site Congregation
What Is the Essence of This Choice?

The essence of this choice is to develop worshiping communities at various sites within a reasonable travel distance of a main campus in an attempt to reach various communities of people or target groups. Often the activities offered at each site will differ according to the needs of the community or target group and according to the capacity of the primary congregation to provide leadership.

This model is most often employed when a base congregation sponsors satellite worshiping communities or congregations but maintains an organic, collegial, or partnership relationship with the various locations. At the same time, many variations of this model exist.

Some multiple sites are within the same geographic community and are simply developed out of the necessity of having a place to do different types of worship, discipleship, and fellowship that cannot be accommodated within the primary facilities. Other sites are strategically located around a metropolitan area to reach same or similar target groups of folks who are attracted to the style of worship, discipleship, and fellowship characteristic of the primary congregation.

Who Ought to Consider This Choice?

Congregations should choose this model if any of the following circumstances arise:

- The congregation is out of space in its primary location.
- The church has a strong appeal to people who must travel more than twenty to twenty-five minutes on Sunday morning to get to its location.
- Members want to reach communities of people or target groups who are significantly different from the primary congregation.
- Members want to venture out with a radically different congregational model than they are now practicing without disrupting their current pattern.

Also, in some congregations the leadership feels that it needs to relocate, but the congregation is not ready to accept this choice. The congregation then starts worship services in other locations to enable them to continue to grow while the core congregation takes time to consider their longer-term choices.

Is the choice to worship at multiple sites primarily a choice for very large congregations? Absolutely not! Any congregation who would consider a second worship service, and that is generally done by the time a congregation reaches 80 to 85 in worship attendance, could conduct that worship service at a different site if it would enhance the style, quality, or ability to reach a chosen target group. It is an excellent method for midsize congregations to expand their ministry.

What Are Strategic Transition and Change Issues to Address?

Worshiping at multiple sites allows for experimentation with radically different worship, discipleship, and fellowship styles. It allows for a schedule of activities that competes with or compliments the schedule at the primary campus. It empowers a congregation to reach diverse groups of people that they could not reach because of the bounded culture present at their primary location.

Worship at multiple locations also allows for a primary congregation to partner with congregations that are generally smaller, very focused on whom they are seeking to reach, and in need of a relationship with a larger congregation for the provision of various support services to carry out their ministry. This has been an effective model in urban areas for a multicultural partnership of congregations. Harmony can be maintained as the ministerial staff from the primary location also provides leadership at the satellite locations. Often the satellite locations are created because the primary location is out of space or because the satellite location is more than twenty to twenty-five minutes away. In such cases the senior pastor may choose or be asked to preach regularly at two, if not three, locations.

What Are Essential Resources to Have Available to Embrace This Choice?

The congregation must determine clearly defined target groups of people for each site A passion for reaching people at and around all sites must be part of the DNA of the congregation. It is too expensive to maintain multiple sites without a primary desire to grow the congregation and reach additional people for active participation in the congregation.

Do not forget to dialogue with congregations who made this choice at least five years ago to determine what to do and what not to do. A lot of resources can be lost while making poor decisions as part of this choice. Great demographic reports for all sites will be helpful in planning the programs, ministries, and activities to be held at each location.

The congregation should have a realistic understanding of present leaders who will stay or leave once the focus is on multiple sites. Also, intentionally recruit leaders who will invest themselves in each site. The leadership core at each site, as well as the congregational staff, would benefit from the services of a Christian leadership coach.

Choice Eight–Metropolitan Regional Congregation
What Is the Essence of This Choice?

Choose to become a congregation that seeks to appeal to people from a large region of the metropolitan area. Such congregations will offer 24/7/365 programs, ministries, and activities that address the real needs of real people in real time from womb to tomb.

Who Ought to Consider This Choice?

Before attempting to realize this choice, congregations need to already have 500 people in average weekly attendance. They should be located in a fast-growing context with numerous transportation means and routes that make travel to the congregation site easy. To qualify for this choice you must be able to attract people who must travel more than twenty to twenty-five minutes on Sunday morning to reach your facilities.

What Are Strategic Change and Transition Issues to Address?

These congregations must be able to think and act in a manner that will produce a congregation larger than ones with which 80 or more percent of the members have ever been affiliated. Multiple worship services with multiple styles must be embraced. Decision-making must be staff-initiated. In such complex congregations the laity must relinquish their decision-making authority and give permission for decision-making to professional staff and leadership. This "permission-giving style" must be a basic method of ministry functioning in such congregations.

What Are Essential Resources to Have Available to Embrace This Choice?

Readiness, including a sense of urgency, must be demonstrated in various ways. It is essential to discover and dialogue with congregations who made this choice at least ten years ago and have been able to sustain it. Congregational leadership must know and understand the strategic actions this choice calls for.

A vision that includes a big, holy, almighty set of goals must be incorporated into a future story of the congregation's potential. This congregation has to understand the need to be faithful, effective, and innovative in all major programs, ministries, and activities. Coaching for numerous leaders of these congregations from a Christian leadership coach will add great value to the resource base.

Choice Nine–Social Service or Special Purpose Congregation

What Is the Essence of This Choice?

Choose to determine that which is most unique and satisfying to the congregation as a social service or special purpose congregation, and pursue it. A social service approach focuses on three or fewer social ministry or social action causes around which the congregation develops major emphases. The goal is that the congregation becomes known for these emphases throughout its geographic region. A special purpose congregation may focus on a demographic niche or two that most or all the congregations within the geographic region ignore.

Who Ought to Consider This Choice?

Congregations who have developed unique styles of programs, ministries, and activities that are more important to them than is reaching a certain geographic community should consider this choice. The term "unique" characterizes many elements of these congregations. They also place a high priority on quality.

What Are Strategic Transition and Change Issues to Address?

Being a social service congregation involves engaging in ministries to the social, physical, and psychological needs of people in the congregational context. The congregation sees itself as a social ministry outpost that serves its context and various target groups unconditionally.

A special purpose congregation focuses on a special purpose; target group; social, political, or religious cause; or on a unique characteristic of the congregation. Some special purpose congregations focus on certain lifestyle characteristics of niche demographic groups.

A university context congregation, particularly if it is located on the campus, is a special purpose congregation. A congregation that focuses on a specific social justice or moral issue is a special purpose church. A senior-adult-focused congregation is a special purpose church.

What Are Essential Resources to Have Available to Embrace This Choice?

A highly focused passion combined with a deep sense of urgency are essential resources for this choice. Social service or special purpose congregations must clearly identify their focus and quickly become known as the expert congregation in this focus in their geographic region.

These congregations should discover case studies of other congregations who have embraced this choice and dialogue with them to understand the signs of health and strength of such congregations as well as the strategic actions that can be the most effective.

Leadership may be a significant strategic challenge for these congregations, as it will require persons who desire to provide strong servant leadership for the causes the congregation embraces. The leaders must be able to have their own emotional and spiritual needs met through their involvement in the congregational causes. For this reason, coaching from a Christian leadership coach should be a high priority for these congregations.

Choice Ten–Multiple Worshiping Communities Congregation

What Is the Essence of This Choice?

The essence of this choice is to intentionally choose to be a congregation that creates and nurtures multiple worshiping communities within an existing congregation. This involves starting new worship services that focus on groups of people whom the core congregation has not been able to reach, but who are located within the context of the congregation. Typically the staff and lay leadership of the core congregation lead the new services with some outside assistance and expertise.

Multiple worshiping communities within one corporate congregation may be as simple as having an early worship service and a late worship service on Sunday mornings, even if they have substantially the same order of worship. It can be as complex as the congregation who projected a future where they would have a minimum of six worshiping communities.

This latter congregation envisioned the following:

- a new interactive, fast-paced, liturgical worshiping community
- a traditional worshiping community characteristic of the heritage of their denomination
- a contemporary worshiping community started to attract the college community from a large university near their site
- a postmodern worship community that would meet on Thursday nights to attract young adults with a nonchurch background
- a bilingual community to address the Korean population that had moved to their area following a particular industry that had relocated into the county
- a bilingual community to address the emerging Hispanic community that had moved from being a transient, seasonal population to permanent resident status

Who Ought to Consider This Choice?

Congregations ought to consider this choice in the following circumstances:

- They have over 125 in average weekly worship attendance and want to solidify their existence as a multiple cell congregation with various worship, learning, and fellowship groupings.
- They have three or more age generations and need to affirm a diversity of methodologies to approach God in worship through a diversity of worship opportunities.

- They find building larger sanctuaries or worship centers is impractical because of the cost of $2,500 or more per seat or because the church has outgrown its available space and property, or when it is actually more effective to start a new worshiping community using the philosophy of multiplication
- They have around 75 to 85 in average weekly worship attendance and want to make the numerical growth passage to 125 or more.

The final choice may be one of the most effective methods to break through this numerical barrier that forms a growth ceiling for more than 60 percent of all North American congregations. Often the natural Kingdom potential of these congregations is much greater, but once they have been less than 85 in attendance for a decade, it is practically impossible to break through that growth barrier without adding a major new component, such as a separate worshiping community.

What Are Strategic Transition and Change Issues to Address?

Diversity is addressed in that each worship experience has the opportunity to address a generation mindset, different life stage issues, and different spiritual development stages. Also, scheduling of the various services allows for multiple, diverse discipleship learning experiences, and the opportunity for multiple, diverse fellowship experiences.

At the same time, this choice allows for one congregational name, one membership roll, one governing board, one budget, one unified staff, one treasury, one set of facilities, one consistent belief and values system, and one Web site. Particularly, it is important to celebrate the oneness of the congregation through common worship, learning, and fellowship experiences throughout the year, with an emphasis on the sense of community that emerges from fellowship gatherings.

What Are Essential Resources to Have Available to Embrace This Choice?

Consistent unity with diversity is the initial emotional and spiritual resource the congregational leadership must possess. The *Enduring Visionary Leadership Community* has to have ownership of and a passion for using multiple worshiping communities to expand and extend the reach of the congregation. Spend the necessary time in researching how other congregations have dealt with the logistics of this choice and have handled the transition of their congregational participants to the point at which they embraced the schedule and style diversities this will bring. Make sure congregational participants are comfortable with reaching new people who may approach their Christian walk different from their traditional way.

The vision within your congregation must be clear at the point of unity in diversity, or this choice may raise significant conflict in the congregation. Some of this conflict may be over the stress of programming and the use of facilities. Some of the greatest stress may come in an unlikely place, and that is the preschool area. Multiple worshiping communities call for larger spaces and more workers for preschoolers, because the preschool space will be used more hours, and perhaps concurrently, by various worshiping communities. Preschool space capacity needs may double.

The congregation should have a realistic understanding of present leaders who relate to various worshiping communities. Many new leaders may have to be developed. Christian leadership coaching will be a great asset to motivate congregational leaders to action in a multitasking style.

Choice Eleven–Multiple Congregations within a Congregation

What Is the Essence of This Choice?

The essence of this choice is to choose to be a congregation that starts or nests multiple congregations within its congregation. These congregations differ from worshiping communities in that they are fully congregational–with their own unique worship, learning, and fellowship experiences identified solely with their congregation.

To *nest* congregations means that you make room for them in the physical, spiritual, and social space of your congregation. It may also imply that at some point in the future they develop their own *wings* and leave the *nest.*

These nested congregations may have a separate corporate entity, denominational affiliation, and belief and values system. Certainly the ministerial staff of each congregation would belong uniquely to them. Another way to phrase this choice is to say that multiple congregations exist within a church, or various Christ-centric faith communities function within one church or congregation.

Who Ought to Consider This Choice?

Congregations within a diverse context that calls for multiple types of congregations to reach various pre-Christian, unchurched, and dechurched groups ought to consider this choice. This choice allows them to reach a new generation and significantly different target groups in terms of race, ethnicity, and lifestyle in a manner that often is not possible within the existing core congregation. Congregations who try to change from within often face great resistance to transition and change.

Congregations may overcome these difficult transition issues by blessing an autonomous congregation through providing them with space in which to meet, and through other tangible and intangible elements of empowerment. Congregations located in areas where real estate and building costs are high should consider an intentional strategy of nesting other congregations who reach noncompeting groups of people.

Congregations who are declining in numbers, but rich in facilities space, should consider nesting other congregations–particularly ones who may be more successful at reaching the new emerging groups of people in the core congregation's context.

What Are Strategic Transition and Change Issues to Address?

Worship, discipleship learning, and fellowship experiences may occur in radically different styles, cultures, and languages. The belief and value system of the various congregations may be different, but still within a range the core congregation can embrace.

Membership is one issue of diversity for new congregations started within existing congregations. Among people born after February 9, 1964, formal membership is not a critical issue. They are simply connected to congregations at various entry and community points. Therefore, diversity will exist at the point of membership expectations. Separate marketing efforts are maintained, with separate logos and identity systems, separate Web sites, separate mailing lists, and distinct target groups.

Relationship experiences or congregational gatherings are the common, regular means for expressing harmony. Intentional experiences should be planned that bring participants from the various congregations together multiple times each year for worship, learning, and fellowship. The leadership of the various congregations should have some common spiritual growth experiences with one another several times a year. Or, they may have a regular share and prayer small group system among them.

What Are Essential Resources to Have Available to Embrace This Choice?

Sufficient facilities space, parking, and a worship, education, and fellowship schedule acceptable to all congregations will be critical, as will a sense that God is leading in this choice. This choice may have more diversity of race, ethnicity, socioeconomics, and lifestyle among the participants than the multiple worshiping communities. As such this option offers a great potential for a clash of cultural values. Therefore, multicultural sensitivity is an essential resource.

A vision for an adult-to-adult relationship between the various congregations must be present. Every congregation, and especially its leaders, must evidence a strong desire for each congregation to soar in a manner that will allow them to move toward their full Kingdom potential. Regular intercongregational fellowship and worship experiences will enhance the ability of each congregation to have the highest quality and quantity of ministry and respect and appreciation for the ministry of the other congregations.

Time spent in researching how other congregations have dealt with various aspects of this choice will pay big dividends in the congregation. A regular dialogue and time of prayer between the key leaders of each congregation may create and maintain the sense of fellowship and common purpose that must be present. A facilitator or Christian leadership coach would be a great asset for their intercongregational leadership gatherings.

Choice Twelve–Multicultural Congregation
What Is the Essence of This Choice?

The essence of this choice is to develop a congregation that is clearly multicultural, and not dominated by a single culture. A number of racial and ethnic groups, as well as various nationalities, are represented in the participating membership and in the congregation's core leadership.

Worship is often diverse, multicultural, and even multilingual. Discipleship and fellowship experiences also represent the full spectrum of cultures attracted to the congregation, rather than small groups breaking off into homogeneous groupings. Evangelism and new member recruitment efforts focus on continuing to reach persons from various cultural perspectives.

Who Ought to Consider This Choice?

Congregations located in a multicultural context should consider this choice. If its context is not also multicultural, a congregation will find it difficult to sustain the multicultural nature of a congregation for more than seven to nine years.

It is easier for a new congregation to embrace this choice than it is for an existing congregation to transition to this choice. Existing congregations may have too much ownership of their former culture, and may—even without meaning to—come across with paternalism to other racial, ethnic, and nationality groups. The core leadership community of a new or existing congregation must be multicultural from the beginning of any multicultural efforts for this choice to be effective.

It is easier to embrace this choice if the pastor's household is multicultural and even multilingual. The pastor's spouse should be of a different racial, ethnic, or national origin and must be actively involved in the congregation. When the pastor is not married, she or he should be multicultural or multilingual. If this is not the case, then the staff of the congregation must be multicultural and multilingual.

What Are Strategic Transition and Change Issues to Address?

Diversity is obviously empowered by the presence of various races, ethnic groups, and nationalities. This presence must be authentic and genuine, permeating all dimensions of congregational life. Any tokenism will destroy the true multicultural nature of the congregation. While quotas for representing each racial, ethnic, or nationality within the congregation in every program, ministry, or activity is not the best approach, significant, obvious effort to embrace the full diversity of the congregation in everything that is done is an essential characteristic of true diversity.

A diversity of racial, ethnic, and nationality groups speaks very positively to a holistic application of the gospel. That allows this model to represent the New Testament church in an ideal form. Multiculturalism also affirms a diversity of approaches to reach people for a Christ-centric faith journey and for involving them in that journey.

Harmony is empowered because it is probable that in the midst of great racial, ethnic, and national diversity there will be a significant unifying or organizing factor. This unifying factor can be a captivating vision the congregation is seeking to fulfill. Such a vision may focus around a great spiritual perspective or a mission goal.

One hunch is that a close analysis of multicultural congregations would show that the clergy and laity leadership of these congregations have a similar socioeconomic, education, or cultural mindset. This common mindset is part of what holds the congregation together. In the leadership dimensions of the congregation it is much more difficult to have a diverse socioeconomic group of folks represented than it is to have a diverse racial, ethnic, or nationality group represented.

What Are Essential Resources to Have Available to Embrace This Choice?

The most essential resource is a commitment to begin, serve faithfully, and end as a fully multicultural congregation not dominated by the habits and practices of any one culture. To do this a multicultural congregation must have at least three cultures represented in significant numbers. Two cultures do not necessarily make for a multicultural congregation.

Second, the congregation must own a vision and core values that supersede all the individual cultures and perspectives or religious expressions. Only this empowering vision can unify the congregation in faithful, effective, and innovative service. Multiple languages and dialects must be spoken in the congregation, and sensitivity to the meaning of words must be a hallmark principle. Programs, ministries, and activities must speak to various culturally relevant ways of learning and relating.

Third, multicultural congregations who serve as models may be difficult to find, but time spent in dialogue with others who have made this choice will enrich your journey.

Fourth, leadership for the congregation must be multicultural from the very beginning and remain that way throughout the life of the congregation.

Fifth, a coach should always be available to help the congregational leadership maintain a unity in diversity stance, style, strategy, and practice at all times.

Choice Thirteen–Congregational Multiplication Movement

What Is the Essence of This Choice?

The essence of this choice is to develop and sustain a strategy of starting new congregations in which the fulfillment of this strategy leads to a self-perpetuating congregational multiplication movement that fuels itself with minimal external pushing from denominational or parachurch organizations.

This best happens when a vision of and dedication to reproducing new congregations is built into the DNA of newly launched congregations. Within seven to nine years from the time a group of new congregations is launched, with reproducing new congregations as part of their DNA, these new congregations can be seriously involved in multiplication movement actions.

Existing congregations may make this choice when they become captivated by a new or renewed vision for launching new congregations. Often these congregations see the multiplication of new congregations as the most effective means of evangelism, new member recruitment, and community transformation.

Within the movement are some congregations who may launch one or more new congregations each year. A few congregations keep a minimum of five new congregations at some point of launch and development into self-sustaining Christ-centric faith communities.

Who Ought to Consider This Choice?

Congregations who find themselves in a fast-growing context, or a significantly changing context, must respond to this opportunity by launching new congregational expressions focused on reaching new residents migrating or immigrating to their area of ministry influence. A few congregations will see this from a global and local perspective and include in their multiplication efforts partnerships with congregations in various parts of the world.

Denominational organizations that are serious about doing their part to expand the reach of God's kingdom will facilitate the launching of a number of new congregations each year equal to at least three percent of the congregations currently affiliated with their denominational organization. If they are successful in launching not only a significant numbers of congregations, but also a grassroots movement of launching new congregations, then their most serious challenge will be to continue empowering the multiplication movement and not to kill it through intentional or unintentional control mechanisms.

It is difficult for denominational organizations to give wings to those things to which they gave roots. Too often, denominations measure success by what they control rather than by what they empower. They particularly love to count new congregational statistics because that masks the fact that the remainder of congregations—as a group—are declining and the denomination does not seem to be able to stop the collective decline.

What Are Strategic Transition and Change Issues to Address?

Only through new congregations can a Christ-centric faith community touch the full spectrum of God's creation. Congregational multiplication movements affirm geographic and demographic diversity, generation distinctions, racial and ethnic pluralism, and lifestyle uniqueness.

No one congregation is pluralistic enough, or sufficiently diverse in its doctrine and methods, to reach all people within its context. Full diversity is best expressed through the fellowship of congregations within a given context, rather than one congregation falsely claiming that it has a ministry for and to everyone.

Many denominational families have an ethos that makes a significant contribution to the overall Christian movement. Through the launching of new congregations within that religious cultural context, the harmony represented by that denominational ethos is maintained.

Faithful, effective, and innovative congregations are most likely to be part of a congregational multiplication movement. They have a healthy spiritual community that, when replicated through launching new congregations, provides a creative harmony that benefits Kingdom work. The DNA of such congregations begs to be cloned in the vibrant spiritual life of new congregations.

Few denominations have a culture of growth and expansion that will create and sustain a congregational multiplication movement. Some denominations do not even have a comprehensive strategy to start new congregations. Such denominations will cease to exist within three generations after they stop starting new congregations.

What Are Essential Resources to Have Available to Embrace This Choice?

The big four are leadership, partnership, finances, and prayer.

First, it takes a large supply of pastoral and lay leadership to create and sustain a congregational multiplication movement. If a new congregation is to have both short-term and long-term success, it will typically need ten to twenty households, of which at least two must be clergy households, who will commit to launching the new congregation.

Few seminaries have ministry preparation tracks that equip clergy and laity to lead in the launching of new congregations. Often skill development and ongoing learning must take place in a lead partnership congregation committed to a congregational multiplication movement. Denominational organizations can mentor and provide resources to these mentoring congregations so they can function as new congregational ministry incubators.

Second, to create and sustain a congregational multiplication movement requires mobilization of a number of congregations equal to 20 percent of the total number of congregations affiliated with a denominational organization. These congregations must be willing to be primary or secondary partners for the launching of new congregations. One-third of partner congregations must be faithful, effective, and innovative congregations who will serve as primary partners for launching new congregations. The second third must be willing to be supporting partners, and the final third must be participants in one or more aspects of the new congregation.

These numbers may seem impossible to achieve. However, that is why the creation of a congregational multiplication movement must be seen as a seven-to-nine-year journey. It will take that long to build the capacity for enough partner congregations. Also, remember that many of these partner congregations will be ones launched during the first few years of the journey toward reaching a full multiplication movement. Within seven to nine years these new congregations can themselves become partner congregations.

Third, a denominational organization must make funding new congregations a priority. No denominational organization can budget for or accumulate sufficient financial resources to pay the launch costs for all the new congregations. However, they can use strategically placed seed money as a magnet to draw other funds from the budget of partner congregations, from individuals from within partner congregations, from members of the new congregations, and from other external resources that may not be immediately obvious.

Fourth, a congregational multiplication movement requires strong prayer support. Such a movement is unlikely to be created and sustained unless a large number of people from at least 20 percent of the affiliated congregations are involved in regularly praying for the movement. A congregational multiplication movement, while very much a strategic process, is also a spiritual process. It is a God thing. It is something that calls for the full heart, soul, mind, and strength of the greater Church. Anything less will be inadequate.

COACHING INSIGHTS

- What approach will work best for you in considering these thirteen choices? Do you need to share all thirteen choices with your active congregation, or at least your *Enduring Visionary Leadership Community*? Or, do you need to choose three possible futures and suggest these to the congregational leadership for consideration?

- Which of these choices seem to be way outside the realm of possibility for your congregation? Which ones make the best sense for the heritage of your congregation? Which two or three would embrace the hope you feel for your congregation?

- It certainly appears that some of these choices could be combined to form a choice that best fits your congregation. Which ones are those for you? How would you go about combining them to capture in one choice the best of what several choices have to offer you?

■ By when will you decide which choice is the one that best fits the collective spiritual gifts, life skills, and personality preferences of your congregation? Which choice is that? By what criteria did you arrive at that conclusion? Will your congregational leadership be convinced by these criteria?

■ Is it possible that none of these work for your congregation? If so, where will you look next for possible choices for your congregation? If these thirteen choices were intended to activate your creativity, where does that new energy take you next? By when will you be ready to share other choices inspired in you by what you read about these thirteen choices?

PERSONAL REFLECTIONS

YOUR REFLECTIONS: What are your reflections on the material presented in this chapter?

YOUR ACTIONS: What actions do you need to take about your life, ministry, and/or congregation based on the material presented in this chapter?

YOUR ACCOUNTABILITY: How and by whom do you want to be held accountable for taking these actions?

CHAPTER TEN

Living into the Future Story of Your Congregation

EXECUTIVE SUMMARY

The purpose of this chapter is to focus on the twelfth step in the future storytelling process, namely, living into the story, celebrating the fulfillment of the story, and regularly updating the story as the journey becomes clearer and the congregation can see farther. Emphasis is placed on keeping the process open, fuzzy, and "chaordic" (that is, characterized by both chaos and order, at the same time) so that it will remain a journey dependent on spiritual leadership, and not become a program or project dependent only on smart—but static—strategy. This chapter also focuses on how to sustain the spiritual strategic journey and to be consistently perfecting the journey.

The story is not the thing. Living into the story is the thing. Being the best possible congregation in your context with a clear vision of your full Kingdom potential is the thing. Making obvious progress toward your current and ever-clearer vision of your full Kingdom potential is the thing.

Everything that has happened to this point in your congregation's spiritual strategic journey is a prelude, an introduction, an overture, a prologue, and a preamble. In rural parlance, everything to this point is "fixin' to get ready to commence to begin to start to do something, maybe." Now it is essential to move beyond the narrative story development to decisive action.

Action involves living into your congregation's story, celebrating the fulfillment of your congregation's future story, regularly updating your congregation's future story, sustaining your congregation's spiritual strategic journey, and perfecting your congregation's spiritual strategic journey.

Action involves the *Enduring Visionary Leadership Community*– composed of the *People of Pastoral Leadership*, the *People of Passion*, and the *People of Position*–taking responsibility for fulfillment of the future story. Fulfillment comes about by making the story come alive, by taking effective action on key empowering action areas that will make the crucial difference in the ability of the congregation to serve in the midst of God's kingdom.

Action involves strategic steps that are open, fuzzy, and "chaordic." Strategic steps are open in that they do not emanate from a bounded list of acceptable actions, but from a creative list of innovative actions. The steps are fuzzy in that they cannot always be defined at the beginning, and must be worked out as implementation is taking place. Chaordic steps are characterized simultaneously by chaos and order.

Action involves several different types of people expressing their support of the story and doing their part to see it fulfilled.

First are people who highly value the meaning and significance of the story and long to see it fulfilled. Out of their deep commitment to the story they will often speak with emotion about wanting to see evidence that your congregation is living into the story. They will easily support changing the story to keep it relevant to the new things God is doing in your midst.

Second are people who are the strategic thinking gurus. They will regularly test the validity of actions being taken based upon whether or not they are staying focused on the key empowering actions that will make a positive, yet critical, difference in the ability of your congregation to serve with ever-increasing effectiveness. They will oppose ideas and actions that do not clearly come out of the story. They may even oppose changing the story to keep it relevant because they will want to stay focused on the original intent and direction of the story.

Third are people who enjoy the rush or the experience of seeing the story being fulfilled. They will bring excitement to the fulfillment of the story. Changed lives resulting from living into the story are of high value for them. They are wide open to changing the story to follow the passion and excitement of the spiritual strategic journey and to tell more vividly what is actually in the process of happening in the lives of people.

Fourth are people who are comfortable with the mechanics of living into the story, and who focus on implementation of the *Future Story Fulfillment Map.* Execution is their middle name. They will help your congregation stay on target with its actions, implementation, and fulfillment. They enjoy calendars, budgets, to-do lists, accountability, evaluation, and reports. As such, they may highly resist the evolving transitions and changes in the story because these mess up their implementation procedures. At the same time, they are probably the most valuable folks to have around for the journey because they hold everyone else accountable for action.

Living into Your Congregation's Future Story

Just in case living into your congregation's future story is not clear or obvious to you, let's state it one more time for the record. Living into your congregation's future story is engaging in regular, continual, intentional actions that are consistent with the goals, benchmarks, or characteristics of your future story. If successful and effective, these actions will pull the congregation forward in the direction of its full Kingdom potential.

Fulfillment Actions You May Take

What are some examples of actions that you might take? Providing such a list is somewhat dangerous because of the tendency to just pick appealing actions off of a list—whether or not they are the actions that will help your congregation fulfill its unique future story. Let's take the risk anyway and hope it does not pollute your efforts. Here are fulfillment actions some churches take to live into their future story:

- Make transitions and changes in the worship services to reposition them to attract a new generation of seekers.
- Hire a different type of staff person called for in the future story to fill a current staff vacancy.
- Start a new Bible study, Sunday school class, small group, or cell group that attracts a new group of people to the life and ministry of your congregation.
- Reorganize the governance and committee structure of your congregation to invest less people and time in the management

structures of your congregation, and more people and time in its ministry systems.

• Develop a new disciple-making process that seeks to help people connected with your congregation grow in the grace and knowledge of our Lord and Savior Jesus Christ. Equally as good is a lay mobilization phase of a comprehensive disciple-making process that seeks to help laypersons identify their spiritual gifts, life skills, and personality preference, and then mobilize these in Christian service in the church and community.

The Function of the Future Story Fulfillment Map

The actions you take must be identified on the *Future Story Fulfillment Map* developed in step eleven of the future storytelling process. Actions you take that are not part of the *Future Story Fulfillment Map* may be excellent actions, but they may also derail the focus of your spiritual strategic journey. They should be rejected.

The *Future Story Fulfillment Map*, like the future story itself, is not a static document. It is a map for the exploration taking place as you travel along your spiritual strategic journey. The tactics and actions of the map will continually transition and change throughout the journey, but you should keep them in place until it becomes obvious that more effective tactics and actions will keep the congregation soaring in the direction of its perceived destination.

The Beginning of Living into Your Future Story

When does living into the future story for your congregation begin? Is there a formal launch? This is part of the beauty of the dynamic, open-system, fuzzy, and "chaordic" future storytelling process as opposed to a more formal, closed-system, rigid planning process. The fulfillment of the story begins happening while the story is being written. It does not wait for a formal launch. As congregational participants are captivated by the vision God has for the congregation, they begin engaging in actions that will result in the fulfillment of the emerging spiritual strategic journey. This particularly happens when the congregation has a permission-giving stance that seeks to empower laity in ministry.

Future Story as Movement, Not Process

In these situations congregational leaders recognize that living into the future story is a movement rather than a formal implementation process. Living into the future story must become the action people are thinking about and doing all the time. It becomes the mantra for the life of the congregation. In fact, one sign a congregation does not "get" the concept of living into the future story is a demand for formal approval. A congregation may make a real or implied requirement that no action takes place until the congregation has formally approved it through its formal governance system.

At a congregation I call Founders Church, their future story included the need to rethink their staffing patterns for their very large congregation. For two years they had been seeking a new children's ministry director, but their future story called for them to seek an associate pastor for young adult families. Such a position would look at the whole family or household in which children are living. This approach places emphasis on the role of the family in the spiritual development of children. Following a failed two-year search under the old staffing model, a new search began with the new model and the sense of urgency and passion created by the new story. Within the first 120 days of formal living into the story, they called to the staff the new associate pastor for young families.

Often new congregations find it impossible to place the story in written form fast enough because it is being experienced and lived into on the fly. In these congregations the future story remains oral tradition for a good while before it is written down. If and when it becomes written, it is probably because leadership has empowered a scribe or storyteller to write the story. A major reason for doing this is to be sure the leadership is clearly communicating the journey to the congregation. Without such a process, it is possible to get a disconnect between the direction the leadership is heading and the direction the congregation perceives it is heading.

The older a congregation is in terms of both how long the congregation has been in existence and in terms of the average age of the average member, the greater the likelihood that a stated or formal requirement will develop that, until something is in the official story, the congregation cannot do it. Certainly, the managers within the congregation will not allow financial resources to be committed to it. These congregations will have difficulty overcoming formal, closed-system process to move to the new ad hoc informal processes of living in the future story of the congregation.

Communicating the Story

Living into the future story involves regularly communicating the story. Use the congregation's Web site, use Web logs (or blogs), use the congregational newsletter, use direct mail to the congregation, use video recordings of people telling stories of the fulfillment of the future story, use storytelling in meetings of the congregation, use one-on-one encounters with congregational participants, and use any other vehicles you can think of to regularly and positively tell of the fulfillment of the future story. This is definitely one of the situations in which the three most important words are *communicate, communicate,* and *communicate.* The future story must come alive for the congregation on a regular basis.

Living into the future story involves regularly praying for the fulfillment of the story. Through the share and prayer triplets the spiritual strategic journey may have been launched in your congregation. The share and prayer triplets, or some other appropriate prayer process, may now be an excellent way to provide a spiritual base for the fulfillment of the story, which can make a vital difference in how well your congregation serves Kingdom issues in the midst of its journey. It is important to be intentional about prayer as a foundational resource for living into your congregation's future story.

Celebrating the Fulfillment of Your Congregation's Future Story

Reaffirm your future story and the spiritual strategic journey through a celebration experience every 120 days. Update the story as the journey becomes clearer and you can see farther. The fun and the faithfulness have just begun. Both the thrill of the journey and the fear of the unknown are taking place simultaneously. Because the fulfillment of the intended actions by a congregation for its spiritual strategic journey begins to happen while the preparation for the journey is still going on, you may already have much to celebrate.

You can best benefit from this principle of celebrating every 120 days by planning a gathering of the *Enduring Visionary Leadership Community* to celebrate places where the future story is being fulfilled. Conduct these celebrations around a fellowship meal or a reception. Use music, use worship, use interaction, use video, use live testimonies, and use other vehicles to empower the dynamic nature of the story to come alive for those in attendance. Record these celebrations in both audio and video form for use in other venues for communicating the fulfillment of the future story and to provide a historic record.

Whom Should You Invite?

Intentionally invite congregational leaders to attend who are not participants in the *Enduring Visionary Leadership Community.* This will continue to show inclusion of the active congregation in the journey and will hold to a minimum gossip that can come from persons in the congregation who for any reason feel excluded from the journey. At best it will allow the excitement and exhilaration being experienced to also captivate their imagination and spiritual passion. Also, be sure to issue through as many media means as possible an open, general invitation to attend to anyone in the congregation who has an interest.

Intentionally invite to these celebrations new members who have connected with the congregation during the past year so they can experience more deeply what is going on in their new congregation. This can be a wonderful part of the assimilation process for them. It helps them know the story behind the emerging story that attracted them to the congregation. Also, invite people who have been attending your congregation regularly, but have not yet formally connected. This may be an excellent way to embrace them within the community of your congregation and cause them to think more about formally connecting as they encounter the future story of the congregation in action.

Specifically invite to these celebrations anyone directly impacted by the fulfillment of a portion of the future story. Ask them to engage in *Vision Fulfillment Storytelling*. This is the telling of the stories concerning experiences in which the future story of the congregation has had an impact on the life and ministry of persons connected with the congregation. This reinforces that the story is impacting the lives of real people in real time.

With Whom Should These Stories Be Shared?

Share these stories with the entire congregation so they can be impacted by the experiences of story fulfillment. Sharing these stories should take place through telling the stories, writing and distributing the stories, and showing the evidence of the impact of the stories. Have people engage in *Vision Fulfillment Storytelling* in the congregation's regular worship services.

Vision Fulfillment Storytelling should also become a new permanent agenda item at the board or governance meetings of your congregation, or at the church business meetings or conferences. Often boards or business meetings begin with presentations and dialogue around management agendas such as minutes, financial reports, and old business items that need to be brought up once more. This approach often leads to setting an unenthusiastic tone for the meeting, particularly if the financial report of your congregation is not positive.

When done well, *Vision Fulfillment Storytelling* can set an enthusiastic tone for even board and business meetings. People involved in the meeting are more motivated to focus on embracing future opportunities when they are impacted by the joy of future story fulfillment. More people can be impacted by the stories of real people than would be the case without the telling of these stories. The future story comes alive, is seen as vital, and is kept regularly in the minds of people involved in making crucial policy decisions for the congregation. It changes the scripts of the dreams and thoughts about the congregation to ones that are positive and future-oriented.

Many congregations have used the *Vision Fulfillment Storytelling* emphasis in their board and business meetings all throughout the journey, even before the future story is initially told. It immediately changes the tone of these meetings. It immediately makes them more joyful and mirrors the concept of worshipful work. It helps to diminish the controlling aspects of management and increase the empowering aspects of vision.

Regularly Updating Your Congregation's Future Story

As a result of the fulfillment of some portion of the story, that part of the story will need to be revised or otherwise updated to keep it relevant to the new things God is doing in and through the congregation. God is actively at work; and when portions of the future story are fulfilled, your congregation can now see the next mountain and its summit. You need to project your story farther into the future with more depth as the elusive destination of your journey becomes farther up and farther in. The future story of your congregation will continually be revised. It is dynamic. It is open, fuzzy, and "chaordic." It is never finished.

Remember, the written future story is not intended to be the story of what God has directed in the past to be done in and through the congregation. Rather it is the story of what God is doing through the congregation in the future. We want to keep up with that story by continually revising and updating the narrative to be congruent with what we discern God is doing and to where it is God is pulling the congregation.

Following each 120–day celebration of living into the future story of your congregation, the *Enduring Visionary Leadership Community* needs to spring into action with a revision, updating, and renewed communication of the story. It is not that they have to do it personally, but that they see that it is done. Perhaps they can empower a core writing group of three to five people to continually revise the story.

Even so, at each 120–day updating several additional types of people need to be involved in revising the story:

First are people who have been impacted by the story and have a *Vision Fulfillment Story* to tell that may further sharpen the story.

Second are people in the congregation whose area of responsibility has been impacted by living into the story, who need to have input to the next draft.

Third are people who have discerned a new twist to the future story and have something that can stand the test of faithfulness to the future story to offer for the writing group to consider.

Fourth are people who have connected with the congregation within the past twelve months who may have a new and fresh perspective on the life and ministry of the congregation.

The results of the revision should be published for the congregation through various communication channels. The "new and fresh" should be highlighted in some manner. The "old and faithful" should be celebrated and appreciated. This revision should be done quickly, perhaps within thirty days, before too much additional progress is made on the journey.

COACHING BREAK

✔ Gaze out the window for a minute. Ponder the situation of your congregation. What images come to mind?

✔ How comfortable are you with the dynamic nature of the future story process? Do you understand the full importance of being faithful to the process of living into the story? Remember it is not the story, it is living *into* the story that takes you toward your full Kingdom potential.

Sustaining Your Congregation's Spiritual Strategic Journey

To sustain its journey, a congregation must ask several depth-exploring questions. How does a congregation remain in the prime of its life through continual focus on the emerging spiritual strategic journey, and the story around that journey? What does a congregation do several years into their journey? Why is it important to reconceptualize the journey every seven to nine years? What must you do to sustain an excellent spiritual strategic journey that is always seeking to reach the full Kingdom potential of your congregation? How do you sustain the excellence of pastoral leadership throughout the spiritual strategic journey?

Remaining in the Prime of Life

How does a congregation remain in the prime of its life through continual focus on the emerging spiritual strategic journey and the story around that journey? "Prime" is that phase in your congregation's life when relationships, programs, and management are all fully developed and expressed. Vision is also fully developed for Adulthood, and begins to diminish in Maturity. All of this is explained in detail in chapter 5.

Several key factors may enable your congregation to remain in the prime of its life.

First, it hardwires into its culture a revisioning process based on the new things God is doing in the life of the congregation. Such revisioning occurs every seven to nine years, or whenever vision diminishes so that the congregation is in Maturity. Rather than assuming that the current vision will always be the correct and effective vision, the congregation embraces the concept of living into a continually changing future story, realizing that about every seven to nine years it needs to take a major new look at refocusing its spiritual strategic journey.

Second, it develops a leadership culture that anticipates and discerns forward, future movement in the journey of the congregation that needs to be affirmed and incorporated into its future story. While leaders need to understand the history and heritage of your congregation, they also need to be able to visualize what is to be built on that foundation. They need to be the type of people who are able to visualize the new World Trade Center towers in place in the lower Manhattan borough of New York City before they are built.

Third, your congregation is not stuck in one time dimension. It has the ability to simultaneously affirm the past, present, and future of the congregation. One-dimensional people often make shortsighted and uninformed decisions based upon their personal digital photo of what the congregation looked like in the past or will look like in the future. The future of your congregation is not a static digital photo with a time stamp on it, but a real-time video of the future life of the congregation being played out in front of you.

Fourth, it hardwires continual learning into its leadership culture. It rewards learning and the sharing of new insights. A congregation that stops learning cannot see far into the future for long. Once it stops learning, it may stop making progress. If that happens, the future story of your congregation toward which God is pulling you moves past you, and you begin falling behind. This creates a small gap at first, but it becomes an ever-widening chasm the longer your congregation is not in a learning mode. Therefore, learning is a foundational issue.

Actions Several Years into the Journey

What does a congregation do several years into their journey? Approximately every three years your congregation should engage in a major effort to rewrite its *Future Story Fulfillment Map.* It is not that the map, if regularly updated, is no longer relevant. It is that the three-to-five-year actions projected by the map will start to be fulfilled, and the necessity exists to project major actions farther into the future. The map, though tested regularly with reality, must always be projected into the future ahead of the actual actions that will be taken.

The congregation's ownership of the actions called for by the map begins to ebb over the years and needs to be reinvigorated. Once again the congregation needs to be captivated by a sense of God's spiritual strategic direction for the congregation. The ownership goes deeper than the future story and includes the specific actions themselves.

Reconceptualizing the Journey

Why is it important to reconceptualize the spiritual strategic journey every seven to nine years? The life cycle and stages of development model teaches us that congregations who are more than one generation old and do not revision every seven to nine years will find themselves moving down the aging side of the life cycle, regularly becoming older and more passive. Therefore, about every seven to nine years it is important for these congregations, which are at least 80 percent of all congregations, to engage in a major overhaul of their spiritual strategic journey to be sure they are traveling in the right direction.

At first you might wonder why there is the need for this if the congregation has been regularly updating its story to stay focused on God's spiritual strategic journey for them. The answer is that no matter how well your congregation does this continual transition and change, it can still develop a group think mentality that does not take a hard look at itself from an outside perspective.

Recently I worked with a congregation whose vision centered around the theme of involvement in missions projects globally. Many areas of the congregation had done a wonderful job of leaping forward in promoting this theme. The spirit and vitality of the congregation had increased over a seven-to-nine-year period in such a way that it had positively impacted every area of the congregation. This is a wonderful, effective, and focused congregation. Among the byproducts of this missional journey were a doubling in attendance, a tripling in the finances, and a ten-fold increase in the amount of resources going into missions work.

At the same time this mission-happy congregation had failed to respond to two reactions to its missions endeavors. They required third-party coaching to bring these issues to the surface for dialogue.

First, most of the missions work had been away from the community or context of the congregation. Now an increasing number of people were ready to invest their newfound zeal in their local context. They wanted to go beyond giving money but did not have an adequate vehicle to do that.

Second, missions involvement had focused on projects the congregation sponsored but the congregation was failing to affirm that many people are called to various missions and ministries involvements that will never become official missions and ministries projects of the congregation. Therefore, a process needed to be developed to affirm the calling and involvement of each congregational participant.

Other reasons also exist to do a major overhaul of the story after seven to nine years. These include the fact that totally new opportunities may emerge not present seven to nine years ago, and so the future story has never reflected these. It would be hoped that a congregation as a whole has matured significantly in its spiritual strategic journey over the years, and may have different perspectives on their journey that call for that journey to be reconceptualized.

Another reason is that even terminology and how people talk about ministry and congregational life can change over a seven-to-nine-year period. An updating of terminology that goes beyond simple editing and revising the future story may be needed. Think about the word *blog*. This was the most important new or emerging word of the year 2004. It refers to a Web log—or "blog"—which is a personal Web site for use in sharing information about which readers can comment. Presidential and other political candidates popularized the use of blogs during 2004. Seven to nine years earlier blogs had not yet emerged as a Web presence. For younger, digitally oriented target groups, a congregation who does not understand the importance of blogs and the dialogue that takes place on blogs may be considered out of touch.

Sustaining an Excellent Congregational Spiritual Strategic Journey

What must your congregation do to sustain an excellent spiritual strategic journey that is always seeking to reach the full Kingdom potential of your congregation? The key to sustaining an excellent spiritual strategic journey is a focus on building capacities within the congregation. Many, if not most, strategic efforts or futuring processes in congregations stretch the congregation beyond its comfort zones, but they do not seek to develop the new capacities or provide a forum for the learnings that will allow the congregation to effectively lead into the future.

A rubber band may be stretched, but too often it snaps back to where it was before it was stretched, or it breaks rather than snapping forward to a new position or being repositioned forward from its starting place. Similarly, the beginning point of a congregational spiritual strategic journey is too often the reference point for the congregation and the basis on which it makes major decisions.

New capacities must be built and new learnings must be embraced. These enable the congregation to see its future as its point of reference and to do so without unhealthy stress and conflict. To do this the congregation must be a learning congregation that continually seeks to hardwire new understandings of how to apply faithful truths to future ministry. Tactically, the congregation must be identifying learning communities on a regular basis that can positively infect the congregation, like a virus, with new learnings on how to live into its future.

Sustaining Excellent Pastoral Leadership through the Journey

How do you sustain the excellence of pastoral leadership throughout the spiritual strategic journey? Learning is also the key here. Congregations should encourage their pastor and ministerial staff to project the future story of their personal ministry while the congregation is pursuing its journey. Then the congregation should provide opportunities for their ministerial leaders to engage in the capacity building and learning experiences necessary to prepare them for the next stages of ministerial leadership. Continually learning ministerial leaders are essential for congregations to be effective in traveling along their spiritual strategic journeys. Few congregations will travel farther than their ministerial leaders can take them. And ministerial leaders can take them only as far as they themselves have learned to go.

Perfecting Your Congregation's Spiritual Strategic Journey

How does a congregation know that the spiritual strategic journey it is sustaining is not yet its perfect journey? What more can a congregation do when it feels it has done all that it can to serve God with faithfulness, effectiveness, and innovation?

This is where the *FaithSoaring* referred to in chapters 5 and 6 comes in. Based on 2 Corinthians 5:7, this is the ability of a congregation to walk or soar by faith rather than by sight. *FaithSoaring* takes a congregation to places they could not conceive of a few years earlier. *FaithSoaring* is when a congregation moves from success to significance to surrender to the next new thing God is pulling it toward. *FaithSoaring* is when a congregation is fully aware of the presence of God in its midst. *FaithSoaring* is when a congregation, even though it loves the comfort of the present, is willing to be embraced by the open, fuzzy, and "chaordic" nature of an unknown and unseen future.

The crazy thing is that this perfecting comes about when the congregation may have just completed what it feels is a long journey to get to where it is pulled forward by God's vision for their future. They have hardwired and sustained their journey and now wonder how anyone could ask anything more of them. Sight often tells us we have gone to the end of all possible journeys or climbed all the mountains left to climb. Can there be anything else? Can God ask anything more?

Where Is There Evidence of Perfecting the Journey?

Perfecting your congregation's spiritual strategic journey may be seen in the congregation that had been very successful in its current location and appeared to have reached its full Kingdom potential. Then they decided to relocate into a growing area, change their name, and change their style of worship, discipleship, fellowship, and ministry to reach a next generation of seekers. These seekers were born after the end of the Vietnam War in 1975,and before 2001. They do not understand all the talk about war because they had never known war. Now with the World Trade Center attack, and Afghanistan, Iraq, Iran, and North Korea, they are rethinking life and spirituality and want a congregation that will connect with their journey.

Sister congregations in the area of this congregation wonder why in the world they made such a radical change. They were already the model and most successful congregation of their denomination in that area. The answer is that God's perfect vision for their journey involved more. They engaged in *FaithSoaring*!

Perfecting your congregation's spiritual strategic journey is seen in the congregation who had been involved in helping to build–and then took the lead in building–several Habitat for Humanity houses. They were a success in their region of the state. They are making a great contribution to this ministry. They engaged in holistic ministry to the people whose houses they were building. This included authentically sharing their Christian faith out of a deep relationship they built with the families. Then, the need arose for a new Habitat for Humanity chapter in their area. They immediately volunteered to take on a lead role, even though they were a small congregation with less than 135 in average worship attendance. They engaged in *FaithSoaring!*

Perfecting your congregation's spiritual strategic journey can be seen in the congregation who has started a few new congregations over the years. Perhaps they were already seen as the role model for their denomination in church planting. Then they become captivated by the desire to launch a congregational multiplication movement in which they would plant multiple new congregations each year and would seek to insert into the DNA of these new congregations the idea that they will become reproducing congregations. Within ten years this congregation and those they have planted were starting several dozen congregations each year. They engaged in *FaithSoaring!*

Perfecting your congregation's spiritual strategic journey can be seen in the congregation who had a wonderful weekday early education program for preschoolers. They were always full and had a waiting list. They did not have to market their program. Word of mouth and the endorsement of several local pediatrician doctors were all the marketing they needed. While already the model for a congregational program in their area, they determined to seek full accreditation, did so within a few years, and then became a teaching program to help raise the level of Christian weekday early education in congregations throughout their region. They sacrificially gave away what they had learned and charged no fees for it. They engaged in *FaithSoaring!*

Perfecting your congregation's spiritual strategic journey can be seen in the congregation who is known for a high percentage of its active youth and adults being involved in one or more missions projects in their local area, throughout North America, and in various places around the world. After many years of taking a few missions trips and embracing a few missions projects each year, missions involvement became the mantra of their congregation. They have truly become a "GlobaLocal" congregation. They engaged in *FaithSoaring!*

Perfecting your congregation's spiritual strategic journey is all about *FaithSoaring*. Your full Kingdom potential is always further up and further in.

COACHING INSIGHTS

- How do you keep the planning process of your congregation alive and not allow it to become the end or destination? What are actions you can take to live into your future story that will be motivating, inspiring, and effective?

- Keeping the *Enduring Visionary Leadership Community* of your congregation engaged, active, and refreshed is an essential part of living into your future story How do you care for their spiritual, physical, and emotional needs? How are these needs addressed in your own life?

- Who are your execution persons within your congregation, that is, the people who will take responsibility to keep the journey moving? These are crucial if your church is going to reach its full Kingdom potential. You must have people who help you show up on time dressed to play because they believe passionately in the journey. Who are these people?

- The *Future Story Fulfillment Map*, if you are not careful, can simply turn into another planning chart. What do you need to do to keep this from happening in your congregation? How can you truly make it a map of your emerging journey?

- When is good enough, good enough? If you have followed the process of this book, you have already done amazing things within the fellowship of your congregation to sharpen its ability to serve in the midst of God's kingdom. Now you are called on to sustain your journey and even perfect your journey through moving into a whole new dimension of ministry. You are not only outside the box, but beyond the box if you fully surrender your ministry to God's ideal will. How do you handle this personally? What assurance and what support do you need for the perfecting process?

PERSONAL REFLECTIONS

YOUR REFLECTIONS: What are your reflections on the material presented in this chapter?

_____

_____

_____

_____

_____

YOUR ACTIONS: What actions do you need to take about your life, ministry, and/or congregation based on the material presented in this chapter?

_____

_____

_____

_____

_____

YOUR ACCOUNTABILITY: How and by whom do you want to be held accountable for taking these actions?

_____

_____

_____

_____

_____

CHAPTER ELEVEN

Coaching Congregations to Pursue Their Full Kingdom Potential

EXECUTIVE SUMMARY

The purpose of this chapter is to focus on the art, science, and practice of coaching as an approach to helping congregations pursue their full Kingdom potential. The focus is on describing and characterizing coaching, talking about the distinctions between coaching and other disciplines such as consulting, and sharing coach approaches and tactics. A distinction is made among approaches to coaching. Coaching may be content rich, contextually relevant, or content neutral. Consulting is morphing to coaching; teaching is morphing to learning; individual leadership is morphing to leadership communities; and expert approaches are morphing to peer learning communities.

Throughout this book we have highlighted the coaching motif. For some readers this is a new approach. For others it is the new word for the same old approaches. To some it is an emerging approach with which they are becoming familiar, but they are having trouble separating it from their image of a coach for a sports team. Also, some people see coaching as a new word with some new characteristics, but they are not really sure how it is different from consulting approaches with which they have become familiar over the past several decades. They legitimately ask if there is really something new they need to understand and utilize.

Is Consulting Dead or Just Not Cool Now That Something New Has Come Along?

Thirty-five years ago I became interested in consulting with congregations. It was fairly new for congregations to be open to an outside consultant helping them with strategic planning. Congregations already used outside consultants for architectural services and fundraising. These were hard, visible issues. For soft, invisible issues such as planning, consultants were not common.

Innovators such as Lyle Schaller, Loren Mead, and Donald McGavran were developing solid reputations as congregational interventionists. Early adapters such as Ezra Earl Jones, Herb Miller, Speed Leas, Carl Dudley, Win Arn, and many others soon began to emerge and popularize this new ministry niche.

Little formal training or certification existed to prepare persons to be congregational consultants. Persons who wanted to be consultants figuratively hung out a shingle containing their name and the word *consultant.* Suddenly they were consultants!

Emerging emphases at Fuller Seminary in California focused on church growth; as did the Yokefellow Institute in Richmond, Indiana, where Lyle Schaller held court, the various offerings of The Alban Institute, and a few other learning settings. Certainly business education models could be adapted, but they also carried the liability of not understanding the spiritual and organism side of congregations.

I developed my initial practices in consulting through many resources. These included research into helping congregations transform, through visitation to dozens of congregations to discover the stories of their transformations, through mentoring from various folks around my seminary who understood the consulting process, through readings in the area of consulting, and ultimately through a doctoral program where my focus was on the development, use, and evaluation of a process for consulting with congregations.

However, my real education came when I went to the Baltimore, Maryland, area where I had grown up. With the sponsorship of my denominational missions agency, I plunged into consulting with congregations in racially, ethnically, and socioeconomically transitional communities.

My systemic, left-brained approach worked reasonably well to provide short-term fixes congregations might eventually use to transform themselves. It was a heavy data gathering and analysis approach that focused both on the congregation and its context. It was an approach that was consistent in the mid-1970s with other approaches being attempted by denominational organizations and by educational and parachurch groups.

Consultant-led strategic planning, and to an extent congregational studies, is an approach that began to fade as the transition to the twenty-first century added a postmodern mindset to the already existing modern and ancient mindsets. By the early 1990s, strategic planning was an approach that was seeing decreasing effectiveness and acceptance among congregations who had a growing percentage of participants born after February 9, 1964–the Sunday night the Beatles first appeared on the Ed Sullivan television show.

Some would say that Lyle Schaller signaled the end of the era of the consultant in 1997 with the publication of his book *The Interventionist* (Nashville: Abingdon Press, 1997), and a *farewell to consulting* learning experience he conducted in Atlanta.

But is consulting dead? No! It is being transformed and reinvented to add coaching to the collection of ways congregations can be empowered to reach their full Kingdom potential.

Is Coaching a Fad or a Way of Helping Congregations Pursue Vital Ministry?

Coaching is not a fad. It is an emerging way of helping congregations pursue vital ministry. A coach approach transforms consulting by seeing congregational leadership as learners who need help along their journey toward transformation rather than as clients who need answers to challenges.

Both consultants and coaches engage in assessment activities. However, a consultant intervenes with fixes or prescriptions, while a coach comes alongside congregational leadership to help them learn the skill sets needed to continually transform. Coaching empowers congregational leadership by helping them develop the capacity to continually live into their future.

The world is much more complex than it was thirty years ago, when delivering the right answer was the goal of consulting. Coaching seeks to help congregational leadership confront the various choices they face, create and dialogue around the possible passages to the future, and confront the critical questions they must face as they navigate their spiritual and strategic journey.

Congregational coaching is a practice of ministry that mirrors a *Paraclete* approach as coaches come alongside congregational leadership to walk with them on their spiritual, strategic journey. A coach is not necessarily an expert in congregational growth or health. Rather, a coach is an informed colleague with a spiritual and congregational bias who helps congregational leadership soar as they live into their future story.

One emerging style of postmodern congregational coaching focuses not only with individual persons, but also on a leadership community of a half-dozen to a couple of dozen people. Coaching congregational leadership seeks to create and nurture the *Enduring Visionary Leadership Community* rather than lead a board, committee, or team. Such communities have as their primary focus a collective relationship to God, to one another, and to the congregation for which they are providing the passionate spark for transformation.

True congregational transformation occurs when congregations understand their full Kingdom potential and can be nurtured as a Christ-centric, faith-based community to journey toward that potential. Congregational coaches who understand how to guide the transitions and changes that lead to transformation are a valuable asset to congregations.

Coaching is an emerging right-brained approach that sees relationships as more important than tasks, significance as more important than success, stories as more important than strategies, experiences as more important than rule books, people as more important than institutions, and soaring with strengths as more important than problem-solving.

Just like consulting thirty years ago, few formal programs in coaching are process-driven. Some formal programs are training coaches to carry out a specific program, project, or process. When this is the approach, the focus is not on coaching a congregation to be reimaged in God's image, but to be reimaged in the image of the creator of the program, project, or process. This is an unfortunate use of coaching.

As was true of the emergence of congregational consulting thirty years ago, some Christian coaches tend to simply carry business coaching models over into the congregation world without a spiritual element as a catalyst that morphs the business concepts into the spiritual arena. Business coaching models will not work effectively for long-term congregational transformation that requires both a spiritual and a strategic approach.

Where Can You Go for Help on Coaching?

If you stay focused on process rather than content, you may not have many choices. One recent book whose first four chapters have merit is *Christian Coaching: Helping Others Turn Potential into Reality,* by Gary R. Collins (Colorado Springs: NavPress, 2001). However, it needs further work as a guidebook that really gets at the heart of the matter in terms of applying the principle of coaching to congregational leadership groups.

Currently, I am connecting to an organization known as Internal Impact (Web site: www.internal-impact.com). Its principal partner, Jane Creswell (e-mail: coachjane@internal-impact.com), has many years of experience as an organization coach inside IBM, where she founded the IBM Coaches Network. She has earned multiple coaching certifications from the business world. More important, she has a lifetime calling as a churchperson, so that she and a half-dozen colleagues are now focusing on helping certify coaches for congregational leadership.

Her current certification process provides potential coaches with five days of classroom learning, three teleclasses, a mentor coach for four months, a *learner's permit* in coaching, and a continuous learning process. This enables them to begin to become trustworthy and experienced coaches with accountability to a larger system and a group of mentoring coaches who have international certification as personal coaches. Her process is congruent with the concepts and coaching values of the International Coach Federation. Jane is currently preparing a book on *Christ-Centered Coaching* that Lake Hickory Resources will publish in 2006.

The best thing that has happened is that, with her coaching, folks to whom I relate through Lake Hickory Learning Communities at Hollifield Leadership Center (www.Hollifield.org) have formed a new emphasis on coaching called VALWOOD Christian Leadership Coaching. Through VALWOOD coaching certification and practice is offered to individuals, ministry groups, and congregations. You may contact them at www.valwoodcoaching.org.

COACHING BREAK

✔ Gaze out the window for a minute. Ponder the situation of your congregation. What images come to mind?

✔ What are the applications of coaching within your congregation? Who are candidates for coaching? the pastor? the staff? the board?

persons with the gift of evangelism? persons seeking to start a new program, ministry, or activity?

✔ Who coaches you? Who holds you accountable, at your request, for fulfilling the actions you say you want to take? How much more effective would your life and ministry be if you had a coach?

Coaching That Is Rich, Contextual, or Neutral

Not all coaching is pure coaching. Much coaching has significant content or a framework. Pure coaching begins with the person, leadership community, or congregation being coached, and their expression of agendas. Three approaches to coaching are content rich coaching, contextual framework coaching, and content neutral coaching.

Content rich coaching seeks to remake the leader, ministry group, or congregation in the image of a body of content, with sensitivity to spiritual understandings. Examples of this are Natural Church Development, CoachNet, Bowen Family Systems, T-Net, and mentoring.

Contextual framework coaching seeks to remake the leader, ministry group, or congregation in the image of God congruent with the unique situation of the congregation or ministry setting. Contextual framework coaching is process-oriented coaching. Examples of this are the process described in this book—spiritual strategic journey—and other process-orientated approaches to planning, discipleship, staff leadership and development, and other forms of ministry-oriented, action-based forms of coaching.

Content neutral coaching seeks to remake the leader, ministry group, or congregation in the image of identified issues of the person or persons being coached. This approach to coaching highlights the idea of a carriage, a stagecoach, a train coach, or coach class seating on our airplane. Coaching seeks to convey people from where they are to where they want to go. Personal ministry coaching, or the coaching of congregational leadership communities, fit this approach.

It is essential that persons coaching others, and the person, leadership community, or congregation being coached, be able to distinguish among content rich coaching, contextual framework coaching, and content neutral coaching. The type of coaching needed is the one most desired by the person, leadership community, or congregation being coached. The purest form of coaching is content neutral coaching. Systems, programs, or project coaching characterize content rich coaching. Persons who are purest regarding coaching would not consider content rich coaching to be coaching in the best sense of the discipline. It is too task-oriented, requires behavior change to learn and stay focused on a certain system, and focuses more on the outcomes than the person. Of course, users of content rich coaching approaches do not perceive their coaching this way.

The Progression from Clinician to Consultant to Coach

Recently a group of congregational and denominational leaders, plus several executive and organizational coaches, gathered for a learning experience. One dialogue topic was the difference between being a clinician, a consultant, and a coach. Here are some of the ideas expressed that may assist you in seeing how different approaches could be applied to your congregation. Each may be relevant to the life and ministry of your congregation at various times and circumstances.

A clinician is a person who is program driven. The training program drives the relationship. Clinicians teach the book. They do not always have real, personal experiences to share. They focus on diagnosis using a manual, and then suggest efficiency steps. The right way to do things using a step-by-step, one-size-fits-all process is an important principle to them. A clinician treats symptoms, rather than causes, and thus provides a fix rather than a solution. They know primarily one way to do things and provide little or no tailoring or customizing. They tend to be perceptual and logical, and focus on a Gospel of Matthew approach.

A consultant is a person who uses a systemic approach involving principles and customization. Consultants engage in assessment and analysis to discover problems and solutions. A strategic planning model in which the outcomes are driven by the model is popular with them. They feel they have the answer to solve your problems or situation, so they come across as experts, but may simply have a briefcase and a notebook. A consultant often brings a solution, but then is not there long enough to see that it doesn't hold for the long term. They tend to be conceptual and logical and focus on a Gospel of John approach.

A coach is a person who focuses on the personal growth and potential of the person being coached. Coaches address issues such as empowerment and enhancement of the client. Initially they assess a person, group, or congregation's situation by asking questions, listening, and being process oriented. Coaches enable rather than tell the answer, and encourage rather than discourage. They focus the client on self-discovery and follow through with implementation. Like the Holy Spirit, they come alongside the client in a covenant relationship as a partner. They tend to be conceptual and feeling and focus on a Gospel of Luke approach.

By the way, while we are on this subject, let's add one more helping process. The newly emerging approach to assisting congregations in reaching their full Kingdom potential focuses around peer learning communities. These work best with excellent pastors, staff ministers, leadership communities, and congregations. Peer learning communities tend to take a perceptual feeling approach to learning that focuses on action and reflection. They also focus on the Gospel of Mark.

The primary transition in helping styles currently is between consulting and coaching. The difference between consulting and coaching is that coaching develops capacity rather than dependency, focuses on self-discovery and learning rather than expert answers and training, seeks to affirm and build rather than do problem solving, seeks to provide encouragement and soaring, is centered rather than bounded, and makes the person being coached the hero rather than giving that position to the consultant or coach. A coach helps the person being coached own the discoveries, rather than having to adopt them.

All three roles—clinician, consultant, and coach—exist today. The current progression is definitely in the direction of coach. The future progression will be in the direction of peer learning communities for persons who demonstrate an ability to learn through insightful reflection of experiences they have been part of and actions they initiate.

Coaching Congregational Leadership by Asking Discerning Questions

Observation of the *Coaching Breaks* and *Coaching Insights* in this book will reveal a heavy bias in favor of asking questions rather than providing answers. Several reasons for this approach are obvious. One I would like to highlight is a belief that God is seeking to impart wisdom and insight to the church body. A role of a coach is to discover and draw out of persons being coaching that which God may be seeking to say to and through them, magnify these discerned truths, point the persons being coached toward action around their discerned truths, and then hold them accountable for effective action.

Questions are more compelling than statements. Pastors, staff ministers, lay leaders, and congregations as a whole seek to answer the questions they are asked. Questions can present powerful learning opportunities through which congregations can build the capacity to handle many of their own situations.

Many congregations will actually seek to change their program, ministry, and activities patterns in response to questions that are asked on denominational report forms. I know, I know; we all hate those forms. The truth is we allow the questions on those forms to frame the culture and practices of our congregation in more ways than we think. Since this is true, what would happen if congregations were asked truly insightful, discerning spiritual and strategic questions?

Questions are an important part of the work of Christian leadership coaching. Discerning questions can suggest areas of contemplation, learning, and action for congregational leadership. They may even introduce perspectives about which congregational leadership had not previously thought.

Here are some questions that might provoke contemplation, learning, and action:

Discerning Question One: Who are the people with the most positive spiritual passion about the future toward which God is leading this congregation? Asking this question should discover the *People of Passion* in a congregation who have spiritually creative ideas about the future of the congregation. Such people and their ideas are the type that can transform a congregation.

The old question that might have been asked in this situation is, Who are the most influential people in the life of this congregation? This question would discover the *People of Position* in the congregation, who may have a great love for the congregation, but not be open to the new things God is seeking to do within the congregation that may take them to the next level of Kingdom service.

Discerning Question Two: Who are the people who give evidence of a growing Christ-centric spirituality that results in a lifestyle of personal surrender and significant service in Christian ministry? Asking this question should discover people who are well on their way to becoming fully devoted followers of Christ and who will contribute to develop a congregation that is spiritually deep and strategically effective.

The old question that might have been asked in this situation is, Who are the people who are most faithful to the adult discipleship programs, ministries, and activities of the congregation? This question would discover the persons who are most involved in the life of the congregation, but it does not guarantee that they are growing as dynamic spiritual leaders, only that they are busy.

Discerning Question Three: Who are the people who connect well with pre-Christian, unchurched, and dechurched people and can effectively share with these people a personal story of Jesus? Asking this question should discover people who have networks that may be appropriately and authentically cultivated to introduce people to a Christ-centric, faith-based journey through local a congregation.

The old question that might have been asked in this situation is, Do you know any lost or unchurched people to whom we need to make a visit? This question would discover persons for a sales-oriented prospect list and assumes that all people respond best to a confrontational or propositional witness or invitation to church.

A Congregational Case Study

"Yeah, I believe we have the *Big Mo*," was the claim of the chairperson of a Future Story Leadership Community in a congregation in the southeast section of a large metropolitan area. Parkview congregation, for the first time in thirty-three years, was experiencing momentum in its spiritual strategic journey. If continued for another two to three years, this momentum was likely to lead to genuine transformation for this congregation.

Thirty-three years earlier this congregation had relocated from the downtown area of its metropolitan area to what was then an exurban area with no development around it and a road that would be characterized as a *"farm to market"* road that brought people from their homes to the congregational facilities. Like many congregations who relocated during the 1960s and 1970s, their dream was the relocation; and their assumption was that if they relocated, they would be able to attract new people from the area surrounding their new site. It was an "if-we-relocate-they-will-come" fantasy. They made no intentional effort reach their new neighbors, but simply assumed they would come.

Over the next three decades they muddled along as a numerically plateaued congregation, subject to various short-term fixes that gave them enough of a periodic morale boost and program fix that they were able to sustain reasonably successful congregational life. They did not achieve a spiritual strategic journey in their new location, and they certainly did not have the characteristics of a movement.

In recent years they have initiated a spiritual strategic journey. Several things made this possible. These included a new pastor, some long-term program emphases finally attracting younger families, significant population growth in their area, readiness for change and transition, an intentional futuring process, and the use of a congregational coach. This new spiritual strategic journey might help them transition from an institutionalized congregation to a congregation with true momentum, and thus to have become a movement.

What are the characteristics of the congregational spiritual strategic journey that are important for Parkview to understand? How has their journey seemed to have created a movement?

Characteristics of This Congregational Spiritual Strategic Journey

Parkview came to understand that congregational spiritual strategic journeys are right-brained rather than left-brained. They are focused on spirituality, values, meaning, significance, character, relationships, experiences, and connections rather than programs, competence, systems, strategies, structures, rules, operational guidelines, and formal governance patterns.

They are focused on creating a movement rather than the completion of a planning process. Any planning that is strategic in nature seeks to create a future story for the congregation. Early in the journey they tell the future story of the congregation, which it then seeks to live into, rather than seeking to push the congregation forward by means of static objectives and goals.

To live into the future, the congregation must create a movement of people that engages in a spiritual strategic journey. It is like Abraham and his kinship leaving his home to journey to a place that God would show him. It is like the Israelites leaving Egypt as a tribe to journey to a Promised Land of which they had heard and to which God would lead them. They had a dream, vision, or dynamic story as to what the journey would be like, but not a clear plan. They knew the God of the journey and trusted that leadership.

Spiritual strategic journeys are centered rather than bounded. A bounded journey is predefined by a downloaded map. All the roads and attractions along the way are known. Effective execution is the only unknown or only variable in doubt. It assumes a stable context.

Spiritual strategic journeys are an exploration more on the order of the Lewis and Clark expedition of 200 years ago across the recently acquired Louisiana Purchase. While there is a general idea of the journey, there are also many unknowns. The excitement is discovering new routes and attractions that add value to the journey. The core purpose is the same, but the methodology and nature of the journey is constantly changing.

Spiritual strategic journeys are dialogical rather than debated. In debated journeys there is constant argument over which routes and side attractions are the right ones to take or enjoy. In a dialogical journey all routes and attractions are valued, and participants in the journey are given permission to experiment and see what new might emerge.

Spiritual strategic journeys involve coaching rather than consulting. Consulting is an expert approach that seeks to make the participants dependent on the consultant's answers or fixes. Coaching the journey motif emphasizes the learning aspects of the journey and is constantly focusing on asking questions that will lead journey participants to discover their own answers that they will remember long past the visit of a consultant.

Characteristics of a Movement within the Congregation

Parkview learned that congregational spiritual strategic journeys that are also a movement originate in the heart, soul, mind, and strength of the congregation. They are *grassroots* in nature. At least 21 percent of the average number of active, attending adults are captivated by a sense of joy, inspiration, deepening relationships with God and one another, and true movement toward reaching their full Kingdom potential as individuals and as a congregation.

Some spiritual strategic journeys miss the point. They are simply a new name given to an old long-range or strategic planning process. They are top-down in nature. They are leader-centric. They do not captivate the imagination of the congregational participants.

Building a spiritual base for the movement through something like share and prayer triplets is essential. As described in chapter 7, these involve three people meeting ten times for 100 minutes over 100 days to share their spiritual and strategic journey as Christians with one another and to share about the spiritual and strategic journey of their congregation. In addition to sharing, they pray for one another and for their congregation, with an emphasis on the future of their own journey and that of their congregation.

Movements are made up of dynamics leadership and learning communities rather than committees and boards. These leadership and learning communities focus on developing movement among a group of people rather than being leader-centric and relying on one person to initiate action.

Movements, at their best, ultimately become self-perpetuating with coaching from a third-party rather than constant pushing by a manager. As long as a spiritual strategic journey requires pushing and managing as the primarily motivating actions, it is not yet a movement.

What about This Congregation's Transformation and Journey Toward Its Full Kingdom Potential?

Parkview has empowered various leadership and learning communities to pursue new ventures that produce some "chaordic" situations and require permission-giving leadership. Pastoral and program staff are regularly and appropriately reminding the congregation of the centering, moorings, or core values of the congregation with which each venture must have some congruence and definite consistency.

Several of these leadership and learning communities have made great progress and have developed movement in various parts of the congregation. Enough movement and excitement seems to be occurring, and has been occurring for the past two years, that the exclamation by the chairperson of the Future Story Leadership Community that they now have the "*Big Mo*" seems to be legitimate.

They are considering programs, ministries, and activities they totally rejected just two years earlier. They are now at a different place in their spiritual strategic journey and see things from a different viewpoint. They are a movement.

By the way, all of this happened at Parkview using a coach approach that focused on assessment and then learning. It was a contextual framework approach toward congregational leadership, and a content neutral approach toward the senior pastor and the ministerial and program staff. Because of this, the learnings have been hardwired into the new, emerging culture of Parkview.

What Is the Role of This Congregation's Denomination?

The role of Parkview's denomination is to affirm the spiritual strategic journey of the congregation and to encourage them at every possible place. Denominational polity in Parkview's denomination means the denominational leadership is directly involved in the calling of the pastor and other ordained staff ministers for the congregation. It is important for the denomination to recognize the significance of what is happening in the spiritual strategic journey and the true movement that exists. The denomination must help the congregation have pastoral leadership that understands and relates to the current journey and the emerging movement. A misstep in pastoral leadership could stall the movement.

It is also possible the denomination could be a resource for the coaching this congregation will continue to need to help it stay in movement. Often congregations declare too soon that they have arrived in their journey and they stall the movement themselves. The illusion for many congregations is that a fix was all they needed and that the radical transformation represented by a solution is unnecessary. Such thoughts are often misguided and abandon spiritual strategic journeys before the movement is self-perpetuating.

Further, the denomination must learn how to use a coach approach to help Parkview and the other congregations related to this denominational judicatory to be involved in *FaithSoaring*. What do you feel should be their first step to fulfill this need?

COACHING INSIGHTS

- What has been your experience with consultants and the consulting process? In what ways has it been beneficial to your ministry and your congregation? Have you experienced it as a short-term fix or as a long-term solution?

- Have you experienced coaching from a Christian leadership coach who seems to understand the process of coaching and to have your goals in mind? How effective has this coaching been for you? Do you see yourself as coachable? What do you feel are the characteristics of a person who is coachable and one who is not?

- When you think of coaching, do you think of a sports team or an accountable relationship, a strong approach or a weak approach, an intervention approach or a learning approach, questions or answers?

- What do you feel are the implications of coaching for how you may function as a leader in your congregation? Can staff members be coached? Can boards and committees be coached? What if you implemented a communities approach? Would you know how to apply coaching in this situation?

- What additional information do you need? What do you need to understand or learn to apply coaching in your ministry? What are you going to do, and by when, to obtain the information, understanding, and learning you need? Do you need someone to hold you accountable for doing this?

- How is your situation similar to or different from Parkview? What additional information do you want to know about what happened at Parkview and other similar congregations? How are you going to obtain this information? Who are congregations you know who have gone through the type of spiritual strategic journey your congregation needs to pursue? How are you going to locate these congregations so you can dialogue with them and learn from one another?

PERSONAL REFLECTIONS

YOUR REFLECTIONS: What are your reflections on the material presented in this chapter?

YOUR ACTIONS: What actions do you need to take about your life, ministry, and/or congregation based on the material presented in this chapter?

YOUR ACCOUNTABILITY: How and by whom do you want to be held accountable for taking these actions?

CHAPTER TWELVE

Pursuing the Full Kingdom Potential of Your Denomination

EXECUTIVE SUMMARY

The purpose of this chapter is twofold. First, we will talk about the role of denominations in coming alongside congregations who are seeking to reach their full Kingdom potential. As a part of this purpose, the five varieties of denominational service to congregations are presented. Second, we will talk about the application of this process to denominational organizations that are seeking to transform themselves.

What Type of Service Do Denominations Need to Offer to Congregations that Will Help Congregations Thrive?

During the past fifty years the types of service offered by denominational and parachurch organizations to congregations has transitioned through various waves. To look at these waves, let's imagine that someone drew a line in the sand, or turned a page, and that service to congregations started all over again with the end of World War II.

Clinician Wave

The first wave of service was the *Clinician Wave*. Methods clinics were very popular during the generation following World War II. Frequently they involved individuals or teams from congregations going to a central location to receive training in a project, program, or methodology being offered. The clinician approach is an instructional approach that involves adherence to rules and standards and focusing of left-brained thinking.

Denominations often rolled out a new program, project, or emphasis every year or so. With each of these they had a notebook, instructors, and implementation checklists. Congregational leaders were told that if they went back home and worked through the checklist faithfully, and did not change anything, the program, project, or emphasis would work for their congregation. If it did not work, then they did not do it right.

Chaplaincy Wave

The second wave of service was the *Chaplaincy Wave*. During the period of 1955 through 1965 a pastoral care approach to congregation life arose partially as a reaction against the high task orientation of the *Clinician Wave*. This right-brained, compassionate chaplaincy approach focused more on the psychological approach to congregational ministry, individual and group counseling, and a deep emphasis on care ministries.

The academic discipline of psychology of religion, emerging out of pastoral theology, plus its application vehicle, pastoral care, surfaced as a strong, positive wave to help congregational participants in faith discovery and stages. Out of this came various approaches to interpersonal relationship groups, and later the multiple variations of the small group movement. Important in this wave was the concept of a comforting presence and maturing emotional systems.

Consulting Wave

The third wave of service was the *Consulting Wave*. During the decade of the 1970s a consulting approach began to emerge in many denominational traditions. Assessment and intervention consulting helped to customize the principles of methods clinics for each congregation, and to use small group processes to help congregations confront issues facing them. Systems, strategies, and structures are hallmarks of this conceptual, left-brained approach.

A part of this wave was the training of thousands of congregational, denominational, and parachurch leaders in various consulting processes that could be customized to the unique situation of congregations. Lyle Schaller was the father or leading figure of this movement, and many people have been influenced by his approaches. He still impacts this movement and other waves during the elder statesman phase of his life.

Coaching Wave

The fourth wave of service is the *Coaching Wave.* This wave, along with the next wave, is still emerging. Both began to emerge during the 1990s. Coaching seeks to turn consulting on its head. Rather than focusing on a directive style that is consultant dependent, it focuses on an action style that seeks to develop the capacity in congregational leaders to navigate the pathways and passages of their spiritual strategic journey as a congregation.

This approach is known in some places as Christian leadership coaching. It involves a style of coming alongside individuals, groups, and congregations that seek to make the congregation the hero rather than the coach. This is not sports coaching, but rather an approach that seeks to convey people from where they are to where they perceive they want to go, or where God is pulling them. While it focuses more on persons than tasks, feelings than thinking, it does have a prejudice in favor of action.

Communities Wave

The fifth wave of service is the *Communities Wave.* This refers to the concept of peer learning communities in which the participants primarily learn from the individual and collective experience of their own lives and ministries. This is an approach for people who are creative and innovative in their thinking and have high skills at applying what they learn into the congregation they lead.

A formal definition for peer learning communities is that they involve congregational leadership peers connecting through multifaceted communities for dialogue, support, learning, and soaring together in ways that strengthen their ability to reach their full Kingdom potential. Often interaction with respected congregational practitioners and twenty-first-century Christian ministry thought leaders will be used as a catalyst for launching peer learning dialogue.

Service Strategies for Thriving Congregations

All five of these service waves are still legitimate types of service for congregations. The question in today's church world is not the validity of various types of service, but which type will help your congregation thrive?

One answer to this question has to do with what type of performance category is most characteristic of your congregation. I suggested in chapter 2 some performance categories. They were *Perfecting Congregations, Pursuing Congregations, Preparing Congregations, Providing Congregations,* and *Presiding Congregations.*

Certain types of learning, and perhaps thriving, are most characteristic of certain performance categories of congregations. *Presiding Congregations* learn best from the *Chaplaincy Wave* methodologies, *Providing Congregations* from the *Clinician Wave, Preparing Congregations* from the *Consulting Wave, Pursuing Congregations* from the *Coaching Wave,* and *Perfecting Congregations* from the *Communities Wave.*

Congregational Performance Categories and Learning Styles

PERFORMANCE CATEGORY	LEARNING STYLE
Presiding Congregations	Chaplaincy Wave
Providing Congregations	Clinician Wave
Preparing Congregations	Consulting Wave
Pursuing Congregations	Coaching Wave
Perfecting Congregations	Communities Wave

But here is the problem. While the congregation as a whole may be primarily in one performance category and best able to benefit from one particular wave, various groups and leaders in the congregation are at various performance categories and able to benefit differently from the waves of service. This is one factor that speaks to the difficulty of leading a congregation through transition and change, and why a singular approach will not work for every congregation. You are a pastor, staff minister, program director, or lay leader. What should you do to apply in your congregation the best type of service that will help it thrive? Here are several principles.

First, realize that an and/both approach is far superior to an either/or approach. This means that a single service wave is insufficient for your congregation. You need to plan to use multiple approaches to learning in your congregation. For example, if you are a *Preparing Congregation,* you should not only use a *Consulting Wave* approach, but also use a *Clinician Wave* approach for work with leaders who need to see it written out in plain language and to have a checklist. Further, you should use a *Coaching Wave* approach for leaders who already get it and desire to soar in their understanding and practice of ministry.

Second, consider using an approach that stretches your congregation one wave ahead from the approach that is most characteristic of your performance category, but not a wave that is two or more waves ahead. The example here is that if your congregation is a *Presiding Congregation,* using a *Clinician Wave* approach, which is one wave ahead, may help systematize and improve some of the work of your congregation. But to use a *Consulting Wave* approach, which is two waves ahead, would be something for which you are probably not ready. It would not benefit your church and would probably frustrate them.

Third, dialogue is essential between the various styles of learning. One of the sources of conflict in a congregation can be the gap between learning styles and services waves utilized. People who learn best by the *Communities Wave* will be a threat to people who primarily know how to learn or be serviced by a *Clinician Wave* approach. The gap is too great. The *Clinician Wave* is four waves away from the *Communities Wave.*

If, however, a *Consulting Wave* approach was used, or even a *Coaching Wave,* then the gap may be small enough not to create unnecessary conflict. The conflict can come from either perspective. The folks who best learn and are serviced by the *Clinician Wave* may feel those who are proponents of the *Communities Wave* are trying to take the congregation to a "chaordic" approach that will take the congregation too far away from their moorings.

From the opposite perspective, the folks who best learn and are serviced by the *Communities Wave* may feel that those who are proponents of the *Clinician Wave* are seeking to control the congregation and not allow it to make progress and be relevant to today's world.

Fourth, it is essential to stretch the leading edge people in your congregation. You cannot hold back their creativity, innovation, and openness to new ideas without losing them. Their thinking outside or beyond the box must be affirmed.

Engage your *Coaching Wave* and *Communities Wave* leaders in learning and service opportunities that stretch them and help them move to the next level of ministry performance. Include methods in their learning for working within the system of a congregation with people who are not yet ready to learn and be serviced at the same level as these leading edge people.

Fifth, stretch yourself as a leader. Continual learning is essential. You must figure out how you personally best learn and are serviced by leadership development emphases, and then seek to stretch yourself to the next wave of learning and service. Your personal growth does not have to be bounded by the system in which you currently minister.

It is possible for you as a leader to grow on one track and your congregation to be growing on another track. This will work as long as you do not feel compelled to impose your wave on a congregation not ready for that type of learning and service. Further, this will work as long as you do not value your wave as being better than the type of learning and service for which your congregation has readiness. When your track and your congregation's track conflict, your focus will most likely turn to your next place of ministry service.

What type of service does your congregation need to thrive? It needs the type of service that fits its unique situation as a Christ-centric, faith-based community, and its distinctive collection of leaders with differing spiritual gifts, life skills, and personality preferences.

Methods of Learning for These Congregational Performance Categories

Congregations in each of these categories tend to learn in different ways the things they need to know to take the next steps in their spiritual strategic journey. Certain methods of learning are characteristic of each congregation's performance category. Certain approaches by denominations to serving these congregations are characteristic of each performance category. Thus, the following methods are performance category appropriate.

Perfecting Congregations tend to learn best through peer learning communities, peer congregational gatherings, dialogue with respected congregational practitioners, dialogue with twenty-first–century Christian ministry thought leaders and with Christian ministry coaches or personal ministry coaches. The average denominational organization has difficulty helping these congregations to learn, because these congregations have often soared beyond the learning frontiers of their denomination. Denominational organizations that are high performance and understand the dynamics of perfecting, can come alongside these congregations through peer learning experiences and coaching.

Pursuing Congregations tend to learn best through peer congregational gatherings, dialogue with respected congregational practitioners, dialogue with twenty-first–century Christian ministry thought leaders, Christian ministry coaches or personal ministry coaches, and relationships with mentoring congregations. Some denominational organizations identify well with pursuing congregations. It is how they also see themselves. Therefore, a pursuing denominational organization can project its growth efforts on pursuing congregations, and each end up helping one another pursue a spiritual strategic journey.

Preparing Congregations tend to learn best by using expert consultants, emulating other congregations who have recently faced the same or similar opportunities and challenges, and through teaching congregational relationships. Too many denominational organizations find themselves identifying with the learning patterns of these congregations. They are overachieving in an attempt to develop the readiness or capacity for great, solution-oriented change in the midst of a church and denominational culture that only wants short-terms fixes.

Providing Congregations tend to learn best from attending clinics at which they learn tactics for the next six to eighteen months of the life of their congregation, and have an instruction book to take home with them with supporting media such as a DVD that explains the take home materials. Denominational organizations often spend too much time helping these faithful congregations to continue their mediocre ministry. Often they do this because of the loyalty of this category of congregations to the work of the denomination and its budget.

Presiding Congregations, if they are open to any learning, tend to learn best from rediscovery of proven patterns of the past. However, their reaction to opportunities to change may well be, "Learning? Who said anything about learning? Especially not something new!" It may seem that any time denominational organizations spend with these congregations may be more time than is justified. However, the people within these congregations are still persons of worth created in the image of God to live and to love. So at least a nominal involvement in these congregations is an important part of the ministry of denominations, as is their power to bless congregational leaders.

Implications for Denominational Organizations

Think back to chapter 3, when we introduced the seven categories of people in a congregation. Not surprisingly, that concept has implications at several levels for denominational organizations.

At one level, denominational organizations need to help congregational leaders to understand the seven categories. Strategies can be developed and resources focused to help congregations nurture the *People of Pastoral Leadership, Passion, and Position,* particularly.

At another level, denominational organizations can help congregations develop plans to provide basic ministerial, spiritual, and program services to *People of Participation, Passivity,* and *Perpetual Care* so that they will not feel neglected when a primary focus develops on the first three categories.

Further, the *People of Passion* and *Position* can be taught and coached in strategies to mobilize ministry to, with, and through *People of Participation* and *Passivity.* Additionally, coaching can be made available to *People of Pastoral Leadership* as they navigate the fuzzy environment of focusing on *People of Passion* and *Position.* Also, congregational leadership can be taught sensitivity to *People of Potential* and how to recognize signs and cultivate interest and inquiry from these persons.

Finally, denominational organizations need coaching in figuring out who these categories of people and congregations are within their district, region, and denominational family. This has the potential to focus their ministry in the most productive areas.

COACHING BREAK

✔ Gaze out the window for a minute. Ponder the situation of your congregation. What images come to mind?

✔ Think particularly about the relationship of your congregation to its denomination and other parachurch organizations. What is their relevance to your ministry? Do they understand how to help you reach your full Kingdom potential? What are specific actions or resources you need from them? Could one thing you need be their assistance in pulling together similar congregations for the type of cluster process to be described next?

Spiritual Strategic Journey Congregational Cluster Process

For denominational organizations that desire to involve multiple congregations in a spiritual strategic journey, the *Spiritual Strategic Journey Congregational Cluster Process* is an excellent emphasis to embrace. This approach involves a minimum of three congregations, and a maximum of seven, determining to go through a spiritual strategic journey process together as a cluster or community of congregations. The optimum number of congregations in a cluster is six.

To learn more about how to schedule a *Spiritual Strategic Journey Congregational Cluster Process,* contact George Bullard at GBullard@TheColumbiaPartnership.org.

Spiritual Strategic Journey Learning Experience

To initiate the process, denominational leaders should approach prospective congregations to dialogue with them about their spiritual strategic journeys. They may want to provide copies of this book to the congregations. The goal at this juncture would be to invite the pastor, staff ministers, and lay leadership from prospective congregations to attend a *Spiritual Strategic Journey Learning Experience* taught by a mentor coach knowledgeable in the contents of this book and the process followed for a cluster congregation spiritual strategic journey process.

Often these are held on a Friday and Saturday. On Friday, only the pastor and staff ministers are asked to attend an all-day presentation and dialogue. The purpose of this session is to introduce them to the content and process of a spiritual strategic journey, answer their questions, and then prepare them to coach their lay leadership who will be attending the Saturday session.

Years of experience indicate that if the pastor, and to a somewhat lesser extent the staff ministers, are not sold on the year-long spiritual strategic journey process, and if they are not committed to lead the congregation in transition and change activities that may transform the congregation, then they will find some way in the middle of the process to make it fail. Therefore, the Friday session is for the purpose of opening up the curtain, letting the pastors and staff ministers look behind it and see the wizard at work, and thus help them to gain confidence in the process.

Often it will be the dialogue pastors and staff ministers are able to have with their peers that will determine their openness to the process. On these Fridays it may also become apparent to pastors and staff ministers that although this is a pearl of great value, their congregation is not ready for it. This can easily happen even if the pastor and staff ministers are ready. A tragedy is when the pastor and staff minister force the process on a congregation that is not ready. The results are not pretty or pleasant.

On Saturday each congregation is asked to bring with them a number of adults equal to seven percent of the average number of active attending adults present for worship on a typical Sunday or weekend. This number includes the pastor and staff ministers who were present the day before. These people are not yet the *People of Passion* in the congregation, but just a group of people who need to hear and dialogue about the presentation. The purpose of this day is to go through the core pieces of content concerning the spiritual strategic journey, take the congregational participants through several learning activities coached by their pastor and staff ministers, and allow the congregations to dialogue about the overall process and get their questions answered.

The day is implemented in such a way that the congregations are already beginning to learn many things about their situation and will be able to return to their ministry setting and engage in some initial transition and change actions. Empowerment and movement are emphasized from the beginning.

After the learning experience, the denominational staff should then work with the congregations to determine who is ready to engage in a minimum of a twelve–month launch for their spiritual strategic journey toward their full Kingdom potential. Those who commit to the process should prepare by determining who in their congregation constitutes the *People of Passion*, which is the seven percent of the average number of active attending adults present each weekend for worship who have the greatest positive spiritual passion about the future of the congregation.

Spiritual Strategic Journey Learning Cluster One

On a scheduled weekend, from late Friday afternoon through late Saturday afternoon, the *People of Passion* from each participating congregation gather for their first cluster learning experience. During this cluster experience they engage in various learning activities that prepare them to lead the launch of the spiritual strategic journey in their congregation. They also spend significant time building relationships and community between congregations. Each congregation introduces themselves to the remainder of the congregations through a short presentation characterizing their past to present life and ministry. Then the other congregations give them feedback in the form of affirmations, challenges, and suggestions.

The *People of Passion* are instructed as to their role as initiating leaders for their congregation's spiritual strategic journey. They make a plan for what they will do over the next 120 days between learning clusters one and two. They share their plan with the other congregations, again for feedback. Then the cluster experience is concluded with worship.

TELECONFERENCES

In the time between learning cluster weekends, a teleconference is conducted twice each month. The pastor and a designated layperson from each congregation participate in the teleconference. Also present are representatives of the local or regional judicatory or denominational organization, any outside persons coaching the congregations, and the mentor coach for the overall process.

The general pattern of the teleconferences is that each congregation shares their celebrations, challenges, and questions concerning how the process is going in their congregation. After each congregation has shared, then the mentor coach leads a dialogue on the questions that have been raised, reviews materials appropriate for this point of the process, and introduces new material for which the learning moment has arrived.

Spiritual Strategic Journey Learning Cluster Two

The second learning cluster happens in the same manner and with the same schedule as the first. This is held approximately four months after the first learning cluster. Occasionally the time between the clusters is more than four months to compensate for heavy holiday times of the year when congregations are unable to complete all their assignments in a timely manner.

The sharing of congregations' progress reports along with feedback from their fellow congregations is the highlight of the first day. During the second day a workshop is conducted on how to write the future story of a congregation, which focuses on the twelve steps in the future storytelling process. Then follows the development of plans for the next 120 days, and the sharing of these plans and feedback. Finally, the *People of Passion* engage in the worship of God and dismiss. Over the next four months the teleconferences continue.

Spiritual Strategic Journey Learning Cluster Three

Four months later the congregations gather again under the same circumstances and schedule, with the same patterns of sharing and celebration. This time the new content is the sharing of the future story of each congregation and the initiation of the plans of each for living into its story.

Following this learning cluster, teleconferences are held for four additional months to coach the congregations in the direction of living into their future story. By this time the congregational coaches and the denominational staff should be able to continue the process for any additional needed time. After four additional months the congregations should be living into their story and celebrating the new insights as they see their potential with greater clarity.

Expected Results of the Process

How many congregations should be expected to experience significant transformation as a result of this process? It is difficult to predict. It depends on several factors.

First, how many of the participating congregations were truly ready for a spiritual strategic journey according to the explanation covered in chapter 2?

Second, how many congregations were free of unhealthy conflict just beneath the surface, so that unnecessary conflict did not occur when the stress of transition and change began to grow within the congregation?

Third, how many congregations have pastor, staff, and lay leadership who have the courage to take the risks necessary to leap forward in their spiritual strategic journey?

Fourth, how many congregations have the quality of Christian disciples who are able to form an empowering *Enduring Visionary Leadership Community* in such a way that they can discern the leadership of God and apply that leading in an effective way in their congregation?

When you know the answers to these questions, then you will begin to know how many congregations experience transformation through this process.

Pursuing the Full Kingdom Potential of Your Denomination

Is it possible for the congregational process described in this book to apply to denominational organizations? Absolutely! In fact, many of the dynamics are the same. The key difference is that denominations that transform are those that figure out how to sacrificially serve congregations and help them to transform, rather than focusing on the transformation of the denominational organization itself.

What part of the process described in this book for congregations also works for denominational organizations? First, denominations need to be thinking about their full Kingdom potential. Their perspective on their future needs to focus on a God-inspired future into which they are seeking to live. *Faithfulness* is a key word for many denominational organizations. The difficulty is that this generally means they are focusing on the past rather than anticipating the future.

Second, denominational organizations need to cultivate people with passion for the work of the denomination, engage in spiritual processes that build up a sense of Christian purpose, develop leaders who understand emerging denominational dynamics, and engage in learning regarding strategic actions.

Third, they need to identify the *People of Executive* (as opposed to *Pastoral* at the congregational level) *Leadership*, the *People of Passion*, and the *People of Position*. The numbers and percentages differ from those of congregations, but the principles are the same. These identified people form the *Enduring Visionary Leadership Community* for the denominational organization.

Fourth, they need to address a series of denominational issues for generative dialogue. They should begin by having the *Enduring Visionary Leadership Community* assess the denominational organization according to these issues.

Fifth, denominational organizations have a life cycle similar to the life cycle of congregations. It is important to assess the current location of the denominational organization on the life cycle so that next steps are obvious.

Sixth, denominational organizations often have exceptionally powerful future stories that speak to a wonderful, yet generally unrealized, potential. Developing a dynamic, flexible future story is an essential part of pursuing the full Kingdom potential of a denominational organization.

Seventh, consistently living into their future story is the greatest challenge for denominational organizations. Too often, they get sidetracked by political or special interest issues. At other times they allow heritage to block hope in the way they conduct their day-to-day operations.

I recognize this is a brief and inadequate overview of the application of the congregational spiritual strategic journey process. The expectation is that it provides a peek into the possibility for using this process to engage in denominational transformation. The future of denominational organizations may be a lot brighter than many people have predicted. If the future of denominational organizations is as bright as I see it, then the possibility that thousands of congregations will be transformed is a prediction of bright sunlight for the twenty-first–century church.

COACHING INSIGHTS

■ It is essential for your congregation to benefit from the type of service that will best empower it to thrive. Discernment, discovery, and development of that type of service will be the best benefit to your congregation. A denominational organization that understands how to customize services for a congregation is a great gift to congregations.

■ What have been your life and ministry experiences with the five types of service waves offered by denominational and parachurch organizations to congregations? What has been the experience of your *congregation* with the five types of service waves offered by denominational and parachurch organizations to congregations?

■ Through which of the five types of service waves do you personally thrive? Through which of the five types of service waves does your *congregation* collectively thrive? What are the three primary types of service waves represented by the leadership of your congregation? With this information in mind, what should be your next steps over the next 30 days, 120 days, and 365 days?

■ What do you see as the value of engaging congregations in a learning cluster for the launching of their spiritual strategic journeys? In what ways will this strengthen the process? Are there particular challenges to this approach? What suggestions would you have for how to do learning clusters of congregations in your area or region?

■ What do you see as the heritage and hope of your denominational organization? In what ways would the spiritual strategic journey process assist your denominational organization with its transformation? What are the characteristics of the hope you feel for the future of your denominational organization?

PERSONAL REFLECTIONS

YOUR REFLECTIONS: What are your reflections on the material presented in this chapter?

_____

_____

_____

_____

_____

YOUR ACTIONS: What actions do you need to take about your life, ministry, and/or congregation based on the material presented in this chapter?

_____

_____

_____

_____

_____

YOUR ACCOUNTABILITY: How and by whom do you want to be held accountable for taking these actions?

_____

_____

_____

_____

_____

Notes

Chapter 1: Understanding the Full Kingdom Potential of Your Congregation

[1]Charles E. Smith, "The Merlin Factor: Leadership and Strategic Intent," *Business Strategy Review* 5, no. 1 (Spring 1994): 67–68.

[2]C. S. Lewis, *The Last Battle,* The Chronicles of Narnia, Book 7 (New York: Harper Collins, 1984), 196.

[3]Ibid., 207.

[4]Ibid., 210–11.

Chapter 2: Preparing Your Congregation for a Spiritual Strategic Journey

[1]I am grateful for the insights of persons who helped develop readiness materials for the Pursuing Vital Ministry effort in North Carolina for many of the suggested activities for spiritual preparation. More of their work can be seen at www.PursuingVitalMinistry.org.

Chapter 3: Navigating the Spiritual Strategic Journey of Your Congregation

[1]The concept of the *People of Passion* and their ability to impact the entire congregation was inspired by the writing of Malcolm Gladwell, *The Tipping Point: How Little Things Can Make a Big Difference* (Boston: Little, Brown, 2000). Gladwell indicates that 6 percent of the people in a given social network are capable of infecting the entire system with the virus of change.

[2]The concept of 21 percent of the active participants in an organization being able to provide leadership for the entire organization was inspired by hearing Everett Rogers talk about his book, *The Diffusion of Innovation,* 4th ed. (New York: Free Press, 1995).

[3]This concept of the *Enduring Visionary Leadership Community* came together for me through hearing Jim Collins talk several years ago about his book, Jim Collins and Jerry I. Porras, *Built to Last* (New York: HarperBusiness, 1994). The concept that captivated me was that charismatic (meaning magnetic personality) visionary leaders are a liability that organizations can overcome over the long haul by concerted effort. Rather than such a visionary leader, a congregation needs an *Enduring Visionary Leadership Community* that can be carriers of the vision long past the leadership era of the current leader. This leadership structure would allow congregations to continually soar in the direction of their potential.

Vital ministry is not about plans, programs, and paradigms. It's about...

NET Results

Effective Ideas for Pursuing Vital Ministry

Net Results magazine delivers effective ideas that work from local church leaders, columnists, coaches and consultants. Six print and/or six electronic issues each year.

Features methods, theology and motivation from men and women immersed in helping congregations from more than 80 denominations reach their full Kingdom potential.

Plus Exclusive articles by Dale Galloway, Tom Bandy, and Senior Editor George Bullard, not available anywhere else.

It's like having a firm of internationally recognized experts on retainer for just pennies a week!

"Coaching Corner" questions help you get the most from each issue.

Bonus "Byte-Size Net Results"- emailed articles easy to forward to your colleagues.

For more information and/or to subscribe:
www.netresults.org
e-mail: netresults@netresults.org
phone 806/762-8094, ext 103.

To access a FREE sample issue of Net Results Online go to www.netresults.org/sample